MINISTRY WITH YOUTH ON THE MARGINS

MINISTRY WITH YOUTH ON THE MARGINS

Serving Teens with Trauma, Disabilities, and Mental Health Issues

Mike Severe and Laura Widstrom

Baker Academic
a division of Baker Publishing Group
Grand Rapids, Michigan

Published by Baker Academic
a division of Baker Publishing Group
Grand Rapids, Michigan
BakerAcademic.com

Printed in the United States of America

Library of Congress Cataloging-in-Publication Data
Names: Severe, Mike, 1974– author | Widstrom, Laura author
Title: Ministry with youth on the margins : serving teens with trauma, disabilities, and mental health issues / Mike Severe and Laura Widstrom.
Description: Grand Rapids, Michigan : Baker Academic, a division of Baker Publishing Group, [2026] | Includes bibliographical references and index
Identifiers: LCCN 2026003181 | ISBN 9781540970305 paper | ISBN 9781493456369 ebook | ISBN 9781493456376 pdf
Subjects: LCSH: Church work with youth | Church work with teenagers | Church work with victims of crimes | Church work with people with disabilities | Church work with the mentally ill
Classification: LCC BV4447 .S464 2026
LC record available at https://lccn.loc.gov/2026003181

The names and details of the people and situations described in this book have been changed or presented in composite form in order to ensure the privacy of those with whom the authors have worked.

Cover design by Tammy Myers

Baker Publishing Group publications use paper produced from sustainable forestry practices and postconsumer waste whenever possible.

26 27 28 29 30 31 32 7 6 5 4 3 2 1

To all the children who have graced my home,
thank you for sharing your joy and struggle.

—Mike

In loving memory of Pastor Patty Anderson,
who taught me to wade into the waters of ministry
whether or not I was confident of my footing ahead
because the Holy Spirit was with me.

—Laura

Contents

Introduction

Mike's Story

Several years ago, I (Mike) fostered a tween girl who had experienced extreme abuse. She was brilliant and well-liked. Her elementary Sunday School teachers raved about her inquisitiveness and engagement. As she moved into her teens, the state offered me the option to adopt her. Unfortunately, the process took years, and as she entered mid-adolescence, she became overwhelmed by her childhood trauma. The trauma manifested in violent and highly sexualized behaviors at school, eventually leading her to an adolescent behavioral health hospital. As I navigated the hospital stay, I repeatedly provided information to her church and invited the youth pastor to call or visit to engage with my pre-adoptive daughter. This young teen had gone to every youth event for two years prior to her hospitalization, yet she never received a call, visit, or follow-up from the church during two separate weeklong hospitalizations.

Laura's Story

Four years ago, my (Laura's) family was forced to relocate out of state after a job change. The context of the move was difficult. One piece we grieved was leaving the church we had attended for over a decade, where my then nine-year-old son had attended since he was a toddler. My son was adopted from foster care, bearing the impact of abuse and neglect as well as multiple mental health diagnoses. He is on the autism spectrum with high support needs. He also has bilateral hearing loss and is globally delayed in all areas. The church we left had rallied during his time in foster care and lengthy court battles. The church had grown with him, each year assessing how to best meet his changing needs as church leadership looked at staff and space. They set aside age-level expectations in favor of individualized care and discipleship. He wasn't put in the kindergarten classroom simply because he was kindergarten age. Rather, the question was "In what space and with what teacher will he be best served?" My family felt safe and loved by our church community.

Moving to a new community necessitated the search for a new church home. A multitude of factors went into that search, high on the requirements list being a willingness to accommodate the unique needs of my son, who was then in children's ministry but would age out in a few short years and need a youth ministry willing to think outside the box.

It became part of my weekly routine to call a local church and ask to speak to the children's pastor, explaining that our family was new to town and looking for a church home and that we had a child with disabilities and relevant functional needs. I would ask to learn about the children's ministry and then to share about my son, to see if the church would be a welcoming place to visit and have an inclusive atmosphere. I always asked to stay with my son, at least initially, to make sure that he was navigating well and to watch for situations and stimuli that might promote dysregulation, also known as "triggers." While my son's triggers were inconsistent, various stimuli, including loud noises or being asked to complete a task he felt was too difficult, could prompt negative behavior as a reaction.

One week, I spoke with a lovely church secretary who assured me she would pass on the message to the children's pastor within the hour. I was surprised to receive no return call from this church, a church that had a good reputation in the community. The absence of response communicated to me that my family was not welcome, which felt like the antithesis of everything Jesus taught but nevertheless narrowed our list of possible church homes.

Another church invited our family to visit following my phone call. It had a church member available throughout the morning to help my family navigate, but I watched the staff and volunteers allow my son to wander the space instead of inviting him to participate. The volunteers seemed afraid of him, choosing to take a hands-off approach. In this setting, as a parent and professor, I could have invested time with the volunteers and staff to train them in best practices. Perhaps after several months, I could have left my son in the hands of the volunteers in order to attend adult worship. While possible, that sounded exhausting.

The church where my family landed responded promptly to my phone call, and in conversation together, the staff and I made a game plan for our first visit. I would stay with my son to support him and to help the volunteers and staff learn about his specific support needs. On the day of our visit, we were warmly greeted, and the volunteers did not back away. They came up, engaged both of my children, and included them in the morning routine to the fullest of each child's abilities.

The church also boasts a summer schedule of family activities. Participating in these events gave my family an easier transition, as staff and volunteers could get to know my son while I participated alongside him. By the time school started, just a few weeks after our initial visit, I was able to leave my son and attend adult worship. The staff and volunteers invested time in building relationships with my son, engaging him personally. The children's pastor engaged in ongoing conversation regarding adjustments and accommodations. Sometimes I would get a thumbs-up at the end of a Sunday morning. At times when I was needed, staff responsibly communicated, whether in person or by phone, text, or email. The ministry staff knows where I sit for worship, but rarely do I get called out to provide support for heightened needs.

Four years later, my son has, with support, transitioned to youth group, where he typically has good experiences. But his favorite place is still children's church, where we began. While his age-level peers attend adult worship weekly, it remains a significant stretch for my son. The system we have negotiated is that on the first Sunday of the month he attends the main worship service with me. This provides acclimation to the "big church" worship. On the other Sundays, he serves as a junior leader in kids' church. He runs errands for the children's pastor, sets up supplies and snacks, and is present for the music and message, which is more on target for him developmentally.

Each Teen Is Unique, Each Teen Is Important

We (Laura and Mike) are currently youth ministry professors. Being parents of children with disabilities and other specialized support needs, as well as being former youth and children's pastors, we (Laura and Mike) have learned to look at church spaces with intention. There is no cookie-cutter plan or blueprint that equips churches to meet the needs of every individual who has experienced trauma or lives with a disability. This book offers broad categories in which church staff and volunteers can build awareness—categories we can use to start conversations with families about how to help their youth engage in meaningful ways as well as theological reasons to frame why it all matters. When we grow in our awareness of what could be a barrier preventing someone from joining our worship community, we begin the journey of removing barriers and finding creative ways to accommodate all of God's children.

I (Laura) actively serve as an advocate for my son. I called ahead before all our church visits and was upfront about the challenges that would come with us through the door. Not all parents are as forthcoming. Sometimes the needs of an individual are less visible than those in my son. Sometimes a teen arrives for youth group on their own or as the guest of a peer, and a youth pastor finds themself building a plane as they fly it, learning how to minister to that teen through some measure of trial and error. But because welcoming matters in the business of youth ministry, it is essential for youth pastors to build their toolbox with tools of compassion and wisdom to accommodate every teen who comes through their doors.

As coauthors, our investment in this topic is personal. We write to equip youth pastors, including our own youth pastors, who have a heart for loving God's teens and preteens. The church can effectively and practically welcome teens who have experienced trauma or who have a diagnosed disability: youth on the margins.

A Few Important Notes: Abuse Prevention and Permissions

A few notes are in order about the stories and recommendations in this book. In all cases, the recommendations and best practices recommended here should be conditioned by the reader's church or organization's abuse prevention policies. We ask the reader to carefully apply ideas given here through the lens of protecting teens, volunteers, and staff by following best practices and organizational policies in this area. For example, any suggestion for one-on-one mentoring does not mean the child is left alone with a lone adult.

Also, all our stories come with permission of those involved, including our own children. Names and identifying details have often been changed to protect privacy.

Outline of This Book

The book is laid out in three sections: theory, practices, and pearls of wisdom.

Part 1: Theory—Foundations and Need

Part 1 outlines the motivation for ministry to those on the margins through theological and sociological lenses. It sets the foundation for the methods in part 2 and the issues in part 3. Chapter 1 is a call to reach youth with trauma, with disabilities, and in foster care. It outlines the missional nature of youth ministry and its potential to reinvigorate the church's mission to those who live on the margins of society and the church. Chapter 2 calls us to the margins and offers definitions that can sharpen our vision to see the scope and impact of trauma and disability on teens. Chapter 3 focuses on the theology of the *imago Dei*, the image of God, and begins to show how our theology impacts practice. Chapter 4 addresses sin and suffering for those who serve teens with a disability or trauma. It outlines a brief theology of disability and then develops theological principles into axioms that can guide our ministry practices. Chapter 5 discusses the place of hospitality and extending God's welcome as a fundamental orientation for ministry to teens. It also outlines a series of common tensions and mistakes that waylay hospitality and threaten a healthy philosophy of ministry.

Part 2: Practices and Programs

Part 2 of this book addresses the practical methods and needs of a ministry that serves teens on the margins. Chapter 6 discusses and describes trauma, adverse childhood experiences, and related issues. Here you will find five pillars of trauma-informed care for ministry to teens.

Chapter 7 outlines four common approaches or models of ministry: "zero," "the 1:1," "separate space," and "hybrid." Each of the four is described and evaluated for strengths and weaknesses in various contexts. Chapters 8 and 9 address welcoming teens into a physical space (8) and program (9). Each chapter offers numerous suggestions and helpful information for creating a trauma- and disability-informed facility and programming.

Part 3: Pearls of Wisdom—Topics and Tactics

Part 3 offers topics and tactics. These pearls of wisdom each address a very specific question, need, situation, or ministry context. Here you will find an easy reference for many common issues as you develop a ministry for teens on the margins. Vitally important information on how to refer teens for counseling, help siblings of children with disabilities, teach, and manage permissions are just a few of the practical nuggets in this section.

Our prayer is that you learn to think differently using good theology and research in part 1. In part 2 you will learn to practice trauma-informed ministry that impacts teens and makes space for all teens. In part 3 you can find quick-reference wisdom and answers to tricky and common questions. Let's dive in.

PART 1

Theory—Foundations and Need

1

Who Is in the Boat?

> We men and women are all in the same boat, upon a stormy sea. We owe to each other a terrible and tragic loyalty.
>
> G. K. Chesterton, *The Collected Works of G. K. Chesterton*, vol. 28

When I (Laura) was in high school, I was part of a close-knit youth group of about a dozen. One summer, when we were doing some mission work at a camp, we got into an argument. Everyone was tired, and tempers flared. After dinner, our youth pastor took the group on a pontoon boat ride on the lake. Perhaps he thought it would be soothing, but the argument raged on. Relationships faced irreparable damage, and our youth pastor realized it was time to step in. Out in the middle of the large lake, he stopped the engine and tucked the boat key into his pocket. When we asked what he was doing, he stated, "It is time to settle the issue, and we are not going back to shore until it is finished."

Several of my peers discussed jumping overboard and swimming to shore, but very quickly everyone realized the gravity of the situation. We had a wonderful group dynamic, and this argument was chiseling away at its integrity. On that pontoon boat, one by one, each of us was given a turn to voice our thoughts and feelings while everyone else remained silent. Soon, it became evident that the feelings of some had been overlooked, and the voices of the more timid had been squelched; all of us soon remembered that at the end of the day, we dearly loved each other. While it felt like eternity, about ninety minutes spent floating on Sawyer Lake called our youth group to account. We realized that every person in our community mattered. Together, we worked to create a plan that was agreeable to all and honored all. When the pontoon boat finally pulled up to the dock, the call to live at peace was cemented in. "Pontooning it" became a common phrase in the youth group. Anytime tensions flared, someone would suggest it might be time to pontoon it again, reminding everyone that we were all in the boat together.

Some of the magic on that pontoon boat was a coming-of-age story, one in which youth group members began to step beyond their egocentric mindsets. However, the story also has a clear parallel to the broader church today. The church lives out its calling in real time, and given the pace of life, we sometimes overlook the feelings and needs of those in our community: maybe someone who has come through our doors, or maybe someone who has yet to approach because they are not quite sure they are welcome. A local congregation does not typically have the opportunity to board a pontoon and spend time on a lake, although we may know some elder boards that might benefit from this method occasionally. Just as the youth group failed to pause and notice the needs of fellow members, sometimes the church does the same. Together we can learn to listen, disciple, and reach teens. The following pages will equip and inform pastors, youth ministries, and parents as they work with teens on the margins.

Prophetic Youth Ministry

Youth ministry often serves as a pioneer of the church, noticing needs or going to places and engaging people the church might otherwise choose to avoid. Young people are frequently at the margins of both society and religion. In the past, to reach kids in their spaces, youth pastors would take up activities that were at the time deemed "morally dubious"—like skateboarding, rap, or video games—and spend late Friday nights at football games. These formerly shocking ministry activities have now become commonplace, to the benefit of the church.

Christ describes the church as made up of aliens and strangers (Heb. 11:13). However, the church should not see as strangers those who are orphaned or disabled, or who present themselves in socially atypical ways. Atypical people should feel at home in the body of Christ and a local congregation. As such, the church's work with youth has continuously sought to broaden the boundaries, expand the table, and welcome all who need to hear the message of Jesus. Hope, family, and inclusion are central to the gospel and the ministry of nurture with teens. This work of including and welcoming youth has often required leaders, shepherds, volunteers, and parents to work outside the normal structures of the church: beyond the walls and out onto the sidewalks, the alleys, and the byways. The stranger and the alien are familiar in the prophetic work of youth ministry.

The prophets of the Old Testament called the people of Israel back into alignment with right belief and practice. They were not always popular for this message and call. Being a prophet is often a dangerous and challenging task. Today, youth workers sometimes find themselves thrust outside the walls by the church itself. Youth ministry can become too difficult, costly, or uncomfortable for some in the pews. At a youth conference talk, the late youth ministry pioneer Mike Yaconelli shared the story of a local congregation in which "the elders were shocked to see the junior high kids sitting on the curb, reading their Bible and smoking. I'm thinking to myself, *If I were in that church, I'd bring in that youth worker and say, 'I don't know what you're doing, but you deserve a raise if you can get kids who are smoking to read the Bible!'*"[1] Even when the church ignores or is hostile to needy teens, again and again youth workers go to where the church is not yet present and seek after the sheep. Unfortunately, in our experience, elders are more likely to reprimand a youth pastor for teens smoking near the church than to resource or encourage a creative, effective, and inclusive ministry model.

I (Mike) once held an event during which some teens in gangs wrote with markers on bathroom stalls in church. I often present this scenario to church leaders in training events and conversations. Church leaders responding to the scenario are happy that a youth pastor is reaching teens but almost always suggest that the youth pastor would be better off "reaching them somewhere else." After more than a decade of discussions, the responses still surprise me. The elders regularly suggest reining in the youth pastor or renting the YMCA and doing ministry there instead of in the church building. Conflict created by effective ministry is an unfortunate pattern for those who reach to the margins.

However, by rejecting pioneers in this way, the church may give itself a gift by marginalizing people working with those on the margins. The physical structures, patterns, and expectations circumscribing the typical churchgoer no longer confine these leaders. God's mission forces the church to change, adjust, and become more in line with the broader work of God. Youth ministry has often been at the margins, seeking those who are unreached or even considered unreachable.

We suspect that you care deeply about youth—all youth. We suspect you are one of those people who reach out to the margins. You also likely have some specific needs and concerns in mind. This book is for you.

1. Mike Yaconelli, "Mike Yaconelli Tribute," posted October 30, 2013, by Youth Specialties, YouTube, 4:22–4:41, https://youtu.be/n5zIgH17tzQ?t=262.

Defining the Margins

The two largest unreached people groups in the United States are those with disabilities and those in foster care. While youth ministry, at times, has led the charge to reach those on the margins, there remains much room to grow. Chapter 2 will carefully define disability, mental health, and foster care. Here in chapter 1, we will outline the needs associated with and prevalence of disabilities, mental health conditions, and foster care placements among adolescents in the US. According the Centers for Disease Control and Prevention, 28.7 percent of US adults have a diagnosable disability.[2] Further, as reported by the Substance Abuse and Mental Health Services Administration in 2023, 23.1 percent of US adults—59.3 million people—experienced mental illness in the previous year.[3] The significant overlap between these groups compounds related concerns and complexities. Church attendance is significantly lower among those with disabilities or mental health conditions. Additionally, families of those with disabilities also are less likely to attend church.[4] These loved ones and their families, even when taking into account the overlap between disability and mental health, constitute a significant minority of the US population and an even higher proportion of teens. In 2022, "an estimated 49.5% of adolescents had any mental disorder. Of adolescents with any mental disorder, an estimated 22.2% had severe impairment and/or distress."[5] The occurrence of mental health disorders in the US touches half of all teens.

Those affected by trauma are another significant population. A trauma response can negatively affect physical growth, child development, relationships, reasoning, and moral decision-making.[6] Trauma tends to spread and manifest

2. National Center on Birth Defects and Developmental Disabilities, "Disability Impacts All of Us," infographic, Disability and Health Data System, U.S. Centers for Disease Control and Prevention, April 14, 2025, https://www.cdc.gov/disability-and-health/articles-documents/disability-impacts-all-of-us-infographic.html.

3. *Key Substance Use and Mental Health Indicators in the United States: Results from the 2022 National Survey on Drug Use and Health* (HHS Publication No. PEP23-07-01-006, NSDUH Series H-58), Center for Behavioral Health Statistics and Quality, Substance Abuse and Mental Health Services Administration, November 2023, https://www.samhsa.gov/data/report/2022-nsduh-annual-national-report.

4. Erik W. Carter, Michael Tuttle, Emilee Spann, Charis Ling, and Tiffany B. Jones, "Addressing Accessibility Within the Church: Perspectives of People with Disabilities," *Journal of Religion and Health* 62, no. 4 (2023): 2474–95, https://doi.org/10.1007/s10943-022-01508-6.

5. Kathleen Ries Merikangas, Jian-ping He, Marcy Burstein, et al., "Lifetime Prevalence of Mental Disorders in U.S. Adolescents: Results from the National Comorbidity Survey Replication–Adolescent Supplement (NCS-A)," *Journal of the American Academy of Child and Adolescent Psychiatry* 49, no. 10 (October 2010): 980–89, https://doi.org/10.1016/j.jaac.2010.05.017.

6. Melissa T. Merrick, Derek C. Ford, Katie A. Ports, et al., "*Vital Signs:* Estimated Proportion of Adult Health Problems Attributable to Adverse Childhood Experiences and Implications for Prevention—25 States, 2015–2017," *Morbidity and Mortality Weekly Report*

in a variety of unpredictable and often unrelated ways. It can cause chronic and recurring physical issues, even incapacitating a child or adult.[7] Trauma often leads to behaviors and risk-taking that lead to other mental, physical, relational, or legal problems.[8] There is no current count of the number of children and youth experiencing trauma, but the effects can be overwhelming.

For a final set of statistics, we will consider foster care. For the past five years, the number of children in foster care in the US has ranged from 328,947 to 407,332.[9] According to the Bureau of Justice Statistics, more than 17 percent of incarcerated adults have been in the foster-care system or lived in a mental health facility, group home, or residential treatment facility.[10] About 70 percent of young men and 40 percent of young women who exit foster care as legal adults are arrested at least once by age 26.[11] A thirteen-year-old boy in foster care has a 1 percent chance of being adopted and an 82 percent chance of arrest, conviction, or incarceration by age 18.[12] By definition, every child entering the foster system has significant trauma due to death of a parent, abuse, or abandonment.

In summary, trauma, mental health conditions, and disability affect tens of millions of teens—and tens of millions of others when considering the

---

68, no. 44 (2019): 999–1005; Jack P. Shonkoff and Andrew S. Garner, "The Lifelong Effects of Early Childhood Adversity and Toxic Stress," *Pediatrics* 129, no. 1 (2012), https://doi.org/10.1542/peds.2011-2663.

7. P. P. Schnurr, J. S. Wachen, B. L. Green, and S. Kaltman, "Trauma Exposure, PTSD, and Physical Health," in *Handbook of PTSD: Science and Practice*, 3rd ed., ed. M. J. Friedman, T. M. Keane, and P. A. Resick (Guilford, 2021), 462–82.

8. R. F. Anda, J. B. Croft, V. J. Felitti, et al., "Adverse Childhood Experiences and Smoking During Adolescence and Adulthood," *Journal of the American Medical Association* 282, no. 17 (1999): 1652–58, https://jamanetwork.com/journals/jama/fullarticle/192056; S. R. Dube, R. F. Anda, V. J. Felitti, V. J. Edwards, and J. B. Croft, "Adverse Childhood Experiences and Personal Alcohol Abuse as an Adult," *Addictive Behaviors* 27, no. 5 (2002):713–25; C. S. Rodgers, A. J. Lang, C. Laffaye, et al., "The Impact of Individual Forms of Childhood Maltreatment on Health Behavior," *Child Abuse and Neglect* 28, no. 5 (2004): 575–86, https://doi.org/10.1016/j.chiabu.2004.01.002.

9. "The AFCARS Dashboard," Children's Bureau, Administration for Children and Families, U.S. Department of Health and Human Services, 2025, https://tableau-public.acf.gov/views/afcars_dashboard_main_page/mainpage.

10. "Survey of Prison Inmates Data Analysis Tool" (state and federal prisoners; socioeconomic characteristics; ever lived in foster home, agency, or institution), Bureau of Justice Statistics, January 8, 2016, https://spi-data.bjs.ojp.gov/dashboard. See also Emily D. Buehler and Tracy L. Snell, "Survey of Prison Inmates," Bureau of Justice Statistics, January 8, 2016, https://bjs.ojp.gov/data-collection/survey-prison-inmates-spi.

11. Mark Courtney, Amy Dworsky, Adam Brown, Colleen Cary, Kara Love, and Vanessa Vorhies, *Midwest Evaluation of the Adult Functioning of Former Foster Youth: Outcomes at Age 26* (Chapin Hall at the University of Chicago, 2011), 93, https://www.chapinhall.org/wp-content/uploads/Midwest-Eval-Outcomes-at-Age-26.pdf.

12. Courtney et al., *Midwest Evaluation*, 93.

impact on immediate family. The intersection of trauma, mental health, and disability is the new margin, the church's next mission field.

Why Consider Disability and Trauma Together?

This book will engage practical ministry for youth with disabilities, trauma, or both. Our (Mike's and Laura's) children are in that third category. We have both fostered and adopted children with physical disabilities, mental health conditions, and social disabilities; our children have also experienced loss of family and other trauma. Because our and many other families' stories intersect with both disability and trauma, we are deeply concerned about the church's work in these two areas. Our children need a church that is wider and willing to go to the margins and be welcoming.

Why consider disability and trauma together? First, we believe that ministry to these groups is the pressing and unmet need in our culture and the church. Ministry to this group may be one of the best possibilities for revitalizing the church's work. As stated above, the margins of trauma, mental health, and disability represent over half of the total adolescent population in the US.

Second, disability, mental health, and foster care often overlap. All children in foster care experience significant trauma. It is also true that many also have mental health challenges, developmental delays/disabilities, and physical challenges. Fetal exposure to drugs—more common for children in foster care[13]—can result in daily experience with disability and trauma for a teen.

Third, this topic is deeply personal. We have both fostered and adopted children who experience disabilities and trauma due to the environment they once lived in or the choices their birth mother made during pregnancy. A counselor with significant experience working with children in foster care explained to me (Laura) that as a general rule, children come into care delayed two years behind their peers. In many situations, ground can be made up with time in a loving and supportive home where the child's needs are being met. Children of traumas such as abuse or neglect may always lag behind their peers and need extra support into adulthood. "In contrast to the estimated 4% to 10% prevalence of developmental delay among children in the general population, published rates of delay among young children in foster care are reported to be as high as 60%, with 57% exhibiting language delays, 33% showing cognitive problems, 31% displaying gross motor difficulties, and 10%

13. Lenora Marcellus and Dorothy Badry, "Infants, Children, and Youth in Foster Care with Prenatal Substance Exposure: A Synthesis of Two Scoping Reviews," *International Journal of Developmental Disabilities* 69, no. 2: 265–90, https://doi:10.1080/20473869.2021.1945890.

experiencing growth problems."[14] We believe that a meaningful relationship with Jesus Christ can be a significant component of healing for the children and youth who have come through our homes. We want to see churches equipped so they can effectively be the hands and feet of Jesus to kids like those who have been part of our families!

Many people live on the margins in some way. Here, we are not attempting to address every marginalized or at-risk group. Conversations should be occurring about violence, poverty, incarceration, racism, and many more areas. The current focus will be on two primary groups: youth with disabilities and youth with trauma. This margin is at the center of our work as the body of Christ. It is our belief that youth ministry at this margin can transform the entire church.

The Mission of God and the Margins

Pursuit. Hound of heaven. Searching. God is a seeking God, one who watches and runs to the wayward son. God describes his own character toward the marginalized in Ezekiel 34:16: "I will search for the lost and bring back the strays. I will bind up the injured and strengthen the weak." He came to seek and save. God's vision of the church rightly instills our own vision with bringing, binding, and strengthening imagery. The church is to be like God, as the vehicle of God's work in the world. *Missio Dei* is a theological term for God's mission to the world. Missiologist Van Sanders writes that "when kept in the context of the Scriptures, *missio Dei* correctly emphasizes that God is the initiator of His mission to redeem through the Church a special people for Himself from all of the peoples (τα εθνη) of the world. He sent His Son for this purpose and He sends the Church into the world with the message of the gospel for the same purpose."[15] It is striking that God is looking for a special people drawn from all people. Yet there is an unfortunate irony. Those who have functional support needs—which were once called "special needs"—such as youth experiencing a physical or mental exceptionality, foster care, or trauma, are not widely present in the church.

What if we considered foster care and disability to be as important as the 10/40 Window? While most unreached people groups live within a rectangle

14. Laurel K. Leslie, Jeanne N. Gordon, Katina Lambros, Kamila Premji, John Peoples, and Kristin Gist, "Addressing the Developmental and Mental Health Needs of Young Children in Foster Care," *Journal of Developmental and Behavioral Pediatrics* 26, no. 2 (2005): 140–51.

15. Van Sanders, "The Mission of God and the Local Church," in *Pursuing the Mission of God in Church Planting: The Missional Church in North America*, ed. John M. Bailey (North American Mission Board of the Southern Baptist Convention, 2006), 24.

between latitudes 10 and 40 degrees north, stretching from North Africa to Japan, there is a population of tens of millions nearby, including our neighbors, some of whom may never enter ministry buildings or programs. Those on the margins are often excluded systemically, a deep sadness and shame of the church today. One of the most unreached groups in the world are living down the street and should be just as important as those in the 10/40 Window. Our integrity and obedience as disciples are at stake if we send missionaries and money to distant continents while thinking we can ignore uncomfortable margins at home. These people are also God's mission; he desires to draw them to himself through the church. God's desire for the margins is not a second mission, a special mission, or simply a part of the primary mission. All people are at the core of God's work. There are no margins for him. God will not exclude any people group from being his people.

A Call to the Church

Historically, the church has been working on the margins, supporting rights and advocating for justice and freedom. In this tradition, we can be primary agents in the work of transforming the culture to see all people as valuable, irrespective of money, race, or nation. All people are eligible to be part of society and God's kingdom. If nothing else, all people should marvel at Jesus, for he has transformed the concept of dignity by welcoming all people as part of the human family and inviting all into the family of heaven. We should rightly credit the historical church with helping revolutionize the world's view of women as more than property and taking a stand in support of civil rights. Consider Christian leaders such as Martin Luther King Jr., William Wilberforce, and Ida B. Wells. We remember them for their bold application of Christian belief to confront social dysfunction, to battle for justice, and to embrace marginalized groups.

Unfortunately, the modern church is now behind broader culture in engaging specific at-risk populations. We have withdrawn from the marginalized. The church needs new pioneers to transform itself, just as it transformed itself in the past. The world still needs youth ministry: a youth ministry of the old kind, one that expands our horizons to the margins.

The above observations are not new. Countless people have called the church to return to a robustly Christian witness by working with "the least of these" (Matt. 25:40), and many amazing theological,[16] philosophical, and

16. Wesley W. Ellis and Michael D. Langford, eds., *Embodying Youth: Exploring Youth Ministry and Disability* (Routledge, 2020).

anthropological[17] resources highlight a strong Christian tradition and foundation in engaging orphans and people with illnesses or disabilities. The church is intended to care for those at the margins. This concern is evident from the times of the Old Testament, through the New Testament and early church, to today. We hope to fulfill this intent by mobilizing a group that we believe is most likely to cause change within the entire church, to stretch the church's imagination and practice caring for those who are the least cared for. Youth ministry's pioneering spirit has the vital potential to transform the church today by acting on the creative and evangelistic impulse at the core of the youth ministry movement.

The goal of this text is not simply ministry to people on the margins but also ministry *for* and *with* them. The church is weaker without their gifts, and they have significant contributions ordained by God for the body, a primary topic of chapter 3.

A Ministry with the Margins

Again, ministry is not only *for* but *with* people. David's Promise, a local congregation's day ministry for adults with developmental disabilities, illustrates how. A Michigan community had an excellent special education system, a system so good that families would move from outlying areas so their children and young adults could benefit. However, once the adults aged out of programming, many with a disability had no support and nothing else to do with their time. Their parents, many at retirement age, were forced back into the role of full-time caregiving. When David's Promise began, the vision was not simply to be a caregiving service. A core value was to ensure that participants had regular opportunities to participate in meaningful ministry. As the leadership team brainstormed how to do ministry *with* people with disabilities, several beautiful ideas were born. One idea was rooted in the church's biweekly food distribution program, which served hundreds of families in the county. While the church was able to secure bulk quantities of nonperishables, it was unable to provide families with fresh produce. Perhaps the adults in David's Promise could plant and tend gardens with the intent of donating the food they grew. Several of the group members used wheelchairs or had mobility issues, so kneeling in a traditional garden was not feasible. However, a wheelchair or chair can reach raised beds, and so members of the church built raised garden boxes.

17. John Swinton, *Disciples and Friends: Investigations in Disability, Dementia, and Mental Health; Essays in Honor of John Swinton*, ed. Armand Léon van Ommen and Brian Brock (Baylor University Press, 2022).

The adult participants at David's Promise, along with their leaders, now plant and tend to their vegetables throughout the summer months every year. When the harvest comes, they share with the recipients of the food pantry. The congregation is better able to meet its community's needs because it engages and involves those with disabilities. Conversely, this scaffolding allows a group of adults with functional support needs to contribute to their church and their community. These adults are actively engaged in service and outreach to their community as part of the local congregation. They are not simply a population to serve but co-laborers in the work of Christ in that location. The result is meaningful ministry and fulfillment of an unmet need.

The church should also be in ministry *for* people. Access and justice are often withheld, either intentionally or inadvertently, from children in foster care or with a disability. Isolation and lack of opportunity are rampant, often for the whole family. Several years ago, the Center for Autism Spectrum Enrichment (CASE) invited me (Laura) to bring my children to participate in a group organized by Terri Pardee, a university psychology professor and colleague who had adopted children with major trauma and therefore had personal experience raising children with significant support needs. The formation of this group was influenced by Pardee's hypothesis, supported by her experience in the field of psychology and as a parent, that many children and youth on the autism spectrum have limited opportunity for extracurricular activities. Families felt isolated because of their children's and youths' needs, and the parents stood to benefit from teaching and support. Through CASE, Pardee empowered college students to engage with children and youth on the autism spectrum. CASE pairs youth and children one-on-one with college students in a group setting to participate in games, snacks, a Bible lesson, and activities through which they practice social and emotional skills. The one-on-one relationships allow individualized attention to needs within the group setting. Older disabled youth participate in an additional life skills curriculum. While the children and youth engage in these programs, parents meet with Pardee or other local experts to explore relevant topics.[18]

Numbers grew quickly after the group's inception as the community responded to CASE. Pardee recruited more college students to facilitate the growing numbers, and as she did, she determined to expand the program's reach. While initially focused on those on the autism spectrum, Pardee chose to extend the invitation to families whose children had experienced major trauma.

18. While she has not published her experiences with CASE, Pardee has given a number of presentations sharing ways in which the group positively supported children, youth, and their families.

This is what prompted my (Laura's) invitation. My boys, who were five and six at the time, had been adopted two years prior from a tumultuous foster care background. At first, I questioned the CASE curriculum's applicability, as my younger son had not yet been diagnosed with autism. Pardee assured me that the program was very much applicable. As mentioned, major trauma often results in significant delays in social and emotional areas, just as autism can. Children with trauma either are currently in an unhealthy situation that is delaying their development or are expending so much energy navigating past trauma that, in many cases, they trail behind peers physically, emotionally, or socially. Pardee asked me if my children would benefit from social- and emotional-learning lessons and the mentoring of a college student. The response was a quick yes! The overlap of needs between disability and trauma was evident. Trauma and disability often go hand in hand, and the church often engages with both at the same time unknowingly.

Youth who have experienced significant trauma and youth with a physical or mental health challenge certainly have different types of needs. Yet the overlap of trauma and disability produces specific needs and the necessity for special care. These youth need a little extra grace to engage alongside peers. The way that grace is packaged varies from person to person, but it is a package of grace nonetheless. Further chapters here will equip you to extend grace, package love, and offer support as you invite youth to come aboard your boat. Extra grace, love, and support often create powerful moments of the gospel in real life, making Christ visible.

Making Christ Visible: Lived Theology

Here is an illustration of how theological truth can be made physically visible. Foster children often have no choice whom they live with, what school they go to, or whether they get to see their parents. Many foster children have control over only one thing: what they will or will not eat. This has led to some "fun" situations in my (Mike's) household and a few unusual piles of food found in bedrooms. Foster children may take food they want to eat now and, instead of eating it, stash it away in case the food supply eventually runs out. Called "hoarding," this is usually a response to neglect. One formerly unhoused teen began hoarding food when he started to live in a stable home. His new family was significantly wealthy and owned a host of restaurants. When they discovered the hidden food, the father drove the teen to one of his restaurants, introduced him to the manager, and told his employees that if his son was to come to the restaurant, he could eat anything he wanted, free. He was a big teen; free food was certainly a substantial investment. However, not only did this act stop the food hoarding, but it also embodies the gospel. Imagine the Good Father saying, "All this is mine; this is my child; all that is mine belongs to him." God says to his people, "You will be completely taken care of, without exception and with abundance." The Father then asks those of us who have received this inheritance to do likewise. Making a Taco Bell run after youth group for snacky teens is not the only way to fulfill this command. Our call is even more important: a call to full acceptance and advocacy of those on the margins.

Powerless children need advocates who care, listen, advocate, understand, and fight for the resources and rights of children in their community, school, and local congregation. Showing care could be as simple as adjusting the physical layout of a youth room to allow access for those with a physical disability. Listening could mean creating a safe place to share their story. Advocating may be providing a presence in a court hearing as the spiritual caregiver to a teen facing a juvenile court. Understanding might mean training and familiarizing people with these needs so that cultures can change and everyone can have a place on the boat (a turn of phrase that will be further explored). Fighting might mean helping a foster family find a court-appointed special advocate (CASA) who can speak directly to a judge when a state social worker seems to be promoting an agenda that is counter to the best interests of the child.

Four Barriers: Ableism, Individualism, Immunity to Change, and Scarcity

We need a perspective change. Clearly, there are some barriers to ministry among those with disability or trauma. While later chapters will engage specific models and techniques, a perspective change is necessary first if those models are to be fruitful. Here we will address four specific problematic perspectives that must be adjusted prior to creating or launching programs. These assumptions can be addressed through biblical teaching and preaching that challenge the biases present in a local congregation. The following four barriers are great enemies of the inclusion of those on the margins: ableism, individualism, immunity to change, and scarcity.

Barrier 1: Ableism—Same Lake, Different Boat

It is common to hear the statement "Everyone is in the same boat." This phrase conveys the idea that all humans have a fundamental set of needs, a shared core of humanity—that no matter the differences, we can and should identify with one another. It likely intends to highlight people's common traits, their shared human experiences, and the need for solidarity across differences. As mentioned earlier, Christianity has been one of the most significant forces in the world elevating the value and place of all people. However, this amazing and necessary perspective that values every person may make it difficult to see the individual needs of each person.

"Why are all the beautiful people always up front leading in youth group?" I (Mike) had a youth pastor friend who was asked this question by a teen in his youth group. Initially my friend was defensive. After reflection and likely a bit of work by the Holy Spirit, he was crushed. The popular, the lovely, and the so-called normal had become the norm for the face of the ministry. This is an example of ableism, or discrimination in favor of nondisabled people. Ableism is the first barrier that requires a perspective shift when considering marginalized people. Ableism often creates an expectation of "normal" that does not allow for variance and variety. A youth program that is ableist, even though it is likely otherwise designed for care and safety, might reinjure teens who are already excluded from other aspects of society. What is meant to help teens can instead make painfully clear that not everyone is in the same boat. My youth pastor friend had created a culture and program in his ministry that expected all teens to look and behave the same. Instead of including marginalized teens, he had only allowed those who fit a particular social model or level of physical attractiveness to be in leadership.

Stephanie Hubach uses a metaphor to describe her experience with her two sons, one of whom has Down syndrome. Hubach suggests that "We are all in the same boat" is inaccurate if used to state that all people have the same experiences. She suggests that many people may be on the same lake, but not all are in the same boat. Experiences and capabilities among teens are very different. "We share a common story but the details of our life experiences and our life circumstances may vary significantly," she says.[19] The human story is essentially the same but not experientially the same. Ableism dismisses the reality of those we are trying to serve.

Barrier 2: Individualism—Exclusion or Embrace

Individual experience currently reigns supreme. This cultural emphasis on individualism is the second great barrier to perspective change. Moral codes no longer define *good* or *true*. Not even power or money guide individuals most forcefully anymore. The idea that "I am the captain of my own boat" is a core cultural tenet. Something is considered *good* if it is good for me, if I benefit, or if I think it true. Those outside me are at best useful for my

19. Stephanie O. Hubach, *Same Lake, Different Boat: Coming Alongside People Touched by Disability* (P&R, 2006), 37.

own ends; at worst, they hinder me in my pursuit of my ends. Friends give "likes" or "follows," making friendship a commodity for my own desires or enrichment.

Consider what this view does to those who are considered "inconvenient" or who are marginalized. Rampant individualism threatens not just those outside the norm but the entire social order. Society does not exist as an abstraction. Individuals, families, and associations make up real relationships. When individuals act solely in favor of their own interests, their own boat, they slip into a decadence that undermines all social relationships in favor of personal good. Yale professor Miroslav Volf states that "*otherness*, the simple fact of being different in some way, has come to be defined as in and of itself evil."[20] Most human atrocities begin by dehumanizing the other, all in favor of personal benefit.

This decadence is not benign. Volf states that "it may not be too much to claim that the future of our world will depend on how we deal with identity and difference. The issue is urgent. The ghettos and battlefields throughout the world—in the living rooms, in inner cities, or on the mountain ranges—testify indisputably to its importance."[21] Hubach explains that in search of comfort and affinity, we see ourselves in our own lake, protected and purposefully isolated.[22] Instead of reaching out, the church acts as a protection against the outside world. Most people resist any difference that disrupts and challenges the mirage. Those who have experienced trauma or have a mental health concern are often not comfortable in the church because the church is not comfortable with them.

Disability and trauma are difficult challenges to our complacency and identity, to our very sense of self. The church can seek exposure to the hard realities of those who think and act in ways we cannot comprehend. Instead of exclusion, the call is to embrace our enemies. The call to love is difficult. How can we love an enemy if we cannot even create space for the unlovely or the awkward? The call is to "welcome one another, therefore, just as Christ has welcomed you" (Rom. 15:7 NRSVA). Chapter 5 will address a theology of hospitality in relation to those on the margins that attempts to counter our own sin and culturally driven individualism. One way to look at the margins is by asking the question "Who gets to be in the boat?" The church is not a group of isolated islands or independent sailors charting their own ruggedly individualistic courses.

20. Miroslav Volf, *Exclusion and Embrace: A Theological Exploration of Identity, Otherness, and Reconciliation* (Abingdon, 1996), back jacket copy.

21. Volf, *Exclusion*, 14.

22. Hubach, *Same Lake, Different Boat*, 37.

Barrier 3: Immunity to Change—Built to Include

Beth Guckenberger, director of Back2Back Ministries, tells a story about a foster home she engaged with in her work with orphans and vulnerable children. The foster parents were patient, caring, and persistent. The home was fun and had amazing relationships and rigid structure, with scheduled family time, homework time, dinnertime, craft time, potty time . . . you get the idea. A new boy in the home resisted both the care and the rigorous scheduling. Two weeks after placement in the home, at dinner one day, the boy hurt another child. The family lost control, likely from pent-up frustration. When staff showed up to help, some of the children were yelling and things were flying through the air: There was total pandemonium. Everyone was in chaos. In the middle sat this boy, still at the table and finally calm. Smiling. A worker asked him what he was experiencing, and he said, "I did not understand this family, but *this* I understand." Chaos was his native language.

In many cases, we tend to think we are bringing a gift to those to whom we minister. However, this child exposed faults in the family system. The helpful organization and family rules were keeping chaos at bay. The family had developed a highly refined defense mechanism that helped insulate its members from the pain and difficulties that life presents. Precision, predictability, plans, and process were all in place. Normally these types of defense mechanisms are good and allow us to function, holding back known and unknown threats and uncertainty. Yet these defense mechanisms also immunize us against change, fear, and pain. Unrestrained, such defense mechanisms can prevent growth and even kill the family or group through the very methods intended to protect it.

Eminent Harvard researcher Robert Kegan calls this "immunity to change."[23] We know from personal experience that foster care, disability, and trauma are very difficult experiences to engage. Yet the margins hold a hidden gift. In the midst of the chaos they sometimes involve, we can see our own systems more clearly. We have been coping to compensate for a weakness that must now be addressed. Confronted with who we are, we must repent and change. Without this confrontation, we continue to inoculate ourselves against the growth and wholeness God offers. Much like the family that kept chaos at bay through planning and order, we must confront dysfunction hidden under a careful mask. Hubach shares that "90% of people do not know how to act around those with disabilities, and 70% say that they experience fear when

23. Robert Kegan and Lisa Laskow Lahey, *Immunity to Change: How to Overcome It and Unlock Potential in Yourself and Your Organization* (Harvard Business Press, 2009).

they see persons with disabilities."[24] What if youth ministry on the margins could help people confront their fear or, more importantly, obey Jesus's command, "Do not be afraid" (Matt. 10:28 NIV 1984)? We must embrace different values that create different systems, moving us away from defensive postures to welcoming ones.

Barrier 4: Scarcity—The Boat Is Bigger

One of my (Mike's) favorite movies is *Hotel Rwanda*. Neither a lighthearted nor a peppy movie, it is a tale of genocide. This story journeys with a Rwandan hotel manager named Paul who moves radically away from a self-protective stance during the Rwandan genocide of 1994. Initially Paul hoards favors to protect those in his inner circle. Early in the movie, he is completely unwilling to expand the boundaries of his world to accept and identify with those who are not in his immediate circle of family. Ultimately, exposure to extreme need forces open his heart and hands. Paul's responses to the extreme danger in Kigali move from careful protection of those closest to him to risk-taking on behalf of others, from hoarding resources to irresponsible generosity. He moves from claiming that the life-saving space in the hotel he manages is limited to understanding that "there is always room." Like Paul earlier in the film, maybe we do not engage the margins because we are afraid there is not enough room in our boats.

A scarcity perspective, the fourth barrier to ministry at the margins, is a belief that there is not enough to go around. Anthropologist George Foster called this type of belief system "the image of the limited good."[25] "The limited good," or a scarcity mindset, is the belief that when one person receives something I need, it limits my ability to receive that good myself. Endless stories tell of people destroying neighbors' crops because those neighbors' crops were so fruitful. The belief that there can only be so much harvest leads to the logical-seeming but incorrect conclusion that when one person succeeds, another must fail. Countless stories also tell of churches turning away from "those kids." I (Mike) have seen elders unable to imagine funding youth outreach while rebuilding a $180,000 church steeple. I have often felt the need to challenge the salvation of those who invest massive quantities of money in buildings while refusing a $500 youth outreach activity, but we often do the same thing in our own ways of thinking.

24. Hubach, *Same Lake, Different Boat*, 32.

25. George M. Foster, "Peasant Society and the Image of the Limited Good," *American Anthropologist* 67 (1965): 293–315.

Do we see culture as zero-sum, as occupying an environment of scarcity and violence in contested areas? When we adopt this view, we end up in culture wars or stained-glass bunkers from which truth grenades can be thrown, with little risk of upsetting our own lives and experiences. Often the rules of politics are all or nothing. The motto becomes "I cannot win without you losing something." This is also true of politics in the church. Yet playing to win at the cost of the other is very different from playing to change the game. If we are to move to the margins, we must move away from a scarcity mindset. Youth ministry can regain its prophetic voice in this way.

One of my (Mike's) colleagues, Julie Borkin, describes living out of a limited-good or scarcity perspective in a devotional presentation she shared with the faculty at the university:

> And here's the insidious part: in a lot of ways I thought I was being purposeful—working to stay on mission with my job and priorities—but instead I had shifted to creating my own version of what to do and how to do it. I had fallen to a very transactional understanding of God's promise in Isaiah 40:31, "They that wait upon the LORD shall renew their strength" [KJV]—trying to believe that I was waiting on Him but really wanting Him to function as my holy gas pump rather than attending to what it might mean to wait on Him and be captivated by Him, wanting to know Him and be with Him even if it meant that I had to release some [of my programs and definitions of success]. In sum, I stopped being on mission and started being about myself—in fear, in speculation, worrying about the future, stuck in my thinking.[26]

If God is just a "holy gas pump," we cannot experience his effusive generosity. The scarcity mindset holds us captive and promotes conformity to this world instead of alignment with the activity of God. Removing a scarcity mindset requires a renewing of the mind and a shifting of the vision of the work. We must go from program to people, from efficiency to relationship. We must be those who receive as well as being those who give.

Many envision the church as a lifeboat. But whose boat? God's plan to rescue people demands being on the lake and inviting others into the boat. We would like to pose two nuances to this metaphor. First, what if the church today is a rescue ship, but that ship abdicates its responsibility by making a certain kind of person in the lake unwelcome or avoided? That would be a fundamental failure of the mission. Second, what if the very people we think we are rescuing are actually able to rescue us? The margins confront different

26. Julie Borkin, faculty devotional delivered at Taylor University faculty meeting, February 16, 2023, Taylor University, Upland, IN.

abilities, biases, and fears and are powerful teachers as we engage there. Maybe the hand being offered in help is truly being held out to us. God holds out his hand to us through those with disability and trauma.

A Call to the Margins

We must find the courage to get in the boat of God's activity. Maybe our view that we are the rescuers is keeping us from being part of the larger story God is painting. Perfect programs that are not attended or even accessible by those on the margins may exhibit a veneer of success while hiding failure. Ultimately, God's rescue boat is for those of all languages, tribes, abilities, and traumas. Will we get on God's boat or try to build our own? It is time to get in the boat of God's activity in our lives and the world around us. We are going to "pontoon it" together. Welcome to the margins. God has been waiting for us here.

QUESTIONS TO PONDER

1. Reach out to a family in the church that has a teen on the margins. Ask about the ways in which the church has welcomed them, presented barriers, or both.
2. What extracurricular activities are available in your community for teens with disabilities? Are there opportunities for the church to expand existing opportunities or to fill a gap?
3. What is the visitation policy for clergy members and youth pastors in the local youth center, foster home, or detention facility, and what is your church's abuse-prevention policy for such visits? If you were to visit a teen in one of these facilities, what would be your goal as you connect with that youth?
4. If one of your youth group kids were to break their leg, it would be natural to share the injury story. What would it look like, with the individual's permission and guidance, to share the story and explain best supports for teens on the margins?
5. Borrow a pair of crutches or a wheelchair. Begin in the parking lot of your church and explore what it feels like to navigate into the building, to the sanctuary, the restroom, and the youth room. What barriers did you encounter? In what ways could you consult those with a disability to help your space become more accessible?

2

The Call to the Margins

Seeing and Defining the Need

Our goal in this chapter is to help those who shepherd teens move from "ignoring and ignorance" to a place of understanding. First, we will explore the biblical mandate to reach to the margins. Next, we will define and briefly describe foster care, disability, and trauma. Finally, we will consider inclusion, justice, and Americans with Disabilities Act (ADA) compliance. We will close the chapter with a story about Sam, whose experiences with the church led him to embrace his gifts and leadership in the body.

"Open Our Eyes, O Lord"

I would like to confess a biased blindness. However, I (Mike) am not an unobservant person. I ask questions, not accepting status quo. I have lenses I use to see more clearly and help me understand my environment. This understanding has come through international travel and multiple degrees in fields of study, including psychology, sociology, theology, and anthropology. Yet I have still been blind quite regularly. About that kid who was looking for someone to notice them in youth group. That leader who was volunteering because they were lonely and did not really have a passion for discipling teens. My teen daughter telling me that she needed someone to listen and not fix. Blind too many times, I experienced one situation that was memorably shocking.

As a youth pastor in a small rural town of twenty thousand, it was possible to know the hangouts for teens. Each restaurant had its best menu items, and there was the cafe where everyone went after school. I (Mike) also learned the places of hurting and abandonment. I knew where the high school seniors on "work release" would play disc golf and smoke weed before the end of the school day. I knew the family that constantly had at-risk teens couch surfing as they ran from abusive situations. I thought I saw.

Then came Jimmy. Jimmy was a young adult with cognitive impairments who was mostly nonverbal. He wandered into my church one Sunday morning. He seemed a bit lost, and so were we. We did not know what to do with Jimmy, and he could not really tell us why he had come. Ultimately, we learned he lived nearby, and we made sure he made it back to his apartment. His home was practically next to the church. I then discovered it was in a government apartment building that provided housing and services to those with disabilities. This completely floored me. I could see the building from my office, maybe a three-minute walk past the YMCA next door. I had walked daily to my office, past the high school—which was the focus of all my energy—and around a corner to the church building. I spent many hours renting the YMCA for youth events or seeing if we could get 158 bouncy balls simultaneously propelled in a racquetball court. Jimmy's home was literally one of the few large structures in the entire town I had never entered. The residential facility was filled with people who had no access to the church, were often alone, and lived a three-minute walk from our building.

Our church sprang into action. Congregants began to meet the residents in the complex. They would pick them up and walk them to church on Sunday. We saw our congregation begin to develop valuable connections and engage in mutual discovery and participation. There were challenges as well. Our sanctuary was not wheelchair accessible. Our programs were focused on teaching and study, and we had few ways for our newly discovered neighbors to participate. We were very happy to have them join us. Yet while we opened our arms, nothing much changed in the building, our programming, or most importantly, our thinking. On the surface my church was welcoming, but it did not create a space for or remove the barriers to our new congregants' full involvement. In short, we had not seen them for years despite their proximity, and once we knew of their existence, we did not see their needs. Ultimately, we did not see our own need, and we were made poorer.

The Margins Become the Center

Worldwide, more than one billion people live with a disability. Many teens are homeless or face mental health crises. Many Christians do not see nor recognize these people as neighbors. The biblical commission is "Go out quickly into the streets and alleys of the town and bring in the poor, the crippled, the blind and the lame. . . . Go out to the roads and country lanes and compel them to come in, so that my house will be full" (Luke 14:21, 23).

Even a cursory glance at this passage should stun and bring some clear conclusions. A couple of important observations: Here Jesus speaks of his desire that the periphery become the center. He is saying clearly that people on the margins are welcome, they should be sought out, and that his tables and his house will be filled with them.

Contrast Jesus's command to "compel them to come" with our ignorance and laissez-faire approach to disabled and hurting teens. One typical approach to at-risk teens and teens with trauma or disabilities is to respond to each situation as it arises. Some teens' situations can be effectively addressed as they occur. This approach can be somewhat effective as accommodations are created as each situation warrants. However, this approach risks missing Jesus's invitation and urgency noted in Luke 14 above. Simply stating "We don't have any kids who use wheelchairs" does not absolve our programs from the need for accessibility. When a youth program has no wheelchair-using participants, it is likely because the youth room is up a flight of stairs, the program has no easy access or signage, or it offers no reasonable accommodations. "Going out" in urgent obedience is not the same as simply responding to situations and problems as they arise. A bare-minimum response is passive; full obedience is active.

In the verses from Luke, Jesus describes how the parable's banquet host, a metaphor for the Father, will live out his desire to fill the banquet by filling it with those who are outcasts. Jesus relates this parable while attending a different banquet, which he contrasts with the parable's banquet. In Luke 14:12–13, Jesus exhorts those hosting meals or banquets to refrain from inviting the popular and the pampered rich. He commands his listeners instead to invite "the poor, the crippled, the lame, the blind" (14:13). These people would have been social outcasts, literally excluded from public and religious life at that time. Instead, Jesus flips the excluded to the center of his ministry, simply affirming earlier statements of the purpose of his ministry:

> The Spirit of the Lord is on me,
> because he has anointed me
> to proclaim good news to the poor.

> He has sent me to proclaim freedom for the prisoners
> and recovery of sight for the blind,
> to set the oppressed free,
> to proclaim the year of the Lord's favor. (4:18–19)

Luke means for us to see that Jesus intends his ministry to encompass people who are poor, imprisoned, blind, or oppressed (Luke 4:18–19). Jesus harshly critiques those who exclude any of these groups to advance their own social standing and honor (14:12–14). He then presents a vision of the kingdom in which it is populated seemingly solely by people who are poor, disabled, injured, or blind (14:21–23).

Danger and Invitation

Strikingly, Jesus's teaching in Luke is not primarily about disabled people but rather about those who attend the banquet and those who are ultimately locked outside. Though invited, the proud and the rich fail to enter while those on the margins are earnestly sought and brought. This parable can teach us at least two key kingdom ideals: First, we are in danger of missing the banquet. The table is set, the invitations sent, and the exhortation complete. There is a strong implication here that if we are at the table, we are among those who are poor, injured, or disabled. The more we deny the existence and resist the healing of our diseases the more others find the kingdom ahead of us. Second, while the parable's exhortation to "bring in" (Luke 14:21) is directed at the host's servant—a metaphor for an angelic messenger—we too are sent on God's mission as his people. This mission is to make a people for God. We participate in the mission by actively, intentionally, and compellingly bringing the message to those distant from God.

This work on the margins calls us to dangerous and uncertain places. Ministry is reckless and for rebels, modeling this irresponsible love of God. The margins are also the place where we can see God break through our safe and quiet assumptions. God is found in deserts, in the wilderness, and among the outcasts. We must be bold enough to follow. Imagine a student who makes the first move and comes to a youth event. If a student cannot make it up the stairs, we have failed on multiple counts God's imperative to go to the margins and bring them in.

The implications here are paramount. An evaluation of our ministry philosophy and preparedness is in order to ensure we are in alignment with Jesus's values and plan. Are our tables set and ready? Are we creating straight paths for those to come? Are we out on byways and alleys actively seeking those

God has commanded us to find and bring? We have already told of Mike's experience with Jimmy, someone who came to the church when the church was not ready.

Beyond Ignoring and Ignorance: Half the Sky Is Missing

There is "sky" in every direction. Half the sky is beyond our perception because the earth completely and irrevocably blocks our sight. It is rare that I learn what types of things I am unaware of, just like my church did not see Jimmy or his neighbors. I never think about the other half of the sky because it is always hidden from me. I am literally unable to view it or interact with it in any way. It still exists and is vital and beautiful.

Children's ministry expert Scottie May and coauthors state, "In spite of the many accounts in the Gospels of Jesus connecting with 'exceptional' people, people with disabilities are underrepresented in the church."[1] Researcher Erin Raffety completed a study of disabled people in the church and came to a profound conclusion: There are two kinds of approaches to people with disabilities in Christian churches.[2] Groups taking the first approach, representing a majority of churches, simply ignore disabled people because they "do not have any." People with disabilities are a bit "out of sight, out of mind," like they were at my (Mike's) church before we noticed Jimmy. This first perspective is addressed in more detail in chapter 7, where we describe Approach Zero. Rafferty also found in her research that churches that take the second approach try to address the needs of disabled people through programming. The language used is one of inclusion, but the programming is often on the periphery and never incorporates core leadership involvement. Here the church ministers to teens in need, in foster care, or with a diagnosis. Approaching disability or trauma as a programming issue often results in ignorance because we fail to see the real need or the real person behind the need. This perspective is more fully addressed theologically in chapter 3. The image of God certainly calls us beyond ignoring and ignorance. It calls us beyond programming and managing symptoms of a problem to a full-fledged participation, one that goes beyond even inclusion and targets true justice.

The goal is to move from ignorance to inclusion, and from simple inclusion to full justice and full participation. If we desire full justice and participation, we must be aware of the various needs and issues related to disability,

1. Scottie May, Beth Posterski, Catherine Stonehouse, and Linda Cannell, *Children Matter: Celebrating Their Place in the Church, Family, and Community* (Eerdmans, 2005), 312.

2. Erin Raffety, *From Inclusion to Justice: Disability, Ministry, and Congregational Leadership* (Baylor University Press, 2022), 22–23.

trauma, and foster care in youth ministry. The following section will describe and define each of these three areas.

Who Is Disabled?: Defining Disability

Disability, trauma, and foster care are not bounded sets with definable and durable membership. A bounded set draws lines to say something is either "in or out," with no dispute. In contrast, the distinctions between sickness, disease, and disability are often thin or nonexistent. Set theory is helpful here. Set theory describes the way a culture sees boundaries or membership.[3] Disability is sometimes a "fuzzy set," one with no hard boundaries but rather a gradient or progression from low to high or from more to less severe in a vast array of areas. As Sandra Rief and Julie Heimburge put it, "Disabilities can cause difficulty with language, memory, listening, conceptualization, speaking, reading, writing, spelling, math, and motor skills—in various combinations and degrees. Each individual is unique in the combination of strengths and weaknesses, and degree of impairment."[4] Therefore, terms like "disability" and "trauma" cannot be static markers or labels that indicate a set group of people with an unchanging membership. It is possible for people to move between categories and labels based on age, genetics, illness, family makeup, injury, or medical care.

For example, a child who is neglected and removed from their birth family may have a medical condition, a potential trauma, and a foster placement. These physical, mental, and social situations may create long-term mental health concerns, but the physical disability and social family instability may be only short-term. Just as a foster child may move in or out of social services, often multiple times, so might a person enter or leave the disability community.

We (Laura and Mike) would like to caution against over-focus on definitions of disease, disability, and foster care with the goal of establishing a concrete conception of membership. A "black or white" or an "in or out" approach often sees trauma, disability, or foster care as a situation that must be addressed through a program or medical intervention. Instead, current thinking on trauma and disability invites us to see a person who has entered a community. It is that community that defines how the person can interact or contribute, not their status as a foster child or as someone with post-traumatic

3. Paul G. Hiebert, *Transforming Worldviews: An Anthropological Understanding of How People Change* (Baker Academic, 2009).

4. Sandra F. Rief and Julie A. Heimburge, *How to Reach and Teach All Children in the Inclusive Classroom: Practical Strategies, Lessons, and Activities*, 2nd ed. (Jossey-Bass, 2006), 168.

stress disorder (PTSD) or another medical diagnosis. More will be said on this as we discuss disability and conceptions of sin and suffering in chapter 4.

We also caution against making concrete distinctions between "high-functioning" and "low-functioning" people. This view of disabilities might prompt youth leaders to simply see people as collections of abilities. A focus on ability establishes a hierarchy of more capable and less capable participants: those who need less or more specialized programming and services. This perspective leads to that thinking that those who are capable serve those who are less capable, and that the most capable lead in the church. As outlined extensively in chapter 3, the outcome of this thinking is that Christian leadership and participation in the church are seen simply as matters of productivity and outcome, ignoring the *imago Dei*, and abdicating the gifting and priesthood of all believers.

With these cautions in mind, it is still helpful to discuss definitions of trauma and disability because these can help highlight and heal misunderstandings, bias, or even bigotry. Tom Shakespeare defines disability as a "relationship between intrinsic factors (impairment, personality, motivation, etc.) and extrinsic factors (environments, support systems, depression, etc.)."[5] This simple definition helpfully acknowledges that disability is not only physical but can, for example, be genetic or mental health related. Through this definition, Tom Shakespeare also notes that a medical or physical issue does not in itself define disability. A society has a significant role in such definitions as specific people interact with the society's environment. A personal state involving health, genetics, or personality is therefore disabling only inasmuch as the surrounding society reacts with exclusion, shunning, ableism, patronizing, or sidelining.

Literature on special education defines children with disabilities as "those who have difficulty reaching their full potential without special help."[6] This definition makes it clear that the "potential" here is related not to limited capabilities of the individual but rather to the necessary resources that may or may not be available to that person. "Special help" is a vast category and might include a crutch; a medication; a caring social network; a braille Bible; or a buddy, assistant, or mentor. As Rief and Heimburge explain, "We must allow children with learning differences to try bypassing or compensating for their weak areas by utilizing the appropriate tools and strategies. It is important to remember that these children do have many strengths along with their weaknesses. They can learn."[7]

5. Tom Shakespeare, *Disability Rights and Wrongs Revisited*, 2nd ed. (Routledge, 2014), 76.
6. May et al., *Children Matter*, 312.
7. Rief and Heimburge, *How to Reach and Teach*, 169.

Now that we have briefly defined disability, we can turn to defining and describing foster care.

Foster Care and Wards of the State

Some of the earliest human references to caring for orphans appear in Scripture.[8] God's mandates to Israel and individuals in the Old Testament are one of the most complete sets of ancient laws recognizing the need to care for those on the margins. The New Testament church provides the world's earliest example of an organized type of foster care. The early church expected widows to raise orphans (1 Tim. 5:9–10) and supported the widow while doing so (Acts 6:1).[9] This process provided care for two of the most vulnerable populations at once. More recently, awareness of children in need and best practices concerning them have been continually evolving. For example, in the United States, Charles Lorig Brace, an ordained minister, led the development of the first foster-home system in New York. In 1854, he moved institutionalized children into families, ultimately beginning a dramatic societal and legal move away from the orphanage model. Brace's movement, the Children's Aid Society, ultimately placed over one hundred thousand children in families. "As a result of the New York Children's Aid Society's placements, sectarian social agencies and state governments became involved in foster home placements."[10] Foster care laws developed to support and supervise children in home placements.

Foster care is for children in need of services who are often wards of the state. The goal of a foster placement with a family is safety, permanency, and well-being. States have a variety of approaches to achieving these goals, but each acts to protect children. Court custody is common until a child's needs can be met in a permanent situation, or what is called a "permanency" situation. Ideally each child would be raised by their biological parents, but this is often not possible due to neglect or abuse, parental incarceration or death, or some other form of abandonment. Foster care is, by definition, a temporary situation, but it can often last for years. Even though the goal of foster care is a permanent family placement, 15,379 children entered adulthood in 2024 without a family, and 70,418 were waiting unsuccessfully for

8. J. T. Fitzgerald, "Orphans in Mediterranean Antiquity and Early Christianity," *Acta Theologica* 23, no. 1 (2016): 29, https://doi.org/10.4314/actat.v23i1s.2.

9. *The Apostolic Constitutions*, book 4, sections 1–2, in *Ante-Nicene Fathers* 7, trans. James Donaldson, ed. Alexander Roberts, James Donaldson, and A. Cleveland Foxe (Christian Literature, 1886), available online at https://www.newadvent.org/fathers/07154.htm.

10. "History of Foster Care in the United States," National Foster Parent Association, accessed February 20, 2026, https://nfpaonline.org/foster-care/history-of-foster-care/.

an adoption.[11] In the past decade, hundreds of thousands of children never found permanency once they entered the system.

Foster Care Terms and Definitions

Explanations of a few variations in the foster system and relevant definitions will be helpful as you navigate information on teenagers' placements and situations.

Foster placement is when a certified foster parent houses a temporary state ward, working with a caseworker to restore family permanency for the child.

Foster to adopt is when an adult seeks to adopt a child and that child is placed in their home. This child would be without biological parents or have biological parents who have lost their parental rights.

A *group home* refers to placement of a child with a variety of legal statuses into a home with several other children in a similar situation; not all children in a group home are in foster care. Some children or teens who live in a group home may instead have another specific need: They may have a disability, be pregnant or parenting, or have a legal or behavioral issue. Group homes come in a variety of types, including the following:

- Transitional: For older teens such as those preparing for independent living, those whose parents are missing, or those teens who have run away. Shelter care is the most temporary version of a transitional group home, with placement lasting only weeks, while other transitional care can last for significant periods of a teen's late adolescence.
- Service/need oriented: Provides specific or unique services for teens such as those who are pregnant or parenting, are homeless, or have a disability.
- Probation: For teens who are in some form of detention or probation placement or have some other legal or court-ordered placement. When a juvenile probation service has custody of a teen, it most often works to place them in the safest and least restrictive environment possible. Such placements can range from house arrest to group homes to detention to incarceration.

Family preservation is a kind of pre–foster care service through which providers, churches, or family members are used to protect the children and

11. "The AFCARS Dashboard," U.S. Department of Health and Human Services, accessed February 20, 2026, https://tableau-public.acf.gov/views/afcars_dashboard_main_page/main page?%3Aembed=y&%3A.

help reduce the likelihood of their legal removal from their families. A family preservation service seeks to prevent the need for children's placement in foster care. Children are not legally placed with these providers; instead, the providers support the family in a specific situation.

A *residential facility* often refers to an institution for teens providing medical, legal, mental health or behavioral services that cannot be accommodated by the above approaches. These facilities are often accessed only through court placement in a foster or juvenile probation situation and usually provide an extended treatment program.

Interestingly, group homes are often run by churches or Christian nonprofits and very willingly participate in providing opportunities for faith development or church attendance. Hershey foster homes and Georgia Baptist foster homes are two examples of this model. Teens in probation, such as those under house arrest or in jail, can also be connected to a church community. Often a volunteer or paid chaplain can coordinate visits to teens or even provide a youth group in a detention or group home setting. Most chaplains can leverage volunteers in their system or help a pastor to connect to a specific teen in some form of juvenile placement. However, the vast majority of teens in these placements, as well as their families, do not engage in any significant way with a faith community.

In the ancient world, the church was set apart as the only group rescuing and caring for children.[12] Christian organizations are still primary providers of foster care, and Christians are still the primary source of foster parents in the US. Yet today the local church has partially abdicated its spiritual care of orphans. It is unusual for local congregations to be involved in detention centers, residential treatment facilities, group homes, or individual foster families' lives.

The ministry implications are somewhat obvious and striking. By engaging with teens in foster care, the church can reach the unreached, bring an end to suffering, and provide justice and advocacy. In other words, it can *be the church*. For example, when the church provides a form of family preservation, it may help parents legally keep their children while preventing the parents' actions from harming the children, leading to forced foster placement. This work maintains Christian witness and protects teens most at risk.

Having briefly developed working definitions of disability and foster care, we turn now to defining and understanding trauma.

12. J. Beaudry, "Orphan (in the Early Church)," in *New Catholic Encyclopedia*, ed. Bernard L. Marthaler, 2nd ed. (Catholic University of America, 2003), 10:674–75, view online at https://cvdvn.net/wp-content/uploads/2018/05/new-catholic-encyclopedia-vol-10.pdf.

Understanding Trauma and Loss

To understand trauma, it is helpful to differentiate between trauma and loss.

Understanding Trauma

"Trauma" refers to an emotional response to a deeply distressing or disturbing event that overwhelms an individual's ability to cope. Simply put, trauma is an emotional response to a terrible event. It often results in long-term negative psychological effects that impact behavior, health, attitudes, and overall function.[13] Note that not all terrible events result in trauma for those who experience them.

Trauma can be classified into several types:

- Acute trauma results from a single incident.
- Chronic trauma results from repeated and prolonged events, such as domestic violence or abuse.
- Complex trauma results from multiple and varied traumatic events that are often invasive and interpersonal.[14]

In chapter 6, which addresses trauma-informed youth ministry, we outline adverse childhood experiences (ACEs): singular or accumulated adverse events that lead to the emotional response of trauma.

Symptoms of trauma can include the following:

- Intrusive thoughts: flashbacks, nightmares, and severe anxiety
- Avoidance: steering clear of reminders of the traumatic event
- Hyperarousal: heightened state of alertness, irritability, and difficulty sleeping[15]

Understanding Loss

On the other hand, "loss" typically refers to the experience of losing someone or something significant. This can encompass a wide range of experiences,

13. "Trauma," American Psychological Association, accessed February 21, 2025, https://www.apa.org/topics/trauma/.

14. "Trauma-Informed Care," Missouri's Early Care and Education Connections, accessed February 24, 2025, https://earlyconnections.mo.gov/professionals/trauma-informed-care.

15. Roberto López Jr., Annamarie B. Defayette, Emma D. Whitmyre, Caitlin A. Williams, and Christianne Esposito-Smythers, "Posttraumatic Stress Disorder Symptom Clusters, Suicidal Ideation, and Social Support in a Clinical Adolescent Sample," *Death Studies* 46, no. 8 (2020): 1814–22.

from the death of a loved one, to the loss of a place on the soccer team, to the loss of relationship. Loss is often associated with grief, which is the emotional suffering felt when something or someone the individual loves is taken away.

Types of loss include the following:

- Primary loss: an initial loss, such as the death of a loved one
- Secondary loss: a subsequent loss that follows the primary loss, such as a loss of financial stability or social connections[16]

For example, as a primary loss, a divorce dissolves the family unit. As a secondary loss, divorce often changes a teen's financial stability, living arrangements, and support network.

Grief reactions can manifest in many ways, including these:

- Emotional responses: sadness, anger, guilt, and despair
- Physical symptoms: fatigue, changes in appetite, and sleep disturbances
- Cognitive effects: difficulty concentrating, disbelief, and preoccupation with the loss[17]

Key Differences Between Trauma and Loss

- Nature of the event: Trauma is often linked to a specific distressing event, whereas loss is associated with the absence of something or someone significant.
- Psychological impact: Trauma can lead to conditions like PTSD, while loss typically results in grief and bereavement.
- Coping mechanisms: Trauma often requires therapeutic interventions like eye movement desensitization and reprocessing (EMDR) or cognitive behavioral therapy (CBT), whereas loss may be addressed through grief counseling and support groups.[18]

16. "Secondary and Cumulative Losses," Coalition to Support Grieving Students, accessed February 24, 2025, https://grievingstudents.org/wp-content/uploads/2021/09/NYL-3B-SecondaryLoss.pdf.

17. Caroline Schoo, Yusra Azhar, Saba Mughal, and Preeti Rout, "Grief and Prolonged Grief Disorder," National Library of Medicine, updated April 12, 2025, https://www.ncbi.nlm.nih.gov/books/NBK507832/.

18. *A Treatment Improvement Protocol: Trauma-Informed Care in Behavioral Health Services* (Rockville, MD: Substance Abuse and Mental Health Services Administration, 2014), https://www.ncbi.nlm.nih.gov/books/NBK207191/box/part1_ch3.box16/.

To summarize, trauma is an emotional response to a terrible event. Trauma is not experienced by everyone. Loss is focused on absence, while trauma is an emotional response often focused on an event or series of events. Loss and grief are universal human experiences, while trauma is a particular emotional response to experiences.

In this definition, we are excluding the common usage "that was a traumatic event," instead focusing on trauma as a response to difficult events. A brief illustration is in order. I (Mike) have led camps for at-risk youth, training them and their mentors in Scripture engagement and designing ministry projects for their neighborhoods. Among my favorite times at these camps are mealtimes, when we just listen to a teen's full story. Often these stories are amazing accounts of resilience, grace, tragedy, and redemption. One young woman continued her story for three straight meals, outlining excruciating details involving multiple rapes, losses, and pervasive poverty. Over the course of the three-week camp, it was clear to me that this young woman had faced more difficulty than entire youth groups combined, yet she remained emotionally healthy, capable, and on mission for Christ. She had experienced adverse childhood events and losses but was not, while at camp, experiencing an incapacitating emotional response of trauma. In contrast, at the same camp, one young woman lost her social media streak because of a camping trip and refused to get out of bed. These stories are not meant to minimize or compare the two situations. Both very likely had experiences that were being stored in their bodies, but the response of each person to the events they had experienced was categorically different.

Therefore, it is important to differentiate between trauma and loss, never to minimize either, and never to rate or compare the validity of people's various experiences with them. Regarding minimizing loss, I have heard adults dismiss and even ridicule a middle school student's loss of a first crush. An adult who makes a comment like "It was just puppy love; you will get over it" fails to consider that this may have been the first nonfamily attachment and the most intense emotional experience of a very young adult-ish brain.

An adult can easily minimize a teen's trauma, but this does great harm to the adult's ability to help a teen. A youth pastor friend of Mike's was driving in the cornfields outside Chicago on Interstate 80. Hitting an icy patch, his car spun out of control. He came to rest facing the correct direction after having done a complete 360 on the freeway. He then continued forward with no hesitation or concern and thought very little of the experience. A few months later he was driving and suddenly felt hot and dizzy, his heart racing. His muscles bunched up, and his hands had a death grip on the steering wheel. His panic necessitated that he pull over on the side of the freeway. Once he calmed down, he saw he was at the same location as his earlier vehicular ice-skating incident. This second incident was months later, in a different season, and he had been cognitively unaware of the location. As Bessel van der Kolk, an eminent trauma researcher, states, the body "kept the score."[19] His reaction was automatic, unconscious, and even stronger than it had been during the original incident. What is even more startling about trauma is that it can generalize, or move beyond, the exact circumstances of the original incident, leaving the body in full protection mode and the mind reeling and disconnected, taken over by an automatic response despite being in what may seem an unrelated situation. To say, "This was no big deal," "He is overreacting," or "No one got hurt" ignores the very real physical experience in the body as well as the emotional effects of the trauma. It is a very real possibility that a teen cannot even remember an adverse experience, but their body may. The emotion is true, even if the event is forgotten or misunderstood. The response is physiologically real, regardless of the details regarding the event.

We do not intend this book to be a manual to treat trauma, and we recommend further reading in this area. The science on trauma is making significant strides. One of the most important pastoral responsibilities is to know when and how to refer a person to a trained therapist, which we address in chapter 19.

Compliance or Cutting Edge: Proactive or Regressive

American society has begun to take the necessary steps to ensure that accessibility is available for those with disabilities. The Americans with Disabilities Act (ADA) was passed on July 26, 1990, as Public Law 101–336, and it became effectively enforced beginning January 26, 1992. The ADA is landmark federal legislation that has opened services and employment opportunities to millions of Americans with disabilities. This law is intended to eliminate illegal discrimination and help level the playing field for disabled individuals. In addition to opening more opportunities for jobs and benefits for people with disabilities, the ADA improved wheelchair accessibility in buildings and on public transit. Increased access to buildings and transportation has meant that people with disabilities have more opportunities to participate in public communities.

One of the duties of the local church is to create an environment where people feel welcomed, connected, and enjoyed. The church is a place where

19. Bessel A. van der Kolk, *The Body Keeps the Score: Brain, Mind, and Body in the Healing of Trauma* (Viking, 2014), 130.

people should feel invited whether or not they have disabilities, but unfortunately this has not always been the case. With the arrival of the ADA legislation in 1990, many churches were required to change their building plans because they were not wheelchair accessible. The church had clearly been unwelcoming to people with disabilities in that they did not have physical access. Most churches wait until they are forced to make the necessary changes to literally open their doors to people with disabilities. Today there are still some churches that are not wheelchair accessible.

Many people with disabilities struggle to feel accepted by a community, or they want to be accepted but have fears about being vulnerable. Many have been made to feel unable to contribute to the group. When physical barriers are in the way, people with disabilities are even less likely to feel connected to a community and, more specifically, the church. Even a teen who does not use a wheelchair understands that a friend who uses one would be unable to attend a church that lacked ramps and an elevator. Teens who want to bring their friends know that an inaccessible church is not ready to receive them. There is a disconnect when young people who use wheelchairs feel more comfortable going to a McDonald's than to church because physical barriers prevent them from entering the youth room. The church should be on the forward edge of accessibility and justice.

Exclusion, Inclusion, Justice, and the ADA

The ADA defines disability quite broadly: It states that people with disabilities include those with "physical and mental impairments, those with a record of impairments, and even those perceived as having impairments, or having experienced discrimination on the basis of a perceived impairment."[20] The ADA does call for justice, but it also moderates that call by limiting the requirement of justice in cases of economic hardship. Economic hardship sometimes excuses the nation and certain entities, notably churches, from full enforcement of the law. This means that one can strive for justice, but justice is not required if the cost is too high.

People with disabilities do not, in many instances, have the right to access. Instead, they have the right to pursue access through advocacy and only then to receive needed accommodations. Actual access and the right to pursue access are very different realities. Engaging in self-advocacy is often necessary if they are to have their needs met. Self-advocacy often requires people to reveal

20. Raffety, *From Inclusion to Justice*, 32.

personal medical information to prove their need for accommodations. The choice becomes access or invasion of privacy.

This ADA process only works if people are aware of their rights and if they, or someone on their behalf, advocate for accommodations. Even when effective, much of the ADA is focused on transportation and employment rights, and the process's requirements for disclosure, advocacy, and awareness frequently act to fully exclude teens from benefitting from the legislation. It is difficult to imagine that many teens would want to highlight an uncomfortable distinction, let alone a disability, and then be willing to fight for their right to be included. And even with advocacy, there is still no guarantee of accommodation, inclusion, or especially justice.

Consider, for example, a need for teen self-disclosure and advocacy within the context of an unfamiliar church. Many older church buildings do not have ADA-compliant bathrooms or wheelchair access to all their public spaces. Only renovating such a building would trigger the requirement to make that building fully accessible. Further, the ADA allows churches to be responsive instead of proactive. A disabled person must ask for help or accommodations—which must be reasonable and not overly financially burdensome—in order to receive them. This is at least in part necessary, as it would be impossible to anticipate and provide for every conceivable type of accommodation. However, when the church has a solely or primarily reactive posture, every person with a need must recognize that need and make the church leadership aware in order to receive the accommodations that would allow them to participate in church activities. Often a disabled teen or their parents must help leadership develop solutions. These are high bars of disclosure and initiative to place on teens.

If inclusion is fundamentally invasive to those with accommodation needs and the organization can opt out of offering accommodations, then inclusion is not very inclusive in functional reality. As we discuss the inclusion of all teens, we are promoting these key ideas that together lead to justice and inclusion: We must be proactive, avoid ableism, be noninvasive, advocate, and significantly change our perspective.

Be proactive: To be proactive means to actively anticipate needs and risks. We cannot know every need, medical condition, or past trauma. However, it is possible to anticipate the kinds of environments, programs, staff training, and physical accommodations that will meet the needs of many teens who are being overlooked by every other area of society. In chapters 7–9 we describe the process of evaluating church buildings and programs, and in chapter 10 we offer ideas for immediately taking the initiative to reach out to and include all adolescents. Being proactive requires us to think outside of ableism.

Avoid ableism: The teen in chapter 1 who asked, "Why are all the beautiful people always up front?" caused a period of reflection followed by a reorganization of the processes of choosing, training, and presenting those in leadership. Ableism means our perception of teens clusters them into a simple, single, homogeneous group. Instead of doing this, we must see teens where they are, which requires some nuance in our listening, questions, and observations. Avoiding ableism forces us to know our demographics, both generally and immediately local. A few simple questions are pertinent here to evaluate this area: How do we create programs that create safety instead of reinjuring teens? Do we allow for variance and variety?

Be noninvasive: Offering a safe, inclusive space that allows for variance and variety should not invasively require a teen or their family to provide information they would prefer to keep private. To make serving someone dependent upon proof of their worthiness of that service contradicts the gospel. In addition, all efforts to protect voluntary disclosures by students must be made, whether such disclosures concern trauma, a medical issue, or a family legal issue. Efforts to protect the privacy of the individual are paramount. Acting proactively to provide basic universal accommodations and avoid ableism can prevent the need for a teen or family to disclose personal details.

Advocate: What does it mean to advocate? In Scripture, "the advocate" could refer to a person or being who speaks on behalf of another. Acts 16:21 and 17:18 refer to Paul's efforts to convince or teach people about Christ. As he teaches, his listeners make the accusation that he is advocating for foreign gods. Teaching and convincing are the focus here, with the end goal being a change of mind. Teaching or presenting evidence is a key form of advocacy. Another relevant biblical image is of Jesus himself, who is called "the advocate." In 1 John 2:1, John says that Jesus speaks on behalf of sinners before God: "We have an advocate with the Father—Jesus Christ, the Righteous One." Jesus performs a legal advocacy, fulfilling a role before God on humans' behalf that humanity cannot perform for itself. The *Theological Dictionary of the New Testament* outlines the biblical aspects of the advocate's role as an authoritative teacher, witness, and speaker in a trial.[21] Christ fulfills this role as our helper and defender before the court of God. We fulfill a similar advocacy role as we teach others about the margins and witness to the need for and potential of ministry at the margins. A margin advocate must also speak aloud in the assembly. As we advocate, we wrestle on behalf of those who cannot always speak for themselves, advancing justice by persuading

21. Johannes Behm, "παράκλητος," in *Theological Dictionary of the New Testament*, trans. and ed. Geoffrey W. Bromiley (Eerdmans, 1967), 5:800–814.

others through reasoned and faithful witness. Training our staff, teaching Scripture that discusses orphans and disability, and using trauma-informed preaching (see chapter 14) are all forms of advocacy.

Change your perspective: Ministry on the margins often requires restructuring the way we define leadership, ministry, and programming. In chapter 3, we will address the theological and philosophical assumptions that underpin healthy ministry on the margins, specifically naming some of the core perspectives regarding the image of God, sin, the priesthood of all believers, gifts for ministry, and leadership in the church.

Inclusion is a step, but it is not the full end goal. Each ministry will likely need to address each of these areas to become a truly just church that reaches beyond legal minimums to invite full participation.

Sam: The Final Question of Accommodation or Leadership

Sam was a great kid. He had an infectious smile and bubbly personality. He reacted strongly to everything. A sad story would make him cry, and he always laughed at my jokes, which means he had a well-developed sense of youth pastor humor. He was always just a little nervous around the other teenagers, he could be a bit relationally awkward or overly focused, and he could miss social cues. Also, Sam loved ideas and discussion. He quickly latched on to the gospel after a year of seeing the church live it out. His atheist father spent the next several years trying to convince him to change his mind about religion. Sam's dad said the church was "really just trying to get people's money." Sam would respond incredulously to his father: "That's not possible! Have you seen Mike's car?" Sam would walk over to my (Mike's) house, stand on the outside porch, tell me the story, and always ask for a Coke.

Sam blended in well enough at youth group but thrived leading in small settings where he could discuss topics and ask questions, and where he did not have to restrain his minor quirks. Even though he was fairly terrible at disc golf, he was fairly good at holding a conversation about important life matters with the other teens while playing. I moved across the country prior to Sam's senior year. But he called me several times looking for schools that could help him study apologetics. He had a gift, a passion. He was seeing success and pursued it as a calling and career.

Sam's autism, although minor and often unnoticeable, was a daily struggle for him. Many would consider Sam a risk in a leadership position or in doing evangelism with other teens. Yet Sam was able to leverage his interest in ideas, and especially his focus, into something that would help others winsomely meet Christ. His thoughtful and unassuming personality disarmed people, and they were drawn to his genuine desire to search out truth. Somehow our fumbling and underfunded small church made a way for Sam to not only participate but contribute and lead.

QUESTIONS TO PONDER

1. Have you had the opportunity to befriend someone who, at first encounter, did not fit within the same boundaries as yourself? How did you move beyond the boundaries, and what have you gained from this relationship?
2. Explore your church community's boundaries of who is welcome and who is not. What would happen if Jimmy wandered into *your* church on a Sunday morning?
3. Discovering Sam's strengths in leadership necessitated risking the status quo on behalf of the church. In what specific ways would your church have to stretch to make space for a teen like Sam?
4. Like Jesus and the woman at the well in John 4, what might it look like to create a church where welcome is universal, where diagnoses and histories of trauma do not prevent love from being extended?
5. What decisions have been made to improve access at your church, especially if parts of the building predate 1990? What decisions still need to be made?

3

Running in the Pews

Thinking Theologically and the Imago Dei

In the winter of 2007, I (Mike) was still new to the state of Georgia but had completed foster placement training in a matter of weeks. At the time, I did not know Georgia was experiencing a double crisis in its foster system. A new law made it possible for the government to prosecute caseworkers who did not make an in-person visit to each foster child in their caseload every month. The legislature was trying to force a fix on a system that had been experiencing neglect and lawsuits. Unfortunately, this law did not come with additional funding to help caseworkers fulfill the requirement. Caseworkers were traveling across multiple counties and often had dozens of children to oversee; they simply could not visit each child each month. The effect of the legislation was that Georgia's department of children's services allowed no new foster placements. I had recently moved to an area near Appalachia. There was plenty of need for the removal of children from dire situations, yet the state had suspended removing children and placing them in the foster system. When I arrived, a three-county area had not removed a single child from a biological family for a period of many months. Until Jamie. Jamie was five and had a little brother who was two. The drugs, violence, and abuse at their residence were so extreme that Jamie's caseworker could not go to see Jamie without a police presence. Jamie and her brother were the first children in many months to be removed from their family. For their safety, the children were taken to a different county and given to the new foster family in town (us). It was a risky situation. When parent-child visits occurred, in another county, we were told to arrive an hour early and take a different route home each time to prevent the children from being followed.

I remember picking up the children from the social worker for the first time. Everything was difficult and extreme. The case managers' and investigators' decision to pull the kids from their biological family would further overload caseworkers. Those officials could face charges if caseworker visit requirements were not met as a result. Unfortunately, the details available about the children were minimal: I knew little about their needs or the full extent of abuses they had experienced. Jamie's little brother, Kyle, was a large kid for a two-year-old, but he could not talk or walk. Jamie, an average-size five-year-old, was wearing one flip-flop, no underwear, a tank top, and toddler-size 2T pants, which we thought were shorts. I remember that Kyle smelled like pancakes but had not eaten lunch or dinner; the mother had run the children out of state to a relative to hide them from the police and caseworkers. We went to a McDonald's drive-through and then to Walmart to grab some basic clothes, diapers, and shoes. I will never forget that shopping trip. Jamie would grab items from shelves—shoes or boxed goods—and try to bite through them, often after tearing them into two parts. We later saw this at night when she would eat puzzle pieces and would tear up and chew on her bedding. The shopping trip became a crisis and thus essentials-only. We headed home with barely enough to function.

Jamie and Kyle desperately needed a bath. As my wife and I tag-teamed bath time, Jamie offered herself to me sexually. When I refused her, she became enraged. She clearly thought I hated her because I did not want to do something sexual with her. As she explained, other men in her life did it that way. So now we were trying to set up the beds, dry the kids off, settle a sexually aggressive child, and talk to a caseworker on the phone about the situation. For the next thirty-one days, every night, Jamie screamed on her bed for up to two hours after she stripped it down to the mattress. According to the caseworker, she had never slept on a bed. It was a complete nightmare. We had to protect other children physically and sexually from Jamie. I slept in the hallway on the floor for several weeks to prevent escapes and issues. The caseworker visited us at our home for the first time about thirty-five days into the placement.

We did not think we could take Jamie to church. She had trauma, behavioral issues, and a disability. We decided to try anyway and called the church office. They told us to come that Sunday. A middle-aged woman was waiting for us. She looked us in the eye, took Jamie's hand, said she had been in special education for sixteen years, and walked off, telling us not to worry and that we should meet her at the children's desk in two hours. We wept with relief and exhaustion for the first entire hour and then attended our relatively new-to-us church's service. A few new friends with young families had arranged for some pizza and for us all to go and play in the park that afternoon. The plan was that following the service, the adults would take turns interacting with Jamie. I was looking forward to my first non-crisis adult conversation in weeks.

The service ended. Jamie had had a fabulous experience in the children's ministry. Now we wept for a second time that morning, this time in thankfulness. The church was nearly empty. While one of the families ran to get the to-go pizzas, we stayed in the sanctuary. My wife and I stood on each end of a pew and used it like a racetrack. The children would run straight down the line, run into an adult at the end of the pew, and be turned around to run down the next row, creating a contained circle of giggles. I held Kyle while he watched the other two children—Jamie and our adopted daughter, age four—run laps before lunch.

I distinctly remember thinking that with the help of our small group, a dedicated Sunday aid for Jamie, and lots of prayer, we could maybe do this. That was when the pastor came over and verbally reprimanded us. He told us that the sanctuary was no place for these children. I sincerely hoped he was acting out of misguided outrage about the "defilement" of a holy space and not referring to the various ethnicities of our children.

This story highlights the difficulty of entering the faith community with a mental health issue, foster placement, or disability. It also emphasizes the power of a single well-trained buddy for a child, one who knows the situation and can navigate the difficulties of trauma or disability in a typical church setting. Finally, this story demonstrates the power of theology for a pastor whose beliefs about the church sanctuary outweighed the needs of a struggling foster family and a disabled child's first-ever day at a church.

The Importance of Theology

Let us begin with the end in mind. This chapter's discussions lead to the following conclusion: *Every theological premise carries a ministry implication.* Jay Kesler, friend of the late Billy Graham and former president of both Youth for Christ and Taylor University, has potently noted, "The theology of the youth worker is ultimately more important than his or her strategy or methodology. . . . Your personal theology will have an effect on everything you do. It will influence the type of message you bring, the response you expect, the progress of the [people] among whom you minister, your method of counseling, your attitude towards others, and how you measure results. In short, all we do relates to what we actually believe."[1] This chapter outlines and discusses various views of disability and theological ideas related to teens on the margins. It is important to be clear why thinking theologically is vital from the very beginning. A person ignoring the theological premises on which they build ministry will be hopelessly driven by the winds of assumptions, often perpetuating centuries-old harms and biases. The foundation of theology is that upon which later practical chapters rest. Ignoring this work and applying quick fixes will result in right practice being twisted by bad theology. We will likely feel good about the harm we are inadvertently doing.

There will be two following movements in this chapter. The first will address three main models of approaching disability. Next, we will consider the theological implications of *imago Dei* on foster care, trauma, and adolescent disability ministry. The next chapter will address theological and philosophical approaches to disability and then conclude with essential core theological premises and how they play out in the practice of ministry.

Making Sense of Disability

How do we make sense of disability and trauma in a teen's life? This section discusses three primary models of disability. Each is a philosophical attempt to deal with the problem of pain and suffering in disability, and, fundamentally, each attempts to describe the source of disability. These three philosophical premises—moral, physical, and social—drive thinking about disability, foster care, and trauma. The moral model describes disability as a primarily spiritual issue. The physical model holds to a strict materialist or medical view. The third model is based on personal and community identity and perceives any problem as fundamentally social in nature.

Moral Model

The moral model is the oldest and likely most common of the three frameworks for understanding disability worldwide. According to this model, disability is often considered a result of moral failings, karma, or sins. The causes of a disability are seen as rooted in the character, actions, or thoughts of the disabled individual or their family; the disability is seen as a sign of divine judgment or as a test of faith. This divine-displeasure view of disability increases social stigmatization, exclusion, and discrimination. Conversely, disability can be seen as a gift of faith or honor, as a grace of God for a

1. Gary Dausey, *The Youth Leader's Source Book* (Zondervan, 1983), 23.

greater good, or as evidence of faith or perseverance. A disabling accident or disease might be viewed as an opportunity to grow spiritually or as evidence of God's trust in an individual. Thus within the moral model, disability can be seen as either punishment or opportunity. The latter concept is reflected in many Westerns, both novels and movies, in which an underdog figure overcomes disadvantage to achieve some exceptional or unique accomplishment. The former appears when a disability is used to represent a villain's evil. The moral model is not unanimous in its attribution of disability to sin, but the religious conversation about sin and faith dominates the moral model approach.

Medical Model

In the West, thinking about disability has become nearly indistinguishably intertwined with thinking regarding health care. The second approach, the medical model, focuses on the expert such as a doctor or psychiatrist. The disabled individual is expected to obey the authority and follow the prescription. This model sees experts attempting to realize two primary goals. The first is limiting the symptoms or pain a disabled person experiences. The second is the desire for the disabled person to be able to function in society. The medical model approaches these goals through clinical language and diagnoses made by experts who have specialized training. It sees disability as a deviation from a norm, and its aim is returning the disabled person to "normal," which could be summarized as fitting in both socially and with regard to physical functionality. This view tends to dominate Western health care and education. The ends here are improving, healing, or curing disabilities, or aligning the functioning of disabled people with that of people without disabilities. These ends are often vital and necessary for disabled people's well-being or even, in some cases, survival. However, an important critique of this model is that many definitions of healing or "improving" are simply to alter a disabled person such that their functioning aligns more closely with society's typical expectations of its other members, usually erasing the disability and not necessarily benefiting the disabled person. While the moral view can often lead to stigmatization, the medical view can lead to the disabled person's loss of agency or to ableism in society.

Social Model

The final model has arisen as a critique of the medical model. The social model rejects the focus on "normalcy" as the primary driver of attempts to address disability, instead focusing on a perceived disconnect between the person and environment. This gap is both physical and social, but its cause is in the environment, not in the disability. According to the social model, the handicaps experienced by those with disabilities are caused by society's views that prevent the full participation of its disabled members. Therefore, in the social model, "the way to address disability is to change the environment and society, rather than people with disabilities."[2] The social model's approach encompasses advocacy both to change laws and to portray people with disabilities as typical citizens and loving family members. The social model brings to the fore important insights that have long been neglected. A disability does not place someone on the margins; society does. For example, in his book *Blindsided by Grace*, Robert Molsberry reflects on his experience of disability not as a medical condition in search of a cure, or as a tragedy to be pitied, but as a cross-cultural adventure like learning to live in a foreign country.[3] The social model brings pertinent and hopeful developments in approach. This view can fail, however, by celebrating pain and suffering through a refusal to acknowledge the complex sources and nature of disability.

There is much debate about these models currently in academic literature. The medical model is predominant in practice today in the United States. The social model appears to be in strong ascendancy in philosophical and advocacy literature. Neither the medical nor social model deal with the spiritual realities acknowledged by the moral model. Theology can help us here by bringing us to a fuller and integrative approach in alignment with God's own action.

As God looks at humanity, he is not drawing lines excluding those with various limitations, family situations, or traumas; possessing particular combinations of abilities; or falling within specific age ranges. God calls his people to the margins in sacrificial hospitality. When we enter the margins, our goal is not to bring people toward the center but to realize that the margins are God's greatest area of concern and most often the center of his work and activity. Our hope is not to de-margin those on the outside but to join God in his work by joining the outcasts. The foolish become wise in him. The childless are fulfilled. Strangers and aliens find their home.

2. Rhoda Olkin, "Conceptualizing Disability: Three Models of Disability," American Psychological Association, March 29, 2022, https://www.apa.org/ed/precollege/psychology-teacher-network/introductory-psychology/disability-models.

3. Robert F. Molsberry, *Blindsided by Grace: Entering the World of Disability* (Augsburg, 2004).

Losing Your Shirt and Remaining in the Image: *Imago Dei* and Its Importance for Practice

As is apparent in the previous paragraph, theology is impossible to avoid in the conversation about trauma, mental health, and disability. This following brief discussion is a concerted effort to let our theology be shaped by Scripture and our practice be shaped by Christ's model.

> Jesus' first recorded sermon proclaimed that God's kingdom was at hand. Then he spent the rest of his public ministry on earth bringing in the kingdom. *Our calling as disability advocates is to carry on Jesus' work so that all people, especially people with disabilities, will be welcomed to the body of Christ and encouraged to use their gifts in ministry.*[4]

Leaders, parents, and pastors do not simply *have* a theology or *teach* theology to others. Our theology plays out in every tangible way imaginable, just as Christ lives his theology in perfect expression. Our goal is to become clear and explicit on Scripture and align our practice, understanding how our beliefs shape all that we do. Since our aim is to align our practices with Scripture, and Scripture asks us to welcome *all* people to the body of Christ and encourage them to use their gifts in ministry, our work therefore must include welcoming people who are on the margins as well as promoting their use of their gifts. The functioning or behavior of people on the margins may not always align with the expectations of people who are not; it is nevertheless vital that we welcome and encourage all people. Two stories will help illustrate.

Mike's example: My foster son thought he had found a way to game the system. Winning by making everyone lose is a common misconception of many children, but especially those in foster care. The thinking goes that if the other person loses, then I must win. Even if I also lose. This is the stuff that makes power battles so difficult in parenting. Usually, a power battle is perceived as a win-lose situation. With trauma it is always lose-lose. The child does not actually get what they want but still perceives themselves as winning because the adult did not get what they wanted either. My home has a simple two-level approach to clothes: clothes for church or school and clothes for work or play. It became cumbersome to have too many rules, such as work, school, sports, church, and play clothes. Just imagine trying to suddenly sort the socks for four new foster children in a new home placement. Keeping rules and laundry simple allows for more conversations about the

4. Thrive (CRCNA), "A Biblical Perspective on Disability and Inclusion," The Network, Christian Reformed Church, December 30, 2009, https://network.crcna.org/topic/justice-inclusion/disability-concerns/biblical-perspective-disability-and-inclusion (emphasis added).

more important parts of life. Once my foster son chose to wear his sleeveless sports jersey underneath a dress shirt to church. His plan, I suspect, was to pull off the "nicer" shirt when no one was looking, and then he would be wearing what he wanted. He was now wearing two shirts and somehow, in the middle of the service, he had not been able to enact his plan. Add in a bit of sensory compulsion, and the result was quite humorous. I looked over and he had taken off both shirts and was struggling with both shirts covering his head. His secret defiance suddenly became very public. Defiance was likely a way to exert power, to win even when losing. He was willing to face being uncomfortable, or being punished, to gain back control he lost when he was separated from his biological family. The result was a sudden no-shirt situation in the middle of the sermon. These behaviors, quirks, and patterns can make us wonder if kids like these can ever "fit it," belong, or be "normal."

Laura's example: In the children's ministry area of the church I (Laura) attend, some of the plastic chairs are blue, and others are black. The chairs are similarly designed but not exactly the same; the first model was likely out of stock when the church grew and needed to add more chairs. The children's worship room has a central area for large-group worship, with tables and chairs off to the sides for small groups. Some of the small-group areas use only the blue chairs. Some use only the black chairs. Children are loosely divided into small groups based on numbers each week. Sometimes the first-grade girls are a group. Sometimes all first graders are a group, so there wasn't a consistent meeting area for everyone. When my son was a participant in the children's ministry, some weeks his behavior did not disrupt activities, but in other weeks it was challenging. The adults unsuccessfully tried to identify the trigger in the lesson format, sound level, or routine. Finally, someone asked my son directly what was causing him trouble. He quickly responded by explaining he did not like the blue chairs. When he was assigned to a group in a blue-chair area, he found sitting uncomfortable, and he acted out his discomfort through difficult behaviors. When he was assigned to a group in the black-chair area, he was comfortable and cooperated well. He had difficulty identifying the issue on his own before he was asked about it. The adults were stunned. The solution was so simple: Assign Laura's son to a small-group area with black chairs; the content of the lesson did not matter. His body would be comfortable, allowing him and others to engage.

It is important to remember that even when a blue chair or uncomfortable clothing trigger dysregulation or a child breaks a rule to gain back power, all children are still made in the image of God. Being in the image or the body of Christ requires neither perfection (aligning with an external standard) nor production (producing a benefit to the group) nor peace (keeping the status quo in place).

We do not need to be perfect, keep peace, or produce any utilitarian value to be God's children. However, we each have a role and calling. Teens do not need to line up with social expectations or conform to ableist notions to be positionally in the church or made in God's image. Quite the opposite: A trauma or disability enables the church to be more fully the community of Christ as we minister to and receive ministry from these teens.

What does it mean theologically to be a child who cannot sit in a blue chair or one whose inner compulsions drive them to engage in inexplicable behaviors? Is our value based on conformity—on "normal" behaviors that seem comfortable to others? Stanley Grenz, a brilliant theologian, notes, "the New Testament cannot be understood in its fullness without taking into consideration what is declared in its pages about the *imago Dei*."[5] If Grenz is correct, then it is also true that discipleship and ministry hinge on a proper understanding of the doctrine of the *imago Dei*.

Imago Dei and the Implications for Ministry

Now is the time to ask the difficult question: Is a middle schooler really human? It feels doubtful some days. Especially at camp. Especially doubtful at night, in a cabin, at camp. Yet, middle schoolers included, the church has stood for centuries on its establishment of the image of God, or *imago Dei*, as a basis for ethics and practice. All people are made in the image of God, no matter their productivity, capability, disability, belief, race, or gender. We hold that even sin does not erase God's image in a person. Yet this is not the only view held by society or even by Christians over time. Various groups have ongoing discussions about the effects of age, cognitive ability, and spiritual position on whether someone is still made in God's image. Three primary philosophies relate to the question "Are we human and made in God's image?"

1. We are human insofar as we are able to fulfill some function or value.
2. We are human insofar as we align with a group or a set of beliefs or propositions.
3. We are human because God has made us and declared us so.

5. Stanley J. Grenz, *The Social God and the Relational Self: A Trinitarian Theology of the Imago Dei* (Westminster John Knox, 2001), 203.

Some philosophies and approaches to humanity and disability, many of them still very current today, align with view one, considering people to be less human or more human depending on how they compare to a standard of action, ability, functionality, or usefulness. This utilitarian approach holds that many people are simply "worshipping animals":[6] that we can separate from our genetics only if we have the ability to obey or to perform particular actions or religious observances and then choose to do so. Thus, humanity is not inherent in an individual but is developed into, and this development can be delayed, missed, or even lost once attained, such as through a disability or life of sin. A person's functionality or contribution is the factor that determines their value. And value determines whether people are treated as humans. View one, then, holds that a person can lose the image of God and that a person can gain or intensify the image by conformity to Christ. The image is externally evaluated and kept or earned by external activity and the perceived value of that activity.

The second view holds that a set of beliefs or belonging to a group marks humanity. Varying from a social norm or holding different views or positions, such as a different nationality, marks one as less fully or not at all human. This approach, simply stated, allows us to demonize our enemies or differences by simply moving a person into the "other" category, removing them from the normal benefits or rights of humanity. If someone belongs to a favored category either genetically or through membership, which is determined by where they were born or what creed they ascribe to, they are part of the in-group and thus human.

These first two positions hold that whether a person is human is defined by an arbitrary social norm. The church is not immune to the first two problematic philosophies. Are we human just because we believe rightly or perform the right religious actions? Is our fundamental humanity conditional based on our relationship with Christ or even our obedience in living out the kingdom? While our eternal trajectory is determined by our relationship with Jesus, most Christian theologies and ethics have strongly rejected both approaches, instead favoring a view that makes God the definer and giver of the image. Views about exactly what God bestowed on us in the giving of his image vary. Yet people cannot arbitrarily draw lines that exclude others from God's image if God is the giver of that image.

Excluding others from the image of God based on a creed, category, or inability flies against fundamental Christian orthodoxy. If infants are not

6. James K. A. Smith, *You Are What You Love: The Spiritual Power of Habit* (Brazos, 2016).

fully in the image of God or are only in the process of becoming human, the ethical considerations are considerable. Infanticide becomes possible. Middle-schooler-icide becomes probable. We open the door for a potential humanity or a lesser humanity, with people proffering their own opinions on who is "lesser" and how much "potential" is necessary.

It might be helpful to define the question being asked here. The primary issue is not *what* the *imago Dei* is or *how* it is transmitted but rather *who* is in the *imago Dei* and *in whose image* we have been made. As theologian Walter Brueggemann said, "We are indeed made in the image of some God. And perhaps we have no more important theological investigation than to discern in whose image we have been made."[7] Applied to practice, it is vital for us to start with God as the image giver and the image himself. Christ becomes our model. The goal is not to exclude those who believe differently or are not holy, but first to understand the image giver as being of the first and utmost importance. This image giver is God himself, and he has revealed himself through his son. A Christocentric approach lends itself to implications for church practice, educational theory, and of course, ministry to teens on the margins. Here Christocentric means that we orient all Scripture reading, theology, and practice to the centrality of Christ. His model corrects our practice, and all Christian theology finds its source in him.

Theologian Karl Barth exhorts believers to this Christocentric view: "As the man Jesus is himself the revealing Word of God, He is the source of our knowledge of the nature of man as created by God."[8] Commenting on Barth, Veli-Matti Kärkkäinen states that the "logic of this simple statement is compelling: If men and women can know who they are only on the basis of the Word of God, then it is only by looking at the One who indeed is himself the Word of God, Jesus Christ, that we can know our identity and nature."[9]

Jesus is the originator of humanity and the ideal human. However, Jesus is not the only human. His humanity is not simply a singularity, a perfect yet impossible moral example of what we should have been. This view has led some to say that we become more human or more of an image bearer as we act like Christ.[10] Even more sinisterly, this interpretation could hold that Jesus is fundamentally different from us and that we only share humanity with him

7. Walter Brueggemann, *The Prophetic Imagination*, 2nd ed. (Fortress, 2001), 8.

8. Karl Barth, *Church Dogmatics*, vol. III/2, *The Doctrine of Creation*, ed. G. W. Bromiley and T. F. Torrance, trans. H. Knight, G. W. Bromiley, J. K. S. Reid, and R. H. Fuller (T&T Clark, 1960), 41.

9. Veli-Matti Kärkkäinen, "Jesus and the Goodness of Everything Human: Why It Matters That God Became the Human Prototype," *Christianity Today*, January 27, 2012.

10. J. I. Packer and Gary A. Parrett, *Grounded in the Gospel: Building Believers the Old-Fashioned Way* (Baker Books, 2010), 13.

and him with us as we do what we are called to do vocationally as humans. In the final consideration, this deficient view tells us that God does not, then, share something with us in the incarnation. Instead, he only shows us what we should be doing. If Jesus were not fully human, and likewise, if people were not fully human, then there could be no knowing in either direction, no substitution, no forgiveness. He would not be able to empathize and be our high priest (Heb. 4:15).

Holding a view that requires a performance, capability, or value in order to be human degrades the example of Christ and attempts to strip people of something God named and was given by God himself. As theologian Jürgen Moltmann said, the result of this line of thinking is that "humans who judge according to ideal images think that the life of one who is blind or dumb or lame or is mentally ill is a reduced life, that is, a life that is less than another. But God loves every human life."[11] We agree with Moltmann. It is highly problematic to hold that people are human or not human based on ability or disability, because of social value or lack of capability, because of youth or age, of health or mental illness, of sight or blindness.

Some modern Christians argue that the "image of God (*imago Dei*) is not some de facto property of *Homo Sapiens* (whether will or reason or language or what have you); rather, the image of God is a task, a mission."[12] This unusual view of the *imago Dei* is accompanied by many descriptions of people as liturgical animals as well as of our ability to "be(come) *human*" as we accomplish our tasks. "The *imago Dei* is not a thing or a property that was lost (or retained); it was a calling and a vocation that Adam and Eve failed to carry out."[13] Most troubling in this view of persons is an *imago Dei* that is task oriented. We cannot agree that we are "animals" being formed and called to become "truly human." We reject this view due to the fatal result this theology has brought in practice as a primary argument for religious genocide or the extermination of those with disabilities.

There is no human on the margins of the image of God. Marva Dawn goes so far as to compare human value with God's: "We honor someone because we think that person is valuable. God goes to great lengths to reveal to us how valuable we are to Him."[14] People are valued not because they are

11. Jürgen Moltmann, "Liberate Yourselves by Accepting One Another," in *Human Disability and the Service of God: Reassessing Religious Practice*, ed. Nancy L. Eiesland and Don E. Saliers (Abingdon, 1998), 116.

12. Christian Smith, *Moral, Believing Animals: Human Personhood and Culture* (Oxford University Press, 2003), 163.

13. C. Smith, *Moral, Believing Animals*, 164.

14. Marva J. Dawn, *Reaching Out Without Dumbing Down: A Theology of Worship for the Turn-of-the-Century Culture* (Eerdmans, 1995), 171.

powerful or powerless but because God chooses to value all people. God demonstrates poignant concern and value to all his people through his word, through his protection, and through his church. As one of my (Mike's) students notes, "People have inherent worth and dignity, not because of specific abilities that they do or do not have, but because they are created in the image of God." Thomas Reynolds addresses this view, stating, "In theological terms, disability need not be denied, decried, or overcome as an incomplete humanity, a defect indicating failure of sin. Full personhood is neither diminished by disability nor confirmed by ability. Instead, it is a factor of the interdependent relationships we share with one another as creatures loved into being by God and in the image of God."[15] Disability does not lessen humanity in any way.

Ultimately Jesus is the model for humanity, and just as we see humanity in Jesus, so we can come to know God through disability. Moltmann describes this unexpected turn: "Through persons with disabilities, other people can *come to know the real, suffering, living God* who also loves them infinitely."[16] Just as each human is declared incalculably full of worth, so we can see the incalculable worth of God by reflecting on his image in us.

All this is not to say that all is as it should be, for there are certainly things humans *are* that they *are not* supposed to be. And more obviously, humans do that which does not reflect the God in whose image they are made. Yet we cannot truly steal the image or destroy it in others. The image of God requires that each person be treated as one who is full of inherent dignity and capable of representing God. Jesus, who is "the image of the invisible God" (Col. 1:15), exactly like God but very much unlike us, became "the image of God" (2 Cor. 4:4), exactly like us.

Imago Dei tells us that God has always valued each person we meet more than we can imagine. God is faithful to those whom he has created in his image, and therefore there are no nobodies. Each person we are confronted with is dearly loved, carefully created, and unimaginably valuable. This doctrine highlights the inherent dignity and worth of every individual, emphasizing that our value comes from being created in the image of God rather than from our abilities or achievements. This perspective can be incredibly comforting and empowering, reminding each person of their intrinsic value and the care and protection that God offers through his word and the church.

15. Thomas E. Reynolds, *Vulnerable Communion: A Theology of Disability and Hospitality* (Brazos, 2008), 42.

16. Moltmann, "Liberate Yourselves," 121 (emphasis added).

QUESTIONS TO PONDER

1. See if you can make a list of ten things about you that have shaped who you are and that a person would likely not learn about you in a ten-minute introductory conversation.
2. If a new teen arrived at your youth group wearing clothes that were visibly not clean, what are five possible reasons? Follow the line of thinking on each potential reason. For each reason, how might that shape your understanding of that person?
3. How can you help the teens in your youth group suspend their assumptions about an individual until they know the deeper layers of their story and experience?
4. How do you explain the *imago Dei* in a middle school boy rolling on the floor as you are attempting to lead a lesson?
5. How can our understanding that Jesus suffered shape your response to a current pain point in your life?

4

Meth Labs, Sin, and Suffering

Core Theological Premises for Ministry

As the youth band leads another verse of the song, Patrick hides in the corner with his coat over his head. He likes music but claims that this is too loud and that he does not like this song. Patrick's primary diagnosis is autism spectrum disorder (ASD). He does not maintain eye contact, and he has repetitive body movements, intense interests, a flat tone, and difficulty navigating social relationships. Patrick's acquaintances assume this is the sum of his story and might conclude his autism is a result of the effect of living in a world marred by sin and the fall, something to be erased in eternity.

However, Patrick's story is much more layered. Patrick was born to unwed parents who each had multiple mental health issues. In addition, Patrick's father had a long criminal history, and domestic violence was part of family life. While Patrick was an infant, his father would threaten to hit him on the head if his mother did not comply with his father's directives. Occasionally, the menacing would increase: His father would threaten to drop Patrick as he held him upside down by one leg. Sometimes Patrick's father made good on his threats.

It took three tries by Child Protective Services (CPS) to get Patrick and his siblings removed from their birth home permanently. At twenty-two months, Patrick could barely walk, spoke about twelve words, had crossed eyes, and had ears so full of fluid that he had hearing loss because of untreated ear infections. Patrick would also experience frequent and aggressive dysregulation, beyond the norm of the "terrible twos."

Interventions began immediately. Surgeries, therapies, counselors, pediatricians, psychiatrists. Patrick is now thirteen. He is in special education at the local middle school, testing at a third-grade level. He has been hospitalized six times, has put holes in the drywall throughout his home, has caused his adoptive mother two surgeries for torn tendons, and takes six medications to manage his attention deficit hyperactivity disorder (ADHD) and aggression. He has shoplifted several times. He has never been invited to a birthday party. His favorite possessions are his blankie and oversized Big Wheel. He likes to watch *Curious George*. He will never live independently.

Church is the place where Patrick feels most welcome. People are kind and patient. They give him opportunities to build relationships and serve. He loves counting the children's offering each week and being trusted with the pastor's keys as he puts it away.

Big Questions

If we are loved, and in God's image, how are we to make sense of the causes and painful effects of trauma and disability? Between our two families, five of our adopted children were removed from their biological parents due to neglect and abuse. Prior to their adoption, one child was returned to their biological mother's home but then removed again after a meth lab was discovered in the home. The depth of physical damage due to drugs, the pain of trauma, and the long-lasting effects of abuse starkly present the reality of sin. Sin and its effect cannot be ignored. Sin is pervasive, reaching into all areas of life, and it is ruinous. However, how do we attribute blame or cause to a disability or trauma? Are all disabilities the result of sin? If not, is God responsible? Glibly claiming that all genetic variations that result in disability, as well as all injuries from natural causes, are the result of direct human sin is as false as blaming God for the presence of sin.

Three Views of Sin and Disability

Three primary views address the causes of disability or the relation of sin to disability: the fallen world approach, the social construction approach, and the integrative approach.[1] Each of these views is focused by a theological lens: *imago Dei*, sin, or an integration of both sin and *imago Dei*. After exploring the importance of a comprehensive view of sin, we will close the chapter by

1. Rhoda Olkin, "Could You Hold the Door for Me? Including Disability in Diversity," *Cultural Diversity and Ethnic Minority Psychology* 8, no. 2 (2002): 130.

outlining a series of theological axioms and how they should guide healthy ministry practice.

Fallen World Approach

According to the fallen world approach, disability is the result of the fallen state of humanity and the presence of sin. In this view, disability is thus a direct result of evil committed by individuals or an indirect result of the presence of sin in the world. Here, ministry tends to focus on mitigating the effects of sin, much like relief work following a flood or tornado. Ministries are primarily limited to reducing the impact of disability on an individual while accepting that it is likely beyond human capability to eradicate or heal disability or its social effects. The primary theological premise of such a ministry would be guided by a fallen-humanity or sin theology, minimizing *imago Dei*.

Social Construction Approach

The next view holds that disability is a social construction. According to this approach, disability should be fully embraced while we fight to eradicate the cultural structure perpetuating the experience of disability. Social stigmatization and exclusion are the core issues to address. Problems associated with disability are not caused by individual sin but rather by exclusion or ableism across cultures or societies. This view would hold that the church has fallen in line with an inappropriate view of disability that attempts to force normalization upon those affected. The social construction approach instead advocates for people to embrace others of all ages, genetics, and mental health statuses. This view tends to ignore the often-staggering medical needs and pain associated with disability while often glorifying disability; for instance, a *Reformed Journal* article suggests Jesus was autistic.[2] Practically, this view plays out by creating a model that is centered on celebrating disability with, at its extreme, no attempt to mitigate its sources and effects. The primary theological premise of such a ministry would be guided by universal *imago Dei* untempered by the acknowledgment of sin.

Integrative Approach

Disability is both "not the way it is supposed to be" and a mystery of God. Some reasons and causes of disability may be beyond human understanding and therefore warrant trust in God and his plan. This approach would attempt

2. Sarina Gruver Moore, "Autistic Jesus," *Reformed Journal*, April 10, 2023, https://reformedjournal.com/2023/04/10/autistic-jesus/.

to alleviate suffering while understanding that suffering has a unique role in God's plan. Each member of the body has gifts given by God that are necessary for the functioning of the body irrespective of ability or disability. Each person has a place in the kingdom and church regardless of capability or performance. The primary theological premise of such a ministry would be guided by holding both premises in tension, fallenness and *imago Dei*.

Discussing Disability Well

If you are like us, you hear uncomfortable and even offensive remarks about the causes of pain, trauma, and disability frequently:

God is just testing you.
You are being punished for sin.
The sins of the parents are visited on the children.
What happened to you? What's wrong with you?
Why are you like this?
You are so inspiring!
If you believed hard enough, you could walk!
Have you tried praying?
I have no reason to complain; just look at what you are going through.
If your God allows this kind of suffering, he is either a monster or powerless.
I cannot imagine having no parents.
I'd rather be dead than face . . .
She's in heaven now, so she can walk again. There are no wheelchairs in heaven.
I don't think of you as disabled. I don't even see your disability anymore.
Everyone has *some* kind of disability.
Actually, there's no such thing as a disability.

While some of these comments are well-meaning, they are all quite often on internet lists of "things to never say to a person with a disability." Though some of these comments are just ill-informed, many can be traced back to an incorrect theological premise and are pitfalls to avoid.

In 1 Corinthians 10:13, Paul states that "God is faithful: He will not let you be tried beyond what you are able to bear, but with the trial will also provide a way out so that you may be able to endure it" (NET). Thus, as theologian Amos Yong explains this verse, "if 'you' are impaired, then obviously 'you' must have been given a special grace to endure such disability."[3] Sometimes people must prove that sin is not at the root of their own "misfortune." At other times, the Christian community often "saints" them, expecting a herculean level of spiritual fortitude. We may even, as youth ministry theologian Amy Jacober notes, begin to revolve the world around a disability or trauma, unknowingly creating an idolatry that dethrones God.[4] We address "glass children" in a later chapter, showing how children can become like glass, or invisible, when a sibling's concerns define the entire family.

Human disability is not the same as suffering. Today a common and incorrect logic pervades our culture. Moralistic therapeutic deism has been determined by sociologists like Christian Smith to be the predominant religion in the United States, having replaced orthodox Christian beliefs for most adults and teens. Remarkably, this religion continues to operate under the name of Christianity although it opposes central Christian tenets. A therapeutic faith assumes God wants us to feel good and thus concludes that all suffering is against God's will. We will not address the full consequences of a therapeutic religion, as they have been robustly discussed in research such as the National Study of Youth and Religion.[5] The disconcerting outcome of therapeutic theology is that disability is seen as suffering, and suffering is seen as evil. It is a small jump to see all disability as evil and often related to personal sin. In this logic, we see the flaw of the common US perception of a therapeutic faith. Normal human limitations like being very young or old, or common impairments such as nearsightedness, are suddenly classified as wrongs suffered or evils to forestall. Natural life stages such as old age must be avoided instead of embraced. A diagnosable disability becomes associated with evil in this logic. A therapeutic faith is an incorrect theology that reduces and demands human flourishing to be equal to happiness and comfort.

The potential actual suffering experienced by those affected by trauma and disability is real and should not be ignored. Suffering can indeed reside in the chronic pain or extreme difficulties faced by a person with trauma or a disability, and also in families' crushed expectations and social stigma. Sometimes the suffering referred to is not experienced by the autistic teen but rather by the caregiver parents due to the loss of their child's social independence, a

3. Amos Yong, "Disability and Suffering?—Pastoral and Practical Theological Considerations," *Testamentum Imperium* 5 (2016): 12.

4. Amy E. Jacober, *Redefining Perfect: The Interplay Between Theology and Disability* (Cascade Books, 2017), 43.

5. "Making Sense of Teens and 'Fake' Christianity: The NSYR in a Nutshell," Ministry Leadership Center, 2011, https://ministryleadership.org/content/making-sense-of-teens-fake-christianity-the-nsyr-in-a-nutshell/.

Western ideal. As we can see, there are many false perspectives that can steer us wrong in our practice and pastoral care.

Amos Yong, in his article "Disability and Suffering?—Pastoral and Practical Theological Considerations," discusses four key ideas in exploring the causes of disability and its relationship to suffering and sin. Consider these as theological guardrails that properly guide theological thinking in relation to sin and disability. These guardrails allow us to avoid many of the pitfalls mentioned briefly above:

1. God's sovereignty does *not* mean God is the direct cause.
2. Though a fallen world, sins are *not* directly linked to disability.
3. All sickness is *not* derived from Satan or demons.
4. Pastoral agents should *not* resort to sovereignty, sin, or Satan as the first or foremost cause of any disability.[6]

Yong notes that disability and trauma are not inextricably linked to sin. It is crucial to understand that disability and trauma are complex experiences that can arise from a variety of factors, including genetics, accidents, age, and environmental influences. Structural evils, such as war and economic exploitation, do not mean that all impairments are influenced by devils. Human impairments are experienced by most people at some point in their life cycle. Associating trauma and disability overtly with sin or demons, especially personal sin, can be harmful and stigmatizing. Some children are in foster care because of an event such as a tragic accident that took both parents' lives. Some teens are in foster care because of sins committed against them. Fetal alcohol syndrome creates profound physical and mental difficulties because of sin, but at no fault of the child. Car wrecks can create profound trauma, not because of a particular person's sin but because of the "way things are." And although things are "not the way they are supposed to be," not all trauma and disability are directly caused by sin, demons, or God's sovereign will. In the case of God's will, God certainly "gives and takes away," but many instances of illness and disability in Scripture are simply cited as being the result of accidents or illness (2 Sam. 4:4; 2 Tim. 4:20).

In contrast to ableism or therapeutic religion, Cornelius Plantinga asks us to face the brokenness of the world with hope and grace. He writes,

> We have been called into existence, expected, awaited, equipped, and assigned. We have been called to undertake the stewardship of a good creation, to create

6. Yong, "Disability and Suffering?," 13.

> sturdy and buoyant families that pulse with the glad give-and-take of the generations. We are expected to show hospitality to strangers and . . . to seek justice for our neighbors and, whenever we can, to relieve them from the tyranny of their suffering. Some of us have been called, in imitation of Christ, to bear unusual suffering of our own. But we have also been called, and graced, to delight in our lives.[7]

In contrast to Plantinga's biblical vision, bad theology holds that disability, suffering, and mental health are solely a matter of heroic suffering or of the need for miraculous cures and often interprets suffering as a consequence of sin.

Additionally, it is helpful to note that all of us are temporarily abled. The disability rights movement has developed a nomenclature regarding those who are "temporarily able-bodied." This term emphasizes dependance at birth returning to dependency on others in old age.

Yong's guardrails helpfully tell us where we cannot go or where we should tread lightly theologically and pastorally. They fight against a social stigmatization of disability or normalization of shallow, feel-good theology. The guardrails point out negatives we should avoid, protecting us from ditches on either side of the road we travel in pastoral care. The following axioms are positive statements of theological premises that should guide and impact all programming, counseling, care, teaching, and ministry. If Yong's principles are guardrails keeping us out of the theological ditches, the axioms in the next sections are the guideposts, the theology that shows us the path forward.

Guideposts for Theology: Axioms for Ministry Design

Unlike many trails in the United States, the European trail system is well marked. I (Mike) was once hiking with a youth pastor from the Czech Republic. The system was prolific, and crisscrossing trails occurred constantly. Even so, he easily taught me the shape and color labels that were used on every trail. It seemed you could traverse Europe from country to country without a map, keeping your bearings the entire way. After a time, we realized that we had ventured into Poland. The trail and direction were clear, even if national boundaries were not.

A pioneer of disability ministry, the STARS (Seeking to Always Reflect the Savior) ministry at College Church in Wheaton, Illinois, is one of the oldest disability ministries in the US. STARS administrators were concerned that

7. Cornelius Plantinga Jr., *Not the Way It's Supposed to Be: A Breviary of Sin* (Eerdmans, 1996), 197.

a whole population was uninvolved in church, and they decided to engage. It would have been possible for them to quickly become lost in the myriad available directions as they blazed this new ministry trail. They began with finding ways to serve those with disabilities and their families. Now, people with disabilities sing in the choir, fully participate in integrated classrooms from children through adult, and work in the church's popular resale shop. They staff their own business to provide funding for their own outings and programs and exuberantly participate in the main service, sometimes on stage. This ministry is lifespan encompassing and not just for certain kinds of disability. All ages have places in which to be ministered to and to participate among and serve the rest of the congregation. College Church displays how clear theology leads to important practice differences.

The following sections present a set of theological principles that mark our progress forward on this journey. In a way, the following chapters are simply working out the implications of these core beliefs in practice. By making explicit the theological principles here, we can align our practice to them. While we have discussed *imago Dei*, sin, and the value of all persons, this list will engage a wider variety of core beliefs that influence and drive practice based on clear theological foundations. This list is arranged not in order of importance, but rather in logical order. The broader and first principles tend to pave the way for the following and more specific later principles. This chapter and the previous one have focused on the personhood and value of all people. This list will draw those premises into church practice.

As you read, note that the theological premises are not specifically or solely about trauma, disability, or orphans. Each of these principles is a fundamental posture guiding how we relate to all people in the world, specifically in the body of Christ. We do not need to find new theological points in order to argue for inclusion, hospitality, service, or equity for any marginalized group. All persons are affected and included. Each point here does have specific relevance to the discussion of marginalized teens, and we will discuss the particulars in light of that audience.

All People Are Created in the Image of God

The first edition of *Everybody Belongs, Everybody Serves: A Handbook for Disability Advocates* notes that "each person has intrinsic value not based on what she can do but on who she is."[8] As Genesis 1:26 says, "Then God

8. *Everybody Belongs, Everybody Serves: A Handbook for Disability Advocates* (Disability Concerns, 2009). Quoted in Thrive (CRCNA), "A Biblical Perspective on Disability and Inclusion," The Network, Christian Reformed Church, December 30, 2009, https://

said, 'Let us make humankind in our image'" (NRSVA). No group can be marginalized or excluded.

Ministry to the Marginalized Is a Fundamental Christian Virtue

It would be difficult to find sections of Scripture that do not highlight God's view of the marginalized, the outcast, or the foreigner. The Old Testament often describes a compelling concern of God using the phrase "orphans and widows." Orphans and widows are not two categories but the bookends of the call of God to his people regarding how they are to treat those oppressed, unrepresented, at risk, and outcast. "The prophets offer a call to justice for those who are wrongly oppressed and marginalized, those on the fringes of society—the downcast and disabled."[9] God's concern and call include all groups, from the youngest orphans to the oldest widows who are excluded and vulnerable.

The Church Is on Mission

The church is on a mission. However, this mission does not originate in the church itself. God's mission, or *missio Dei*, is given to the church. All believers are called by God; therefore, each believer has a mission given by God to fulfill while here on earth. Ephesians 2:10 emphasizes the purposes that God has infused into his people: "For we are God's handiwork, created in Christ Jesus to do good works, which God prepared in advance for us to do." Van Sanders elaborates on the importance and source of this mission in which we take part: "When kept in the context of the Scriptures, *missio Dei* correctly emphasizes that God is the initiator of His mission to redeem through the church a special people for Himself from all of the peoples (τα εθνη) of the world. He sent His Son for this purpose and He sends the Church into the world with the message of the gospel for the same purpose."[10] All teens who are part of the body are part of the mission originated by God and given to his church. Therefore everyone, regardless of race, class, disability, or age, has purpose and significance.

---

network.crcna.org/topic/justice-inclusion/disability-concerns/biblical-perspective-disability-and-inclusion.

9. Sarah J. Melcher, *Prophetic Disability: Divine Sovereignty and Human Bodies in the Hebrew Bible* (Baylor University Press, 2022), jacket copy.

10. Van Sanders, "The Mission of God and the Local Church," in *Pursuing the Mission of God in Church Planting: The Missional Church in North America*, ed. John M. Bailey (North American Mission Board of the Southern Baptist Convention, 2006), 24.

Everybody Serves, Everybody Belongs

These are really one principle, with two inseparable sides.[11]

- In healthy churches, everybody belongs.
  "Above all, love each other deeply, because love covers over a multitude of sins. Offer hospitality to one another without grumbling." (1 Peter 4:8–9)
- In healthy churches, everybody serves.
  "Each one should use whatever gift he has received to serve others, faithfully administering God's grace in its various forms." (1 Peter 4:10)

In light of the mission of God, everyone serves and everyone belongs. This premise is often theologically described as the priesthood of all believers. In 1 Peter 2:9, Peter makes this bold claim: "But you are a chosen people, a royal priesthood, a holy nation, a people belonging to God, that you may declare the praises of him who called you out of darkness into his wonderful light" (see also 1 Pet. 2:4 NIV 1984). Ministry is for the entire body, and each person belongs to God. Elton Trueblood, in *The Incendiary Fellowship*, describes this theological truth: "The ministry is for all who are called to share in Christ's life, the pastorate is for those who possess the peculiar gift of being able to help other men and women to practice any ministry to which they are called."[12] Here we do see a distinction in roles: the body and the pastor. All in the body are made for ministry, and the role of the pastor is to equip each believer to fulfill the ministry for which God calls them. There are no exceptions. All in the body are called to do ministry, gifted by the Spirit, and to be equipped. This premise will play out in significant ways in later chapters as we unpack doing ministry *with* people on the margins as opposed to doing ministry *to* people on the margins.

If you are a church leader, elder, pastor, or youth pastor, we hope you agree and resonate with your role as described by Greg Ogden. Ogden states that the reason for a pastor's knowledge, position, and professional training is to use this "knowledge to equip and deploy God's people in ministry. . . . Equipping pastors are committed to giving away the ministry."[13] The priesthood of

11. The following list is quoted in full from Thrive (CRCNA), "Biblical Perspective on Disability and Inclusion."

12. Elton Trueblood, *The Incendiary Fellowship* (Harper & Row, 1978), 41.

13. Greg Ogden, *Unfinished Business: Returning the Minstry to the People of God* (Zondervan, 2003), 97.

all believers does not allow excluding certain persons in the body from our responsibility to equip and deploy them for the work God has given them. Also note that each person has worth and purpose, but many do not often experience a feeling of that worth and purpose. It is not enough to mobilize teens to fulfill tasks or run programs. Engaging teens with service must allow them to experience the reality of their worth and significance. It is also vital for others to recognize that worth and significance.

All People in the Body Have Gifts

All people with trauma or disabilities have gifts. The Holy Spirit indwells each believer, giving each member at least one spiritual gift for the purpose of ministry. Gifts are not only for those of us who are able to sit in blue chairs or keep our shirts on during church, as we (Laura and Mike) shared in the last chapter regarding our children's challenges. "All believers have spiritual gifts; therefore, each believer receives from God the gifts he needs to accomplish this mission."[14] We do not simply tolerate each person trying to serve: Each is gifted for that service by the Spirit. As Paul notes, "There are different kinds of gifts, but the same Spirit distributes them" (1 Cor. 12:4).

John was a young man with Down syndrome. He participated in youth group and had a winsome way of convincing almost everyone he met, of any age, to try to do a headstand. When John developed this slight obsession, it was quite funny to see other teens, parents, staff—everyone—all attempting headstands at random times before and after church events. I wondered if people did it just to humor him. Ultimately, I realized that John had a way of disarming people and creating an atmosphere where risk, exuberance, and fun were expected. Most people would fail John's never-ending challenges to do a headstand, which he requested of people of all ages and even of people he did not know. The ability to get people to feel safe is a gift of hospitality. John could even make people happy in their abject headstand failure as he would bluntly say, "Not good. Good try." And then just walk away like you did not just embarrass yourself in front of a bunch of people. Normally we would not think of someone who does not own any space and is not in charge of any ministry as being able to exert hospitality. Part of the beauty of those on the margins is that their contributions can challenge everyone's norms and expand our vision to see the full scope of God's work through his people more accurately.

14. Quoted in Thrive (CRCNA), "Biblical Perspective on Disability and Inclusion."

No One Is More Important

My (Mike's) childhood home church did not have a youth group when I was a teen, but it still hit the common big youth-ministry ideas. I remember specifically being taught that my body was a temple and that having premarital sex was defiling that temple. I also remember that smoking was explicitly part of this potential defiling of temples. I remember wondering if those two were related in some way. As a youth pastor I picked up the same teaching line and taught it explicitly out of 1 Corinthians 3:16–17: "Do you not know that you are God's temple and that God's Spirit dwells in you? If anyone destroys God's temple, God will destroy him. For God's temple is holy, and you are that temple" (ESV). So there it was, right in print, to convince my young, impressionable teens: God destroys smokers. Then I had a bit of Greek in school and learned that almost all pronouns in the New Testament are plural. The "southern version" of 1 Corinthians 3:17 is "God's temple is holy, and y'all are that temple." As my favorite waitress for my morning Bible studies would say to us, "What can I get yous?" Just as she emphasized with her Midwest accent, so too is Paul putting an emphasis on the plural pronouns in this section of Scripture. Duane Elmer, a conflict specialist and seminary professor, points out that in 1 Corinthians 3, Paul equates all divisiveness with spiritual infancy (3:1–5).[15] "Wood, hay and straw" are not acts like playing video games and wasting time but are "acts that disrupt unity" (3:10–15).[16] The "costly stone" are acts that "contribute to harmony, affirmation, [and] building one another up, . . . esteeming the other"[17] over self and bearing one another's burdens. "God no longer dwells in buildings but in people by his Spirit," says Elmer. "Each person and each gathering of God's people [is] a holy place."[18] Therefore, unity is far more important to God than we can imagine. John Swinton, likely the preeminent thinker on disability and the church, writes: "Nowhere in the list of grace-filled gifts is one person more important than another, though people have different gifts. Nor is there any suggestion that people need to have a certain IQ score."[19] No one is more important in the body: All are vital.

15. Duane Elmer, *Cross-Cultural Conflict: Building Relationships for Effective Ministry* (InterVarsity, 1993), 29.

16. Elmer, *Cross-Cultural Conflict*, 29.

17. Elmer, *Cross-Cultural Conflict*, 29.

18. Elmer, *Cross-Cultural Conflict*, 29.

19. John Swinton, "Restoring the Image: Spirituality, Faith, and Cognitive Disability," *Journal of Religion and Health* 36, no. 1 (1997): 27.

The Church Is Fractured When People Are Excluded

Each member of the body of Christ is vital for the health of the church. Thomas Reynolds describes the repercussions of this view: "Theologically speaking, then, the body of Christ is fractured when people with disabilities are excluded from full participation in the church. Genuine love is prevented from coming to fruition when physical and social barriers prevent access."[20] The church, as the body of Christ, is one, with many parts. As described in 1 Corinthians 12:12: "The body is a unit, though it is made up of many parts; and though all its parts are many, they form one body" (NIV 1984). The chapter continues, "So it is with Christ. . . . Those parts of the body that seem to be weaker are indispensable" (12:12, 22 NIV 1984). Concluding his argument, Reynolds says, "Differences are good and blessed, the stuff of relationships. Alone we are incomplete; we need each other to be whole."[21] A fractured church body is not appealing to outsiders.

The Church Is Immature When Members Are Not Contributing Their Unique Callings, Gifts, and Functions in the Body

It is not only imperative for the teen who is serving to serve but also a matter of unity and maturity in the whole church. All believers are invited to participate in God's work, and without each member fulfilling their God-given and essential function, we cannot attain unity (see Eph. 4:13). Jesus's prayer in John 17, often called the glory chapter, is for unity. Unity through the expression of the gifts in the body leads to maturity, thus fulfilling our purpose to bring God glory on earth. Without this unity, without all parts of the body, the church is severely hampered in its mission, made immature and limited in showing God to a world desperately in need. Each person is vital. As Paul exhorts us to see, "Now to each one the manifestation of the Spirit is given for the common good" (1 Cor. 12:7). Jesus's request is that the church "be one as we are one" (John 17:11). God is perfect unity as three persons with distinct roles. Just as unity reflects the Godhead, so a lack of unity veils the glory of God. In his important work on conflict in the church, Duane Elmer asks, "Why doesn't God send revival?"[22] The cause is disunity and immaturity. God is made manifest in the body by each member contributing their gifts, offering their service, and pursuing their calling. There are no exceptions. Each teen in foster care, each person with health issues, and

20. Thomas E. Reynolds, *Vulnerable Communion: A Theology of Disability and Hospitality* (Brazos, 2008), 238.
21. Reynolds, *Vulnerable Communion*, 182.
22. Elmer, *Cross-Cultural Conflict*, 27.

each person experiencing a disability is vital to God's plan, the maturity of the church, and the kingdom of God.

It is vital that our theology encompass true care for all teens, especially those raised in meth labs, experiencing chronic mental health illness, or suffering in other ways. We cannot blame all suffering, trauma, and disability on sin, on demons, or on God's sovereignty. These premises keep us out of the ditches. Nor can we ignore the often-catastrophic effect of many of our adolescents' situations. Clear theological reflection helps us define our theological premises that will guide the practice of ministry and being the church to teens on the margins.

Remember Patrick from the beginning of the chapter? How do we make theological sense of Patrick's experience in light of this discussion? The sins of his biological parents significantly impacted his brain and development. There is no need for or benefit to twisting ourselves into the theodicy of wondering why a good God did not rescue him sooner or why healing could not run deeper. Patrick still sits in the corner with the coat over his head, counting the children's offering, an active church attender who knows Jesus loves him.

QUESTIONS TO PONDER

1. Think of a middle school student who likes to "talk smack" or uses one of the phrases from the list at the beginning of the chapter. How can we encourage thinking and phrases that communicate kindness and an understanding of the *imago Dei*?
2. Following a lesson on Genesis 1 and 2, where God is recorded as creating all things good, how would you respond to a teen with a disability who asks whether God created them good?
3. How might we help a teen impacted by the sins of their birth father understand the goodness of God as heavenly father, which is often described in patriarchal terms?
4. When church budgets are tight and staff already work long hours, how can we rationalize including extra time, budget allocations, and training?
5. What are commonly understood beliefs in the theology of your denomination or church that address the cause of disability? If this information is not readily available, what does this teach you about your denomination's approach to those on the margins?

5

Hospitality

Extending God's Welcome

For Ben, everything looks fine on the outside. If you asked him, in a moment of vulnerability, he would tell you that every conversation is a sham. Friendships are more for protection from the void than a serious sense of "being known." The adults in his life—his foster parents, teachers, youth pastor, and caseworkers—say they "know how he feels" and that they "have been there." However, well-meaning comments such as these just force Ben to further bottle up his feelings, frustrations, questions, and anxieties. Ben is not the only teen or young adult who shuts down communication with adults in his life. Chap Clark, among many other researchers, notes that "adolescents have a longing that parents, teachers, and other adults have ceased as a community to fulfill."[1] It is quite possible that every adult in Ben's life has abandoned him in significant and tragic ways. Ben has not arrogantly turned his back on the adult world; instead, no adult has ever invited him in.

Hospitality is the fundamental posture of all Christian communities. We have noted how the church has need of further developing skills to extend this fundamental Christian undertaking to those on the margins. Describing to the community the need for hospitality or the benefits it provides is not enough to convince them to address the needs of hurting, disabled, or disenfranchised teens. Nor is it adequate simply to express the requirement

1. Chap Clark, *Hurt 2.0: Inside the World of Today's Teenagers* (Baker Academic, 2011), 27–28, based on the research of Ron Powers and many others.

to extend hospitality, which might result merely in "guilting" people in the church into action. John Bennett, a theorist on higher education, suggests that "hospitality is a cardinal virtue, an essential requirement for what we are about."[2] This chapter explores the interaction between marginalized teens and hospitality.

How Does the Church Grow?

Many people tout new church growth philosophies, apologetic approaches, and ministry programs as the way forward for the church. How does the church grow and fulfill its mission, whether "to proclaim good news to the poor" or "set the oppressed free" (Luke 4:18; see also v. 21)? What are the ways in which the church grows? To answer, we consider one ancient and one modern example: plague and immigration.

Sociologist Rodney Stark holds a view of church growth that is contrary to more current methods. His extensive research of the early church demonstrates that the early church had very little in the way of programs, seminaries, buildings, professional clergy, or resources. The church was often marginalized and persecuted. So how did it grow? Stark holds that the early church grew, and grew magnificently, through sacrificial hospitality. When plagues came, most inhabitants fled ancient cities. In contrast, early Christians were well-known for staying to care for the sick. Often the sick person and the Christian treating them would die from the plague, but many times, they would live. The recovered sick would then follow Christ. When the rest of the community returned following the crisis, survivors, often including Christian caregivers, would still be present. Through researching this extraordinary care of the sick, Stark is able to track that Christians and their converts gained the ability to live through diseases that would kill others. Through this display of love, magistrates, similar to mayors, came to Christ in the Roman Empire. The disciples' love was evident to neighbors and the world, and it "resulted in substantially higher rates of survival"[3] and the blossoming of the early church.

Immigration is a more modern example of the church fulfilling its mission and growing. The Christian population of North America as a whole is stagnant. Until recently, as the population of the US grew due to both natural

2. John B. Bennett, "Teaching with Hospitality," *The Professional and Organizational Development Network in Higher Education* 12, no. 1 (2001): 1.

3. Rodney Stark, *The Rise of Christianity: How the Obscure, Marginal Jesus Movement Became the Dominant Religious Force in the Western World in a Few Centuries* (HarperSanFrancisco, 1997), 74.

increase through birth and immigration,[4] Christians have been a decreasing percentage of the population. The percentage of Christians in the US appears to have leveled out over the past few years.[5] Nevertheless, there is no county in the United States that has a statistically significant higher percentage of Christians today than it did ten years ago.[6] Many Christians have tried to confront this loss with theology, culture war, or politics. Often these approaches are driven by fear of loss. Loss of prestige, loss of power, or loss of position can be a motivator for action, but God calls us to reconsider our response.

Immigration brings many Christians and non-Christians into the US. Approximately 42 percent of immigrants are not Christian—a number comparable to the percentage of non-Christian US citizens[7]—and about 20 percent of unauthorized immigrants are non-Christian.[8] These immigrants, especially undocumented immigrants, find themselves in a new culture, often with no resources or recourse. When US Christians experience lack of some kind, resources to address it often exist. Many people who immigrate, however, find themselves with nowhere to go and lack the resources they need to survive. Many turn to the church and to Christ in their necessity. The hospitality of Christians for immigrants has helped prevent a decrease in the number of Christians in the West. Non-Christian immigrants are experiencing and meeting Christ through the hospitality of the church, and the faith of immigrants who are already Christian is bolstered by that hospitality as well.

Plagues and immigration are simply illustrations of the power of hospitality and the need for the church to lead in these ways. Pandemics and immigration, once thought to be distant concerns, now touch your church. In the same

4. Kristie Wilder, "New 2024 Population Estimates Show Nation's Population Grew by About 1% to 340.1 Million Since 2023," United States Census Bureau, December 19, 2024, https://www.census.gov/library/stories/2024/12/population-estimates.html.

5. Gregory A. Smith, Alan Cooperman, Becka A. Alper, et al., "Religious Identity," in *Decline of Christianity in the U.S. Has Slowed, May Have Leveled Off: Findings from the 2023–24 Religious Landscape Study*, Pew Research Center, February 26, 2025, https://www.pewresearch.org/religion/2025/02/26/religious-landscape-study-religious-identity/.

6. "Evangelical Protestant—Rankings by Area," The Association of Religion Data Archives, accessed March 8, 2025, https://www.thearda.com/us-religion/statistics/rankings?u=2&typ=2&cod=1.

7. Gregory A. Smith, Alan Cooperman, Becka A. Alper, et al., "Executive Summary," in *Decline of Christianity in the U.S. Has Slowed, May Have Leveled Off: Findings from the 2023–24 Religious Landscape Study*, Pew Research Center, February 26, 2025, https://www.pewresearch.org/religion/2025/02/26/religious-landscape-study-executive-summary/.

8. Ryan Foley, "Most Immigrants Vulnerable to Deportation Identify as Christian: Report," *The Christian Post*, April 7, 2025, https://www.christianpost.com/news/most-immigrants-vulnerable-to-deportation-are-christian-report.html. See also "The Religious Affiliation of U.S. Immigrants: Majority Christian, Rising Share of Other Faiths," Pew Research Center, May 17, 2013, https://www.pewresearch.org/religion/2013/05/17/the-religious-affiliation-of-us-immigrants/.

way, those with disabilities may be the focus of the next movement of God's mission through the church. Hospitality, and those to whom we offer it, are key to the heart of the gospel.

Why Hospitality?

Christian hospitality is based on the divinely sanctioned mutual obligation of all people to help one another. Hospitality involves the offer of protection, the removal of barriers, and self-sacrifice without command or expectation of repayment. Two issues drive the need to consider the place of hospitality in ministry to youth: the fundamental call to Christian leaders and the needs of youth on the margins.

Most Christians are aware of the qualifications for eldership in 1 Timothy 3:2, "Now the overseer is to be above reproach, faithful to his wife, temperate, self-controlled, respectable, hospitable, able to teach." Church leaders acknowledge that they should be able to teach or lead and that they should be respectable and controlled. Yet hospitality seems rarely discussed as a leadership quality.

The qualifications of Christian leaders described in the pastoral letters, such as in 1 Timothy 3:1–7, include hospitality in addition to the ability to take on a teaching role. Don Carson, one of the foremost New Testament scholars of recent decades, observes that hospitality is required of all Christians throughout the New Testament and is explicitly required for leadership in the church.[9] Thus, all believers, especially those who are leading and teaching, are involved in and mandated to engage in hospitality.

Disenfranchised adolescents are a significant challenge in youth ministry, yet teens recognize hospitality. Does someone know my name? Am I able to contribute to the group? Do people notice when I am gone? Teens regularly forget substantial content from a sermon, Bible study, or talk, yet research demonstrates that students do not forget how their teacher treated them. Teens fare much better in situations where they perceive the adults and organizations in their lives "to be concerned about them individually."[10]

Christ as Alien: The Nature of Hospitality

If our ultimate aim is extending an invitation to Ben and millions like him, two paradigms are necessary for understanding hospitality at the margins:

9. D. A. Carson, "The Locus of Authority," in *Evangelical Dictionary of Theology*, 2nd ed., ed. Walter A. Elwell (Baker Academic, 2001), 230.

10. Ernest T. Pascarella and Patrick T. Terenzini, *How College Affects Students*, vol. 2, *A Third Decade of Research* (Jossey-Bass, 2005), 599.

Christ as alien and Christ as host. In the following sections, this chapter first explores the theological foundations of hospitality in Christ as both alien and host. Then, it reflects on a series of conditions that destroy hospitality and, in closing, considers a set of disciplines that enable hospitality.

Scripture has strong concern for the alien. In many cultures and times, all outsiders were automatically considered enemies. The unknown was not an adventure or a final frontier but represented real risk to one's entire family's health and existence. To extend one's hand meant one could not ready a weapon. Then and now, to welcome means to disarm and vulnerably open oneself to the other. In many places, even today, there are essentially two categories: enemy and family. To be a stranger was to be an enemy. To be welcomed meant one is no longer a stranger, no longer a threat, but rather a person equated with family. By offering hospitality to an alien, one renders that person non-alien. Belonging has often meant protection, having a place, and becoming family, with the rights and responsibilities therein.

To extend one's hand is to both offer a welcoming home and extend an invitation to a journey. This applies not only to ancient cultures but also to youth groups and camps. Today, too many youth spaces are "property": properties owned by subgroups that feel they must defend against the sudden appearance of people they perceive as enemies or unfamiliar intruders. Many teens with perceived "issues" or chronic health conditions feel alien in the church. Likewise, a foster child or disabled teen can be viewed as threatening and foreign, an invasion into the domains of other adolescents. Hospitality reverses this violence and is lexically opposite from "alien" in the New Testament.[11] Hospitality is thus the creation of a space within which sociological comfort can enable learning—learning that requires both support and risk. Mitigating risk and offering a supporting welcome are within the scope of the role of youth leader.

Jesus himself is a ξένος (*zenos*), an alien.[12] Jesus is the stranger to whom we offer hospitality. A fundamental principle must guide practice: In our society, marginalized and disabled students are sometimes viewed as aliens or "others," and, as the church, we are required to offer them hospitality. As we welcome teens, so we offer Christ the same. Thus Jesus, in a very real sense, is in our youth ministries, not just because we talk about him. Christ's presence among us does not simply require hospitality but demonstrates God's very nature in a life of hospitality.

11. Timothy Friberg, Barbara Friberg, and Neva F. Miller, "ξένος," in *Analytical Lexicon of the Greek New Testament*, Baker's Greek New Testament Library 4 (Baker Books, 2000), 275.

12. Gustav Stählin, "ξένος," in *Theological Dictionary of the New Testament*, trans. and ed. Geoffrey W. Bromiley (Eerdmans, 1967), 5:20.

Christ Models and Commands

In the Gospels, the work of Jesus rests to a large degree on the hospitality extended to him (Mark 1:29–34; 2:15–17; 14:3–9; etc.). In the parables, he plainly accords great significance to hospitality (Luke 10:34–37; 11:5–13; 14:12–14; etc.). What is even more important is that God's hospitality is an essential part of his message. As Gustav Stählin says in the *Theological Dictionary of the New Testament*, "Condescending generosity is one of the fundamental features in the biblical depiction of God"[13] (Luke 12:37; 13:29; 14:16–24; 15:23; etc.). Thus, it is no surprise that the act of offering hospitality is an act of hospitality to Jesus himself. As we are his people and image bearers, we are to be hospitable as God is hospitable.

The command to extend hospitality applies to all youth ministries just as it applies to all disciples of Christ (Matt. 25:35–36; Rom. 12:13; etc.). Jesus "presents it as a fact in the life of His people."[14] A powerful connection made by the author of Hebrews in 13:2 draws attention not to any reward but "to the possibility of contact with the metaphysical world which hospitality gives."[15] Essentially, a lack in welcoming a foster child might precipitate missing a supernatural encounter. In fact, hospitality may transform the youth room into a liminal space: a place where the veil is thin and eyes are open to God's work and God's presence.[16]

How does this look in practice? In a college course on spiritual disciplines, my (Laura's) students read a text that encouraged intentionality in life practices. Following the reading, students would choose a practice rooted in the book and commit to practicing it for the semester. One chapter that was a favorite with students was on the topic of hospitality. College students are just beginning to own their space, whether in a dorm or apartment, so thinking about hospitality in that space was exciting. One student, a resident assistant, wanted to commit to being present and available to the girls on her floor, but she realized that propping her door open was not enough. Her room was rarely tidy, leaving no comfortable place for a guest to sit. For her hospitality project, she committed to keeping the large comfy chair in her room free from her laundry and therefore always available so a student could come and sit. At the end of the semester, for her final presentation, the resident assistant carried the large comfy chair across campus into the classroom and used it for her seat as she presented.

13. Stählin, "ξένος," 5:20.
14. Stählin, "ξένος," 5:21.
15. Stählin, "ξένος," 5:22.
16. Kenda Creasy Dean, *Almost Christian: What the Faith of Our Teenagers Is Telling the American Church* (Oxford University Press, 2010), 206–7.

With tears in her eyes, she shared about the many important conversations she had been able to have with her residents because she had intentionally created a welcoming space.

God waits among us. To engage a foster child is to make space for human encounter and God encounter alike. Sometimes we need to clean off our chairs and learn new skills to make a place for welcome. Hospitality provides a fundamental connection between teens on the margins and the faith community. Quite often teens must belong before they can believe; seeing and experiencing God comes through the group. Christ comes to earth as a guest and an alien. Consider the tacit indictment and poignant proclamation if hospitality is withheld: There is no guest room, no place for the creator of the earth (Luke 2:7)! May teens of all situations find welcome, just as if they were Christ in our midst.

Christ as Host: The Model of Hospitality

At the same time that Christ is rejected as an alien and stranger, he is also a welcoming host. In stark contrast to Christ's rejection, the psalmist boldly prophesies in Psalm 23:5 that "God Himself prepares the table for His guests and anoints their heads."[17] Christ is portrayed as the humble host of the feast (Mark 6:41–44; 8:6–9) who serves guests and washes feet (John 13:1–7). Ultimately, "as oriental hospitality requires in extreme cases, [Christ] crowns His service by redeeming His guests with His own life (Mark 10:45), giving Himself to His guests as an offering in a way which surpasses all human comprehension (Mark 14:22)."[18] In this biblical motif, the connection between hospitality and redemption is evident. Hospitality—its meaning and achievements—directly connects to the gospel.

It becomes quite clear that "tea and crumpets" should not be the primary image of hospitality. Our primary youth ministry model cannot be dodgeball to attract teens and a sermon to inform them. Sacrificial welcome requires more. As we (Mike and Laura) welcomed hurt foster children into our homes, we discovered that ministry in our living rooms looks significantly different from ministry at an office in a church. It is also much messier, harder, more time-consuming, and vastly more impactful.

Hospitality is fundamental to the follower of Christ, is commanded by Christ, and provides the occasion for supernatural encounter. As mentioned earlier in this chapter (in the section "How Does the Church Grow?"), Stark

17. Stählin, "ξένος," 5:25.
18. Stählin, "ξένος," 5:25.

suggests that hospitality, even to the point of welcoming the sick or dying, precipitated the dramatic rise of early Christianity.[19] Visiting a teen's family and seeing their life, attending a recital or game, or helping them acquire a medical service are powerful testimonies that bring teens into the church.[20] Yet hospitality is not simply a method of evangelism but an actual communication and embodiment of the gospel itself. Just as it is required of all disciples, is modeled by Christ, and demonstrates the very nature of God, hospitality is a primary avenue by which the gospel is lived.

The church's gospel calling is to make disciples. Is it possible that youth programming pales in significance to the fact that the people are living the gospel and welcoming marginalized teens? And not just teens: eternal beings! C. S. Lewis clearly outlines the posture one should hold toward oneself and toward other people: "The load, or weight, or burden of my neighbour's glory should be laid daily on my back, a load so heavy that only humility can carry it, and the backs of the proud will be broken. It is a serious thing to live in a society of possible gods and goddesses. . . . There are no *ordinary* people. You have never talked to a mere mortal."[21]

Figuring out how to include an autistic middle school teen in icebreaker games and recognizing the "eternal weight of glory" seem disparate pursuits. The supreme value in each activity, whether games, small groups, camps, or the experience of trauma and disability, is that Christ shines in a thousand places. Christ shines in youth ministry most often through the margins. One can only ignore the implications of the gospel in youth groups if one falsely accepts that Christ also lived a divided life between his work and worship, between his play and the Psalms, between those who did not require healing and those he healed. It is imperative, irrespective of ability or disability, to recognize the true nature of others and ourselves in the youth ministry setting. As discussed in chapter 3 regarding *imago Dei*, "respect is a bestowal of virtue, a mode of interaction that bestows dignity on the [teen] as a person."[22] Respect is independent of performance, ability, or homogeneity. Hospitable people, action, and space demonstrate respect.

As youth workers, we (Mike and Laura) recognize that most students will forget almost everything taught. I (Mike) sometimes cannot get my middle

19. Rodney Stark, *The Rise of Christianity: A Sociologist Reconsiders History* (Princeton University Press, 1996), 188.

20. Of course, abuse-prevention training and strict adherence to abuse-prevention policies is critical when planning and making these types of visits to teens' homes or activities.

21. C. S. Lewis, *"The Weight of Glory" and Other Addresses* (HarperSanFrancisco, 2001), 44–45.

22. Marshall Gregory, unpublished manuscript presented during Taylor University Pedagogy Seminar 2012, held May 21–25, 2012, at Taylor University, Upland, IN.

school Sunday School class to remember a Bible reference even when it is written on the board in front of them! While teaching is still vital, note what teens will remember: the person. Teens are experts at your attitudes toward them. This raises the question, "To what end do I teach theological definitions, creeds, and prayers if most of the content and facts will soon be forgotten?" Content is an important and integral part of making disciples. We cannot minimize doctrine, yet it is not the center. Marginalized teens make this painfully evident. Content can never take the place of the people who are involved in the process. What if youth services were more about welcoming people than only passing along information? Simple transmission of information is too shallow a goal if it replaces truly walking with those made in the image of God. Teens vitally need hospitality. Hospitality fundamentally acknowledges the fact that information is not the primary element in the room. God is present, and people made in his image are present. Here there can be no satisfaction with mere transmission of knowledge. Hospitality "yields more appreciation for the distinct gifts of the other."[23] Simple transmission of information is a weak discipleship that views information as primary over those loved by God sitting in front of the pastor or mentor. To carry the knowledge of "the other" and their ultimate potential is a gift from God, as Lewis notes, a weight of glory, that can only be lived by humility.

Humility requires a good deal from the youth minister: to make way and to make room. Humility requires the posture that adults, their position or title, and information are not the only significant forces in the classroom. Youth pastors "do not constitute a special subgroup of innately superior human beings."[24] The acts of hospitality force us to acknowledge the other and enter into the same process they are entering: relationship and dialogue with truth in the presence of God. Craig Dykstra, a leading Christian educator, notes, "The spiritual foundation of intellectual inquiry may not ultimately be hubris, but humility in the face of realities that do not finally submit to our fantasies and manipulation."[25] Our calling to humility, patience, kindness, and compassion are the virtues through which knowledge is transformed into wisdom.[26] This view of truth and view of people, including oneself, ultimately enables the practice of hospitality. Hospitality becomes a spiritual discipline that enables our

23. Bennett, "Teaching with Hospitality," 1.

24. Gregory, unpublished manuscript presented during Taylor University Pedagogy Seminar 2012.

25. Craig Dykstra, *Growing in the Life of Faith: Education and Christian Practices* (Geneva Press, 1999), 137.

26. Douglas Jacobsen and Rhonda Hustedt Jacobsen, *Scholarship and Christian Faith: Enlarging the Conversation* (Oxford University Press, 2004), 11.

interaction with God himself through his marginalized people. Kenda Creasy Dean summarizes this well: "In the practice of hospitality, God sends me to strangers in the name of Jesus Christ, who call me to recognize God's image in them and, because we share divine parentage to acknowledge them—in all their glorious strangeness—as my brothers and sisters."[27] Christians recognize God in the presence of strangers in the context of the youth room.

Pragmatically, what does hospitality look like for teens in youth groups? A seasoned children's pastor once shared, "Games are to children what coffee is to adults." And while her ministry focused on those younger than our target in this text, the message holds true. Enjoying play together breaks the ice and gives context for the conversations that connect. Many youth ministries provide a space with game tables: ping-pong, foosball, pool, carpetball, and the like. Just remember to think through accessibility for various mobility issues and avoid highly confrontational games for those with trauma. Some offer video games, especially those that invite multiple players. Youth group begins with free time to play together and then often moves into an organized game that invites everyone to enjoy each other's company.

The Christian Life Through Hospitality

Is there something fundamentally spiritual about welcoming those on the margins? Spiritual activities, such as Communion or prayer, are often seen as the "true" spiritual acts. We can erroneously think that praying before a meal with a child is the sole "spiritual" part of the day and consider mealtime itself just a mess. I (Mike) once had seven foster kids at once around my table. I can attest that there was both a lot of prayer and a lot of mess. Thinking through Christ as alien and host allows us to see his presence in all aspects of life and ministry, such as feeding a foster child. Church fathers demonstrate that the spiritual life is not so complex and not so "spiritual" as some modern thinkers have made it. Eating, offering food, and praying are all spiritual because spirituality is fundamental to our nature. The modern separation of the sacred and the secular has relegated prayer and Communion to "spiritual activities," while feeding children is just a necessary task unrelated to our relationship with God. We cannot divide Communion from the embodied act of eating. Likewise, prayer, as an embodied act, has seven physical postures modeled throughout Scripture.[28] Just as prayer is embodied in the person of the "pray-er," so hospitality is also a spiritual act. As Elizabeth Newman

27. Dean, *Almost Christian*, 33.
28. See Luke 22:41; 18:13; Exod. 34:8; Ps. 63:4; and Mark 11:25 for various examples.

explains, "Hospitality, like all Christian practices," is fundamentally tied to and "grounded in humanity's chief end."[29] As described by the Westminster Catechism, all acts and practices connect "to glorify God, and to enjoy Him forever."[30] Some activities may be more or less significant, but to label them more or less "spiritual" is unhelpful and a misnomer. Spirituality is not something one adds to life as a flavoring to the week on Sunday mornings, nor is hospitality something sprinkled into ministry settings.

Thus, hospitality is fundamentally an embodied Christian practice. The words of Elizabeth Patton Moss illustrate:

> Saint Francis came to preach. With smiles he met
> The friendless, fed the poor, freed a trapped bird,
> Led home a child. Although he spoke no word,
> His text, God's love, the town did not forget.[31]

Hospitality is not simply an obligation or command. It is a view of life, a way of viewing oneself and a way of viewing people other than oneself. We do not hold that hospitality is the ultimate key or the most important element in Christian discipleship, nor is it meant to supplant truth or teaching. Hospitality does highlight the fact that the best type of ministry is to live Christianly. Many pastors, monks, priests, spiritual directors, and desert fathers found that their primary role with regard to the weary pilgrim and seeker was to welcome and to make space both for the truth and for others. This discovery—that one should welcome visitors and make space for truth—is waiting for the youth worker as well. Mikhail Bakhtin, a Russian exiled from his country for his Christian faith, proposes that "we have a responsibility toward all that is 'other' than the self. . . . Any truth we might achieve in life is available only as a relationship: relationship with Christ."[32] Thus the Rule of Saint Benedict can take on new significance in our communities: "Let all guests who arrive be received like Christ, for he is going to say, 'I came as a guest and you received me.'"[33]

This chapter concludes by outlining a series of opposing postures that enable or destroy the Christian practice of hospitality within the youth ministry

29. Elizabeth Newman, *Untamed Hospitality: Welcoming God and Other Strangers* (Brazos, 2007), 124.

30. Matthew Henry, *The Westminster Assembly's Shorter Catechism* (Franklin Merrill, 1846), 1.

31. E. P. Moss, "Sermon Without Words," in *Harvest of Gold*, ed. Ernest R. Miller (C. R. Gibson, 1983), 74.

32. Jacobsen and Jacobsen, *Scholarship and Christian Faith*, 42–43.

33. Quoted in Amy G. Oden, ed., *And You Welcomed Me: A Sourcebook on Hospitality in Early Christianity* (Abingdon, 2001), 77.

setting: performance versus dialogue, owning versus dwelling, and hierarchy versus community.

Performance or Dialogue?

"So should I dance to make them listen?" stated a youth pastor beleaguered by the generational and technological distance between himself and his students. Frankly, please don't. First, few youth workers are likely capable of rehearsed elocutionary performances that touch the unmitigated desire for relevance and changing interests within a diverse teen population. Second, it would harm teens. Today, teens perceive a real and stinging separation from the adult world. Chap Clark, an adolescent ethnographer, has labeled this phenomenon "Systemic adult abandonment."[34] Adolescents and young adults feel as aliens in the adult world, and none more so than those who experience trauma or disability. It appears our society intentionally and systemically alienates youth from the very adults who could invite them into the new and challenging world. While foster children have almost unanimously experienced abuse and neglect from their biological families, many more teens have experienced emotional or physical violence, even within the educational system.[35] Thus, Tim Clydesdale argues that we should "respect, understand, and creatively engage"[36] those for whom we care. Respect sums up the necessary approach to dialogue in ministry.

Imagine a teen, hurt or rejected at every turn, first by his biological family and then via a revolving door of constant rejection by changing caseworkers and foster homes. This teen struggles at school and has limited access to resources like mentors and tutors. Then place that adolescent in a competitive, information-centered, tight-knit, and somewhat insular community called the church. Too often the church asks that people "get cleaned up and presentable" before joining. Often, we fear that the issues troubled teens face are contagious to our good and "normal" teens. This places an extreme burden on a needy and marginalized foster child to perform to a set of expectations they do not understand.

34. Clark, *Hurt 2.0*, 23.

35. Samantha Neiman, *Crime, Violence, Discipline, and Safety in U.S. Public Schools: Findings from the School Survey on Crime and Safety, 2009–10* (NCES 2011-320), U.S. Department of Education, National Center for Education Statistics (U.S. Government Printing Office, 2011), https://nces.ed.gov/pubs2011/2011320.pdf.

36. Tim Clydesdale, "Wake Up and Smell the New Epistemology," *Chronicle of Higher Education*, January 23, 2009, https://www.chronicle.com/article/wake-up-and-smell-the-new-epistemology/.

A performance mentality would only validate a teen's suspicions that no one understands and no one cares. We believe a performance mentality is yet another act of violence, especially when there is ableism creating impossible standards. This violence occurs when we are more concerned with mitigating disturbing behaviors or negative influences on "good" teens from those who are different or troubled than we are with supporting the different or troubled teens. Some marginalized teens will accept the demands of a performance mentality simply because many teens continue to prefer conditional acceptance over rejection. Natural positive reinforcement and a positive group influence is powerful but should not be done for the sake of the comfort of the group. Offering hospitality should be a natural process of first making teens welcome and safe and then facilitating their growth.

In contrast to requiring performance, offering hospitality enables connections between teens as well as between youth and adults. Jennifer Brannock Cox, a professor of communications, summarizes: "I'm not proposing that we dance for our [teens] or even attempt to meet their impossible standards for stimulation. What they want is an opportunity to connect . . . in a way that is meaningful and applicable. I don't think that is too much to ask."[37] Highly structured and controlled programs, overfilled with activity, can reduce the opportunity for relationship and being known. This is just an example of the host of gaps present in any environment that block "connection." These gaps are between teen and teen, teen and God, teen and adult, adult and self, and so on. They may be theological, philosophical, technological, generational, or simply caused by sleep deprivation and over programming. Recognition and appreciation of these gaps is vital. International conflict specialist Mark Gerzon explains that dialogue is built on mutual respect and respect leads to acknowledging difference as a very good part of the natural order established by God.[38] Respect intends to build trust and is perfectly suited for bridging the many "gaps" experienced in the lives of marginalized teens. We recommend allowing teens to tell their stories, to critique the ministry, to ask what they believe. Teens have beliefs and conflicts, yet they pervasively believe that adults do not care or cannot be trusted. Offering true open dialogue is an act of hospitality because it moves youth ministry from being a place to *speak* at teens toward a place where they can be *heard*. God, the teacher of Israel, listens to his people

37. Jennifer Brannock Cox, "Reclaiming the Classroom with Old-Fashioned Teaching," *Chronicle of Higher Education*, April 29, 2012, https://www.chronicle.com/article/reclaiming-the-classroom-with-old-fashioned-teaching/.

38. Mark Gerzon, *Leading Through Conflict: How Successful Leaders Transform Differences into Opportunities* (Harvard Business School Press, 2006), 48.

(John 9:31). To respect a teen is required; to hear a teen is a gift we can offer. Both mutual respect and mutual hearing must be intentionally built into healing Christian environments. In doing so, youth ministries exhibit the gospel.

Owning or Dwelling?

We have considered thus far that Christ is among us in each hurting teen, disabled child, and ministry program. To the degree that we perform hospitality, we welcome him and his truth to be present in our midst. Welcoming is a gospel action and fully recognizes the value possessed by each child on the margins. Now it is necessary to consider the place from which we can offer welcome. Famous Christian spiritualist Henri Nouwen states, "It is obligatory for Christians to offer an open and hospitable space where strangers can cast off their strangeness and become our fellow human being."[39] What does it mean to invite those other than ourselves? To make a space? Space is not physical space alone.

I (Mike) once worked for a college where the *Student Handbook* stated that "the classroom is the domain of the professor." The implication and explanation were clear: Students were to tread lightly on the holy ground of the professor. My word, my thought, and my judgment were law. The students were strangers, foreigners, and aliens. Under the best of circumstances, the students could potentially feel welcomed but knew they did not have ownership. This lecture hall was a place where students neither came voluntarily nor acted comfortably. Students could not bring their full selves to the classroom. It was hallowed ground upon which blessings were bestowed upon those who pleased the king. I do not think it is lost on students that lecture halls bequeath A's to those who please the professor.

In the same way, there are many rules for how a ministry runs, what kinds of questions can be asked, who gets to lead up front, and so on. This approach is ownership oriented and destroys hospitality. Conversely, Nouwen argues that "we cannot change the world by a new plan, project, or idea. We cannot even change other people by our convictions, stories, advice and proposals, but we can offer a space where people are encouraged to disarm themselves, lay aside their occupations and preoccupations and listen with attention and care to the voices speaking in their own center."[40]

39. Henri J. M. Nouwen, *Reaching Out: The Three Movements of the Spiritual Life* (Doubleday, 1975), 65.

40. Nouwen, *Reaching Out*, 76.

Ministry often dwells on ideas, but it is done in spaces, with people. A requisite understanding of teaching is that "space" teaches powerfully. Chapters 6 and 7 address the subtle yet powerful ways we ignore how our buildings and programs are ignoring certain groups. Space, created or simply allowed to continue, is part of a powerful implicit curriculum.[41] Youth ministries must be characterized by "*inhabitable* truths . . . humble confidence . . . relational trust; from individualist knowing to communal knowing and being known."[42] We may only offer hospitality when we have a place from which to extend it.

Space is less about physical accommodations, although it certainly encompasses that element, than about other things. Space is about the interior of the minister and leader and their willingness to open themselves to others. A sense of humility and vulnerability is integral to opening a space. Jesus models a host that offers hospitality in his person and not some physical activity like tea time and crumpets. Here we highlight again how you view teens and yourself. The ministry role becomes far more than dispensing information but takes on the role of host, just as Christ is host and offers much more than information. Christ offers his very self.

Hospitality does not simply offer a physical place. It fundamentally offers oneself. As Molly Quinn, director of the Curriculum Theory Project, explains, "We must actually be there—present, to welcome and receive the [teen]. Herein hospitality does indeed call for a vision of home. . . . This sense of place is not so much a building as a people who are called."[43] Institutions or buildings may provide space but do not offer genuine hospitality. Hospitality "calls us to enlarge our hearts by offering our time and personal resources [the gift of ourselves] . . . and invite[s] others also to bring themselves to curriculum labors we undertake together."[44] This invitation is not simply outward but also directed to oneself. "I must be willing to leave my own safe place and seek hospitality with another, to ask for help and let myself be guided. I must be willing to be the needy, vulnerable, weary traveler as well as the generous host."[45] Vulnerability naturally requires risk. This chapter now turns to this final consideration.

41. Elliot W. Eisner, *The Educational Imagination: On the Design and Evaluation of School Programs*, 3rd ed. (Macmillan, 1994), 95.

42. Rodney Clapp, *A Peculiar People: The Church as Culture in a Post-Christian Society* (InterVarsity, 1996), 186.

43. Molly Quinn, "'No Room in the Inn?' The Question of Hospitality in the Post(Partum)-Labors of Curriculum Studies," in *Curriculum Studies Handbook—The Next Moment*, ed. Erik Malewski (Routledge, 2010), 109.

44. Quinn, "'No Room in the Inn?,'" 109.

45. Margaret Guenther, *Holy Listening: The Art of Spiritual Direction* (Cowley, 1992), 11.

Competition or Community?

Just as vulnerability requires risk for the teen, so hospitality involves risk for the ministry and minister. Hospitality is as much a promise to the teen as it is a threat to the status quo of the ministry. Postmodern philosopher Jacques Derrida describes the risk: "To let oneself be swept by the coming of the wholly other, the absolutely unforeseeable . . . stranger, the uninvited visitor, the unexpected visitation beyond welcoming apparatuses."[46] Essentially, Derrida states that hospitality requires more of us than we can fathom or for which we can prepare. Hospitality in ministry must contain at least two conditions. The first condition is for the minister truly to give herself, and the second is to invite teens as they are. Parker Palmer, an educational philosopher, illustrates the common contradiction of these two conditions.[47] One way ministers give of themselves and meet teens where they are is by facilitating a multidirectional flow of relationship between an object/subject and those engaging it. Diagrams A and B (on p. 84 and 85) model potential flows of interaction. Consider the model depicted in diagram A, which is adapted from Parker Palmer's book *The Courage to Teach*. Here God is an object of study, the pastor or parent is an expert, and the teens are amateurs. The one-directional flow depicted demonstrates that neither the pastor (the expert) nor the teen (an amateur) has direct experience with God; neither are they known by one another. The hierarchical approach of this model focuses on the dissemination of knowledge instead of relationship between people and separates the knowers from one another and the object of study. Note that here teens only interact with God mediated by an adult.

Diagram A not only represents a tiered approach to knowledge and relationships but also outlines the predominant competitive model of Western education and most ministry today. Each teen is alone in their search and connections with God. "Competition makes it difficult to regard others as potential friends or collaborators; even if you're not my rival today, you could be tomorrow."[48] An example of this would be competitive Bible quizzing where teens are pitted against one another to prove their mastery of Scripture memorization as a body of knowledge.

Hospitality is possible when one has a place from which to extend it. Ironically, we are aliens and strangers like Christ and thus homeless until we reach

46. Jacques Derrida, "Hostipitality," in *Acts of Religion*, ed. Gil Anidjar (Routledge, 2002), 361–62.

47. Parker J. Palmer, *The Courage to Teach: Exploring the Inner Landscape of a Teacher's Life* (Jossey-Bass, 2007).

48. Alfie Kohn, "The Case Against Competition," *Working Mother*, September 1987, https://www.alfiekohn.org/article/case-competition/.

our final home. How can one offer hospitality out of homelessness? Christian pastors, parents, and volunteers are indeed aliens and strangers following the one who has no place to rest his head. Yet we can take comfort that we are situated in the communion of saints. The communion of saints, the people of God, is our fundamental identity, and that identity rests in God. Out of this rest in God, the community of God can offer hospitality. Diagram A does not recognize the individual needs of the adolescents or the true nature of relationship; neither does it give an accurate picture of the community of God. This model asks for complacency in teens: for them to sit and absorb while being fed a secondhand experience. Teens interact with God only indirectly, always mediated by an adult. Notice how each teen is separate, an island? This view ignores interaction among the teens in favor of dissemination of information. This model cannot accommodate the varied experiences of the teens we are to serve; it ignores their needs for one another and for direct connection with firsthand truth.

Palmer's second diagram (diagram B) visually illustrates a shift toward the creation of community and direct experience. In this diagram we see that each person is in relationship with each other, no one is separated, and the interactions are mutual. God interacts with and is interacted with by the pastors, the parent, the teens, and others in the church. Each human in the diagram becomes a knower, knowing both God and other knowers. This diagram

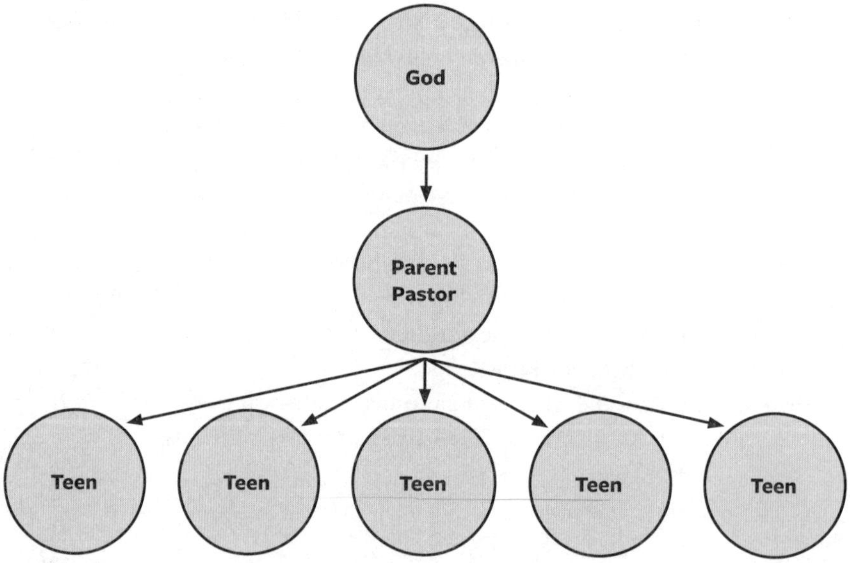

Diagram A

Adapted from Parker J. Palmer, *The Courage to Teach: Exploring the Inner Landscape of a Teacher's Life*, 100.

also presents that each parent, pastor, teen, and other church member connects with one another. One cannot simply disseminate facts to be swallowed without relationship. Here, it is also impossible to see our relationship with God as solely a personal enterprise. We cannot be in Christian community if we are only alone with God and our Bible in a closet. This approach ignores how God works in and through each other person in the church. Diagram B highlights the contributions each teen can make as well as the interconnectedness of the Christian community.

This perspective is necessary for hospitality to function in a biblical manner. In all groups of Christians, all Christians are priests (1 Pet. 2:9–10) and taught by the Holy Spirit (1 John 2:27). To echo Martin Luther, this means that each Christian autistic child, each believing foster child, is a priest. Luther would have called your middle school boy a pope![49] Non-Christian children with trauma are in the image of God and have contributions to make. Hospitality invites both experts and novices, pastors and teens, parents and children to become knowers, fellow learners journeying together. Abba James of the desert states, "It is better to receive hospitality than to offer it."[50] It is only possible to receive hospitality if we do not own the space or the ideas. This posture does

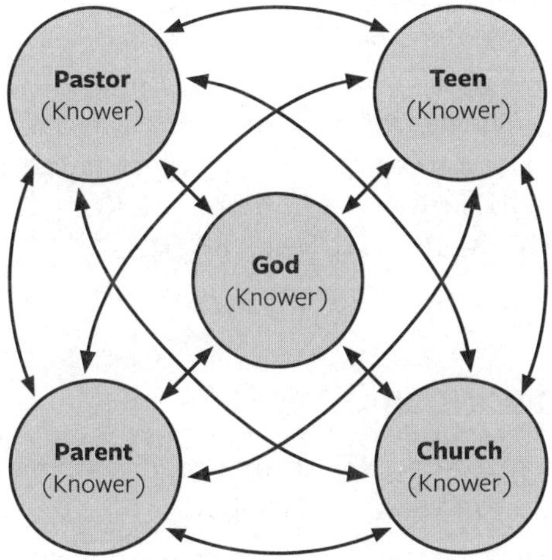

Diagram B

Adapted from Parker J. Palmer, *The Courage to Teach: Exploring the Inner Landscape of a Teacher's Life*, 102.

49. Martin Luther, "The Babylonian Captivity of the Church (1520)," in *Works of Martin Luther*, vol. 2 (Westminster, 1943), 282–83.

50. Abba James, quoted in *The Sayings of the Desert Fathers: The Alphabetical Collection*, trans. Benedicta Ward (Cistercian Publications, 1984), 104.

not remove the need or value of an expert, pastor, parent, or authority figure, but simply places the expert as one of the knowers: A guide who invites teens to a journey together where each participant has contributions to make to the group's growth and progress. Christian leaders become facilitators of the gospel, exploring truth together with everyone in the group. An approach of this nature is not about tweaking our sermons or program methods.

Restored relationships are the core of the gospel, and modeling the gospel is best in community and by recognition of people other than oneself. Christian faith is not simply about knowing things but also about "being known." Douglas Jacobsen and Rhonda Hustedt Jacobsen explain that this includes "Not claiming the truth as if we owned it but living in truth and toward truth as a style of life. Not holding on to our current views as if they defined knowledge for all time but sharing our ideas and ideals with others in the confidence that they will come back to us in improved form."[51] This confidence and trust undergirds hospitality and lets living the gospel in youth ministry become possible. Hospitality is the road to the gospel for marginalized teens. Any space, activity, or program, simply because it contains teens, can become gospel centered.

While hospitality is a skill and gift to develop, this chapter has argued that hospitality fundamentally supports a community centered on the gospel. Hospitality best recognizes Christ's presence among all Christians. Hospitality is a work of mercy, one done by Christ that invites participation as we seek to integrate our faith and our ministry programming. Just as it is required of all disciples, is modeled by Christ, and demonstrates the very nature of God, hospitality is also a primary avenue by which the gospel is lived among marginalized teens. Next we turn to part 2, on living out hospitality and valuing *imago Dei* in specific models and practices.

QUESTIONS TO PONDER

1. Where are the places and who are the people to whom you belong? What indicators help you know you belong?
2. In contrast, when did you feel as though you did not belong? What were the indicators?
3. What does hospitality look like in your context and youth ministry? In what ways is the hospitality of your youth ministry diverse enough to meet the needs of many different teens?

51. Jacobsen and Jacobsen, *Scholarship and Christian Faith*, 182.

4. In what ways does the physical space where your youth ministry meets contribute to or inhibit hospitality?
5. Is creating an ethos of welcome the responsibility of the youth pastor, the adult volunteers, the youth, or a combination? Brainstorm five actionable ideas to contribute to hospitality.

PART 2

Practices and Programs

6

Trauma-Informed Youth Ministry

My (Laura's) adopted daughter is a really good soccer player. She is quick, driven, and because she was exposed to drugs in utero, has high muscle tone. She is usually the smallest on her age-level team, but do not let that fool you! She's the kind of player the coach at my university noticed when she was in kindergarten. My daughter also has some intense behaviors. She does not always listen to or obey instructions from a coach. At times, her behavior with peers can be unsportsmanlike. And there has been more than one occasion when she has taken off in the middle of practice to run across a cornfield. Most coaches would bench her as a consequence of her behavior. The assumption would be that playing time would motivate good behavior, but with my daughter, there is an added variable: trauma. Even though my daughter has been with me since she was two days old and has never had visits with her birth family, she experienced trauma as her birth mother filled both of their bodies with illegal drugs in utero. My daughter experienced trauma again when the mother's voice she had come to know in utero as familiar disappeared and another mother's voice took its place. Benching my daughter would not improve her behavior, and it would cut off access to an important outlet. Leaning into a child's strengths is important. My daughter enjoys being a leader and can organize a group of peers for a scrimmage. She can model a drill or give instructions. Because I know that trauma is a variable that changes the rules in a context where my daughter can succeed, I coach. I coach to manage the variable of her trauma experience. In ministry, we have the opportunity to do the same. We can come to know and understand the needs of the teens we serve and adjust the way we minister to make sure that the opportunities we offer are inclusive to the best of our ability.

Trauma

In chapter 2, we defined three subcategories of trauma: acute, chronic, and complex. Acute trauma occurs from one significant incident. Perhaps someone is involved in a serious car accident or experiences the death of a family member. Acute trauma is a one-time incident that is overwhelming to the brain's coping mechanisms. Following the event, life returns to normal. Chronic trauma, on the other hand, is repeated and prolonged. Examples might include abuse, domestic violence, or repeated exposure to illegal drugs during gestation. Chronic trauma creates an ongoing experience of overload in the brain that affects one's natural coping mechanisms. The third subcategory, complex trauma, occurs when traumatic events have multiple components. Examples include a child's removal from their birth home due to a combination of abuse, neglect, and domestic violence. Any of these experiences—abuse, neglect, or domestic violence—in isolation could be impactful. Layered together, they create a compounding effect. Each of the three subcategories of trauma can become unexpected variables in how we minister to adolescents.

As church leaders work to build relationships with youth, it is important to understand that trauma changes the way the brain functions. Three key areas of the brain are pertinent here:

- The prefrontal cortex controls logic and decision-making and functions metaphorically like a steering wheel in a car. The cortex can be overridden in a flight-or-fight situation, thus relinquishing control to other parts of the brain.
- The cerebellum regulates automatic processes like walking, blinking, and breathing. Many of these processes can be altered when a teen becomes dysregulated and escalated due to a stimuli that reminds the teen of a past trauma, replicating physical and chemical responses from that past situation.
- The amygdala scans for danger, especially ones related to previous dangers. It searches memory and responses, comparing the environment to prior situations. The amygdala becomes physically altered and reduced in the brain, or worn down, by intense reaction, hyperawareness, and

hyperalertness. The amygdala can wither and shrink and needs to be rested. It is like a referee over a ball game. However, in an activated or trauma response the ball game never ends, and the referee, taking no breaks, tires and faces a host of failures or misjudgments.

Once an individual's coping mechanisms are overloaded by a stressful event, they may experience a subconscious fear that the overload will happen again in the future. Their amygdala becomes alert for that situation. Biologically, when the individual encounters situations of stress, they experience an increase in the release of cortisol and norepinephrine and an increase in amygdala function.[1] In brief, when a person experiences trauma, there is an overload of input: more, or more intense, feelings than the brain is designed to process in the moment. To compensate, additional chemicals are released, and the brain shifts into "fight, flight, or freeze mode," in which the nervous system supersedes the thinking brain, shifting into action to protect against the source of distress. A person experiencing a fight-or-flight response will likely notice an increase in their heart rate and breathing. They may begin sweating, their blood pressure will rise, and their digestion will slow as their blood flow is diverted to their muscles for protective action.[2] Sometimes, after the heat of the moment, an individual can be helped to process the experience and come to a better conclusion. For some, the practice of slowing down and reviewing a situation eventually teaches their brain to engage logically in moments of stress and take back control. For others, the nervous system is unable to relinquish control, and while they can engage logically in a therapeutic or supportive setting after the fact, they cannot access that logic in moments of crisis. Medications can help slow reaction time, giving the thoughtful brain time to work, but medications function as a helpful support, not a solution.

In a ministry setting, a teen with a background of trauma might have an interaction with a peer or adult and explode into angry words, become physically aggressive, or both in a manner that is out of proportion to the encounter. In these settings, it is important to find ways and places in which to provide a cooling-down space, recognizing that the teen's brain is not able to process the experience in a thoughtful manner in the moment. Foremost, a change of space separates the escalated individual from the situation physically, as well as separating them from the potential of an audience that might

1. J. Douglas Bremner, "Traumatic Stress: Effects on the Brain," *Dialogues in Clinical Neuroscience* 8, no. 4 (2006): 445–61.

2. *APA Dictionary of Psychology*, "fight-or-flight response," last updated April 19, 2018, https://dictionary.apa.org/fight-or-flight-response.

add fuel to the fire. Walking away also provides time for the brain to begin processing the experience.

Ideally, teens can be encouraged to learn to notice physical signals that they are becoming escalated and to take action in seeking a coping mechanism before the explosion occurs. Sometimes an adult can help notice the physical signals of escalation: clenched fists, rapid breathing, cheeks and neck turning red. A gentle word of observation or an invitation to go for a walk might be enough to remind a teen to notice they are escalating, and that it would be to their benefit to step away. For teens committed to a therapeutic process, responding to early cues can be an important step in growth.

One of my (Laura's) son's counselors encouraged any physical activity that forced him to be present in the moment. Walking, bouncing or dribbling a basketball, and riding a bicycle demand the brain to engage with the present and "catch up."[3] Some teens do well with an assigned space for walking while an adult stays nearby. Other teens need the support of an adult walking and talking with them in order to calm themselves and process.

Opposite to having an outward emotion or aggressive explosion, some teens with a background of trauma will react to an experience by shutting down and losing access to the emotional component of their brain: a "freeze" response. At its extreme, this is considered dissociation. Distancing oneself may provide a feeling of protection to avoid having to process overwhelming feelings. However, shutting down prevents a teen from engaging in life. Another facet in extreme cases is the suppression of a traumatic experience, no longer holding it in conscious memory. Sometimes a licensed counselor can help an individual discover a repressed memory. More often a trauma response creates a "sleeper effect," in which a young person suppresses the memory of the experience for many years until their brain reaches a level of maturity sufficient to process the experience. When the brain is ready, often some stimulus will serve as a trigger to bring the memory back to the surface.[4]

The onslaught of hormones and rapid growth during puberty is difficult for those coming from stable environments, where healthy choices are consistently modeled. How much more so for those who have experienced trauma and for whom a healthy environment was or is missing? Many children can mask their trauma during the elementary years and function well until the

3. Clemens Ley, María Rato Barrio, and Andreas Koch, "'In the Sport I Am Here': Therapeutic Processes and Health Effects of Sport and Exercise on PTSD," *Qualitative Health Research* 28, no. 3 (2018): 491–507.

4. *A Treatment Improvement Protocol: Trauma-Informed Care in Behavioral Health Services* (Rockville, MD: Substance Abuse and Mental Health Services Administration, 2014), https://www.ncbi.nlm.nih.gov/books/NBK207191/box/part1_ch3.box16/.

hormones and rapid brain development during puberty throw everything out of balance.[5] For some, counseling and medication can support them through the difficult years until they gain more mature coping skills. For other teens, the imbalance can become quite significant, particularly alongside emerging mental health concerns that often surface during puberty.[6]

Adverse Childhood Experiences (ACEs)

In 1985, Vincent Felitti, who worked as a doctor at a weight-loss clinic, found himself frustrated by the lack of long-term results for his patients. Many patients would drop out of his program, and in many cases, those who had met their goal initially would later regain the weight they had lost. He began interviewing patients to look for underlying factors inhibiting their weight-loss success. One line of questioning explored patterns of weight throughout life. In a question with one patient, Felitti misspoke and asked about his patient's weight at the time she first became sexually active. Her answer was forty pounds because she was four when her father began abusing her. That response to an accidental question stunned Felitti and served as the first step in unraveling a mystery. Felitti shifted his line of questioning and discovered that a significant number of his weight-loss patients had experienced sexual abuse earlier in life. The physical pounds they carried functioned in various ways as a coping mechanism for the pain.[7]

Felitti knew that another common understanding in science and sociology was that adverse life behaviors come in clumps. For example, a person who smokes cigarettes might also drink alcohol, be overweight, and be unable to graduate from high school. While the clumping was commonly understood, researchers had not been able to articulate why it occurred. In 1990, Felitti spoke at the North American Association for the Study of Obesity, sharing his research and suggesting correlation between early trauma and long-term health quality. While many at the conference disregarded his line of thinking, one colleague, David Williamson, an epidemiologist, shared Felitti's intrigue.

5. Jennifer H. Pfiefer and Nicholas B. Allen, "Puberty Initiates Cascading Relationships Between Neurodevelopmental, Social, and Internalizing Processes Across Adolescence," *Biological Psychiatry* 89, no. 2 (2021): 99–108.

6. Tomáš Paus, Matcheri Keshavan, and Jay N. Giedd, "Why Do Many Psychiatric Disorders Emerge During Adolescence?," *Nature Reviews Neuroscience* 9 (November 12, 2008): 947–57.

7. Jane Ellen Stevens, "The Adverse Childhood Experiences Study—The Largest, Most Important Public Health Study You Never Heard of—Began in an Obesity Clinic," ACEs Too High, October 3 2012, https://acestoohigh.com/2012/10/03/the-adverse-childhood-experiences-study-the-largest-most-important-public-health-study-you-never-heard-of-began-in-an-obesity-clinic/.

Williamson connected Felitti to Robert Anda, a fellow epidemiologist whose own research was exploring the link between depression and heart disease. Felitti and Anda spent a year in conversation and research defining ten categories of adverse childhood experiences, or ACEs, and then produced a questionnaire for preventive medicine patients at Kaiser Permanente. Between 1995 and 1997, more than seventeen thousand people responded to the questions, participating in the study. When the data emerged, Anda described himself as weeping because the correlation was clear, and the rates of suffering were significant.[8]

As the physicians continued to study the data, they realized many patients had experienced a higher number of ACEs, so the questionnaire was adjusted to create a scoring system indicating how many ACEs a person had experienced prior to age eighteen, to explore correlation between a higher number of ACEs and a greater quantity of health problems. Again, the data backed the assumptions of the physicians. Once an individual experienced four or more ACEs, their health risk factors increased exponentially.[9]

Nadine Burke Harris was a practicing pediatrician in an underserved community in California. As she provided care for her patients, she noticed patterns, and in 2008, she read one of Felitti's articles describing a correlation between ACEs and long-term health challenges. Burke Harris became an advocate for the importance of mitigating ACEs in the lives of children as a measure of prevention. She helped found the Center for Youth Wellness in 2012, providing a clinical model for identifying and supporting young people experiencing ACEs.[10] In 2014, she spoke at a TED MED conference in San Francisco. Her talk, "How Childhood Trauma Affects Health Across a Lifetime," has been viewed over twelve million times as of 2025.[11] In 2018, Burke Harris published *The Deepest Well: Healing the Long-Term Effects of Childhood Adversity*, which provides practitioners with tools to identify and respond to the needs created by ACEs. The research of Burke Harris and her colleagues affirms that an individual who has experienced one or more ACEs is not a lost cause. Rather, the data suggests that for a child or teen who has

8. Vincent J. Felitti, R. F. Anda, D. Nordenberg, et al., "Relationship of Childhood Abuse and Household Dysfunction to Many of the Leading Causes of Death in Adults: The Adverse Childhood Experiences (ACE) Study," *American Journal of Preventive Medicine* 14, no. 4 (1998): 245–58.

9. Felitti et al., "Relationship of Childhood Abuse," 258.

10. Center for Youth Wellness, accessed November 5, 2025, https://centerforyouthwellness.org/.

11. Nadine Burke Harris, "How Childhood Trauma Affects Health Across a Lifetime," TEDMED, TED Talk, September 2014, 15 min., 49 sec., https://www.ted.com/talks/nadine_burke_harris_how_childhood_trauma_affects_health_across_a_lifetime.

one consistent, caring adult in their life as they experience and heal from their ACEs, there is a statistically more hopeful outcome for their long-term health.[12] In many families, a parent can serve as the consistent, caring adult, but for families in which no adult is available to fill that role, the church has an opportunity to step in. Youth leaders and caring adults can walk with a teen through their process of healing, much as in the "Life Hurts, God Heals" program model described later in this chapter.

Conduct Disorder

Just as chapter 2 discusses trauma, it also mentions conduct disorders. A teen is diagnosed with a conduct disorder when they display a series of behaviors that oppose social order, often involving breaking laws or harming others with little to no regard for the impact of their choices.[13] While teens make mistakes as they grow and step into their independence, conduct disorders represent the extreme. With therapy and healthy mentoring, many teens can overcome these behaviors and move in a healthy direction.

In cases of conduct disorder, churches need to be wise in avoiding setting up a teen for failure. For example, if money is being collected for an event, teens should not have unsupervised access. Media equipment should be stored in locked areas to prevent unnecessary access. A young youth pastor new to the job did not read the notes left for him from the previous youth pastor about the unique needs of particular youth and took a teen girl with a group to the bowling alley. After paying for the lanes and bowling shoes, he carelessly left the church credit card on a table while he leaned over to change his shoes. The teen, with a known diagnosis, took the opportunity and grabbed the credit card. It was not until a day later that the church was able to unravel the mystery of the missing credit card.

The church can be part of a teen's support by offering positive choices for activity and community. Parents frequently struggle with younger teens who are eager for independence but lack maturity and are still too young for most jobs. While it would always be wise to check local laws and liability, a parent in my (Laura's) congregation made a donation to the church to pay

12. Elizabeth Crouch, Elizabeth Radcliff, Melissa Strompolis, and Aditi Srivastav, "Safe, Stable, and Nurtured: Protective Factors Against Poor Physical and Mental Health Outcomes Following Exposure to Adverse Childhood Experiences (ACEs)," *Journal of Child and Adolescent Trauma* 12 (May 25, 2018): 165–73, https://doi.org/10.1007/s40653-018-0217-9.

13. "Table 17: DSM-IV to DSM-5 Conduct Disorder Comparison," in *DSM-5 Changes: Implications for Child Serious Emotional Disturbance* (Rockville, MD: Substance Abuse and Mental Health Services Administration, June 2016), https://www.ncbi.nlm.nih.gov/books/NBK519712/table/ch3.t13/.

her fourteen-year-old son for ten hours of lawn mowing and yardwork each week during the summer. The teen never knew the true source of the income, enjoyed his first experience of employment, and was lovingly deemed by the church staff the "lawn-tern" instead of intern. On breaks and lunches, he had opportunity to engage with the church staff in the office, building positive relationships. Another church facility manager regularly invites two to three teen boys at a time to help with projects at the church. As they work, they talk, he teaches life skills, and he mentors. In other contexts, adults and teens might be paired based on interest. A retired adult might take a teen out for a round of golf or to the local fishing pond every week during the summer. In a reciprocal way, I (Laura) babysat for a family I met in college who invited me to come early or stay late to share a meal or conversation with the family, offering a blueprint of Christian parenting. Every Mother's Day, the now empty-nester mom from that family sends a note of encouragement as I parent my children. I respond by reminding her how much her influence contributed to my parenting. In each of these situations, care was taken to ensure that abuse prevention practices were followed according to the guidelines of the church. Staff and volunteers completed appropriate training, and adults never isolated themselves with youth.

The Trauma-Engaged Church

In 1946, psychoanalyst and physician Franz Alexander coined the term "corrective experience" to explain the process of re-experiencing a situation with more or better emotional tools and support to "correct" the negative impact of the initial experience that caused trauma.[14] Alexander explained that it can take many corrective experiences to overshadow a negative one. Individuals can be supported by licensed counselors toward having corrective experiences. The church also has opportunity to provide consistent, caring adults to walk alongside teens, often countering an element of upbringing where consistent adult care was missing. As an example, a youth group where I (Laura) previously volunteered would periodically lead a ten-week workshop titled "Life Hurts, God Heals." The curriculum had been adapted from various sources by the youth pastor over the years. Participation was voluntary. Teens had to identify a place of hurt or trauma and be willing to address it from the lens of God's healing love. The lessons were carried out in conversation between the teen and a caring adult mentor trained in abuse-prevention practices.

14. Franz Alexander and Thomas Morton French, *Psychoanalytic Therapy: Principles and Application* (Ronald Press, 1946), 66.

They used the "Life Hurts, God Heals" materials and committed to the teen for the duration of the program.

An important skill for teens navigating their way to adulthood is the ability to develop healthy interpersonal skills. This development has been stifled by our culture's overreliance on technology, but it is a place where the church could meaningfully enter into a teen's life. Teens are in the trenches of learning how to initiate and maintain relationships with both peers and adults.[15] As puberty begins and paces differently in each teen, there is a discrepancy in interpersonal growth from one teen to another, causing some to lag. Teens must learn to navigate increased nonverbal and social cues, as well as recognize the values and beliefs of others. A teen who is overly egocentric may miss important cues and hurt the feelings of another. At times, a teen lacking appropriate awareness of others can behave like a bull in a china shop, crashing through social situations in pursuit of what they want and unaware of whom they might be hurting in the process. While infrequent moments of this type might be standard for the typical teen navigating puberty, there are also those for whom this bull-in-the-china-shop approach becomes the norm. These intensely hurtful behaviors damage the relationships they desperately need to navigate adolescence, all becoming a vicious cycle.

The church has an opportunity to help teens practice meaningful interpersonal interaction with both peers and adults. For many teens, youth groups are the one time in their week when they have intentional face-to-face conversation on topics that matter in life. Youth group gatherings often include time for unstructured hanging out, as well as time for small-group conversation guided by adults through intentionally constructed questions. Exploring different topics, youth pastors can invite and guide healthy discussion in which differences of opinion are welcomed and explored. Respect can be taught through sportsmanship during game time and for differing viewpoints during times of teaching. Adult leaders can look for times to engage with their teens, modeling how to play, and even lose, a game of ping-pong without hurtful "smack talk." Adult leaders teach by example as they check in with teens each week, following up on issues of concern. "How did that math test go?" "Were you able to talk through that misunderstanding with your friend?" These conversations teach our teens that in the body of Christ, we matter to one another. When one of the youth leaders battles cancer, with their permission, we can all wear bracelets in support for the duration of their

15. Jennifer H. Martow, Jessie A. Heaman, and Margaret N. Lumley, "The What, Why, and How of Adolescent Interpersonal Goal Setting Following a Growth Mindset Intervention," *Journal of Adolescent Research* 40, no. 1 (2022): 3–43.

treatment. When one of the teens in our group experiences loss following a house fire, we can be the first to collect donations, with the family's input on what items and quantities are needed. We can also model care through prayer as we teach youth to pray for the concerns of their peers, of course with permission and taking care not to make a teen's private concerns public. When Jordan prays for the concern of Sam at youth group, he is more likely to think about those concerns during the week and to check in with Sam on his own for an update, communicating healthy care for Sam. The church has the potential to function as an interpersonal-skill boot camp when there is strong engagement between youth and healthy adults, in youth group and even as youth are integrated into the larger body of the church.

The Five Pillars of Trauma-Informed Care

Finally, how should the church approach relationship building with a teen who has experienced trauma or ACEs? Simply put, trauma-informed care is just good care, and trauma-informed ministry is just good ministry. Trauma-informed ministry is a ministry that reduces trigger points, but even more, it propels all students toward discipleship. The final section of this chapter outlines how trauma-informed youth ministry facilitates safety, trustworthiness, peer support, choice, and collaboration.

Safety

Safety is defined by those we are serving. To be safe means, in part, that a person is not in a fight-or-flight state. "To breathe and be" without flight or fight allows a teen to move out of survival mode. Then they can do internal work like processing, sharing, or building healthy coping skills and relationships. Safety is wide-ranging, but examples include ensuring the proximity and availability of caring adults, providing leadership and care in alignment with church safety procedures, and properly labeling the locations of bathrooms and entrances. We must consider smells, sounds, temperatures, and textures as variables contributing to a safe experience for a teen with a sensory processing issue. Identifying and accommodating needs associated with safety are outlined extensively in chapter 7.

An annual downhill ski day was a staple on my (Laura's) youth ministry calendar. We would partner with several local churches to get the best group rates and travel about ninety minutes from home for a teen-friendly ski experience. We encouraged our teens to invite friends, making it an outreach event, and beginners were welcome if they participated in the ninety-minute "ski school" to learn the basics. As a skier myself, I loved the event and spent the day traversing the hill to check on kids at all levels. Inevitably, someone would experience a minor injury not needing outside medical attention but ending their day, perhaps a twisted knee. Sometimes the temperature would be unusually cold, and kids would need to take breaks and warm up. I never wanted to be the leader trapped in the lodge, so after a year or two, I dreamed up the role of "lodge parent." I recruited youth group parents, trained in safety practices, who would accompany us on the trip but not ski. Lodge parents would be introduced to the group and then set up camp in the ski lodge with a bag of card and board games. They might bring a book or some knitting, but they were available to be home base for our group should anything go awry. A middle schooler takes a hard fall and wants to be done for the day? They can hang out with the lodge parents! The sixteen-year-old gets overly hot and doesn't want to spend two dollars opening their locker to stash a layer? They can leave it with the lodge parents! Some first-year teens are cold? They can play a round of Uno with the lodge parents, all while the trip leader continues their role of traversing the hill, which holds its own importance. In some regards, all of youth ministry would benefit if we had lodge parents on standby, the extra adults intended to offer the ministry of presence and safety.

Trustworthiness

Trauma arises from a situation that is overwhelming and unpredictable. A welcoming element of church ministry can be predictability. When a group meets at the same time every week, aside from major holidays, it becomes something consistent for a teen to count on. When adult leaders show up consistently, they become people a teen can count on. When the rules are fairly and consistently enforced, both safety and trust are developed. When the schedule of events during youth group or Sunday School is similar each week, even that can become a trusted element.

Interpersonal boundaries allow people time to grow and build trust. Leaders enforcing boundaries, such as following basic safety and supervision rules, reinforces trustworthiness and safety. Ritual, tradition, and predictability are strong and important elements in trustworthiness.

To help convey trustworthiness and predictability, youth groups can print their monthly calendars to provide activity dates, times, and details to teens and their families. Calendars can be distributed online, posted on social media, printed in the church bulletin, and sent through postal mail. Schedules or the order of worship can be posted on the meeting-room wall or on the screen during gathering time. Teens can be periodically reminded of the protocol for inclement weather. My (Laura's) youth group took its cues from the local school district for Wednesday-night activities. If the local school district closed or canceled after-school activities due to inclement weather, church would also cancel that evening. While an unexpected cancellation can be dysregulating, teens who know the criteria and are able to watch the weather forecast can prepare themselves.

Peer Support

Springtide Research Institute's research on adolescents notes that teens need to be named, noticed, and known.[16] While this begins with physical space and caring adults, it must extend to peers as well. Does each teen have the chance to have others know their name, to be missed if they are gone, and to experience a sense of belonging and love from the group? Trauma-informed ministry must provide opportunities for these things to be developed. Teens desperately seek to interact with peers at the same life stage. Even more important is for them to connect with others who have been through similar situations. Providing opportunities for interactions with teens with similar stories is vital. In the church, teens should be able to find a group that believes their emotions, even if the facts are unbelievable or uncomfortable. Being the only foster child or teen with a physical disability or mental health diagnosis can be further isolating to a teen who may already be experiencing disconnection in life. Belonging comes before believing, and knowing they belong comes through being with people like themselves.

Choice

A fall field trip to a corn maze sounds fun to many, but for a handful of teens who exist on the margins, that kind of experience could include several potential challenges. A youth might need to prepare mentally for a change in schedule, a bus or van ride to a new location with unfamiliar resources, and the possibility of Halloween elements feeling scary. Being proactive, a teen might bring a fidget toy, a comfort object, or noise-canceling headphones. There were some teens and parents in my (Laura's) youth group who would carefully read the calendar ahead of time, reach out with questions, and make intentional choices not to attend particular events because of how they might experience them. While we missed those teens, their forethought

16. Springtide Research Institute, *Belonging: Reconnecting America's Loneliest Generation* (2020).

in knowing their own boundaries likely prevented uncomfortable emotional dysregulation. Youth pastors should plan to be proactive and reach out to families for whom an aspect of the calendar might be concerning in case a well-meaning parent is behind on reading mail or an inattentive parent misses the information altogether. There are always surprises in youth ministry, so it can be helpful to have a team of trained volunteers ready to offer a "plan B" option as needed, whether that is a pair of adults available to step out of a discussion or activity with a youth or to offer an alternative activity for a handful. In a setting like the corn maze, a pair of adult leaders created a "home base" for the group around a bonfire. As kids completed or took breaks from the activities for rest or regulation, there were welcoming adults present to greet them.

Collaboration

Many of our teens who have experienced trauma come with atypical behaviors that can be off-putting in our efforts to forge relationships. Many of these behaviors originated as coping and survival tactics but linger even if their environment has stabilized. Youth pastors can collaborate with parents to determine the source and function of the challenging behaviors and prioritize what behaviors to address. One middle schooler with special needs has a checklist of about eight desired behaviors he is working on during youth group time. These are behaviors that help him engage in healthy ways with his peers and put him in the right mindset to encounter the group's topics and teachings. At the end of every session, he and a leader tally his checkmarks for the night. A goal has been set that, when reached, will earn him a reward that is meaningful to him. Some of the positive behaviors that earn him checkmarks include leaving his sibling alone, staying in the same space as the group (he is a wanderer), sitting in the chairs when the group sits for teaching or small groups, and engaging peers with only fist bumps and high fives (he hugs in uncomfortable ways). This teen is highly motivated by rewards, even no-cost rewards such as spending time with a mentor, and through mutual collaboration on his goals, he is helped to engage in appropriate ways with his peers and adult leaders.

Collaboration should also take the form of adjusting leadership structure and representation. Are the conventionally beautiful, "normal," or popular people always up front? In chapter 4, we made the case that ministry is not done *to* or *for* teens with trauma or disability but *with* them. What might it look like to collaborate and receive input and leadership from teens on the margins in your context?

An example of missed collaboration opportunities occurred last summer when two brothers attended different church-based camps. One came home and was physically aggressive for several days because of lack of sleep and poor nutrition from his choices to indulge in the freedoms offered. The other came home and became quite ill, also from indulging in the freedom to refrain from sleep and proper nutrition. While the days away were a wonderful break for the family, the reentry for both boys was awful, prompting the family to question whether sending them to camp was worth it. In hindsight, conversation about the needs of each brother with a point person at each camp could have made provision to hold each to a basic standard of sleep, hygiene, and nutrition.

Building relationships with teens who have experienced trauma takes extra commitment, extra consistency, and extra grace, but the *imago Dei* does not come with caveats. The image of God dwells in each person, despite their circumstances. Each traumatized person is worthy of our time and attention so that we come to understand the impact of trauma on their life and so that we can lean into all of our resources to create a welcoming space for them in the church. As illustrated in many of our personal stories in this book, the work can be exhausting. There are times where all of the good intention and intervention cannot change the life trajectory of a teen during the time we have with them. But we can rest in knowing that despite the challenge, we offered our best to affirm the *imago Dei* in every teen who walks through the doors of our church.

7

Four Models of Ministry

Unlike their expectations for a family dinner or a birthday party requiring an RSVP, church staff never know who will arrive for a Sunday service or evening youth group. Most churches do their best to accommodate groups of varying sizes with the resources available, and in many situations staff can adjust to support the needs of those who attend. The concern is whether a congregation can adequately communicate welcome and inclusion to everyone who comes through their doors.

When I (Laura) served as youth and children's ministry director at a local church, a new family came to visit one Sunday morning. They had several children and youth across the age span, so I began showing the family the church's systems and room locations. The youngest child was a kindergartener who used a wheelchair. I counted it as prevenient grace—grace provided before I realized I needed it—that the kindergarten room was a wheelchair-accessible space, so I was able to direct the family to the elevator and introduce the child to his teacher. Had the child been one year older, this would not have been the case: The elementary-aged children were participating in a rotation model in which they moved to a new room each week for their lesson while the teachers remained stationary for the unit. Several of the rooms being used were in the older portion of the church building, which was not wheelchair accessible. The experience served as a wakeup call. How uncomfortable it would have been to explain to the family that their child could not access the classroom for his group! Surely the family would have felt unwelcome and would likely not have returned. Following that experience, I determined that I would no longer use inaccessible spaces on Sunday mornings. There had been no warning that a family with a child who used a wheelchair was coming, and offering a welcoming atmosphere was very important to my church. The outcome was that the accessible spaces became a bit more cramped, and volunteers had to be more creative in their use of spaces. But in the end, the inconvenience was worth it for knowing, with confidence, that all classroom spaces were physically accessible and ready for visitors each Sunday morning.

Overview of the Four Models

Churches can be creative in their approaches to "making things work" for members of their faith community when resources are limited. Looking broadly at church ministry, we can identify three main approaches to ministry with individuals on the margins. We call these Approach Zero, the One-on-One (1:1), and Separate Space. A fourth possibility is a hybrid that uses two or more of the approaches in tandem. Next, we will briefly overview each approach; then we'll spend the rest of the chapter detailing each.

Approach Zero occurs when a church does nothing to intentionally accommodate an individual with functional needs beyond what is most typical for the general public. If no identifiable member of a youth group requires accommodations for a disability, the need to plan for accommodations can exist off of staff and volunteers' radar. An Approach Zero mindset occurs because people on the margins are often ignored, whether unintentionally or deliberately. Thus, in ministries that take this approach, programming, access, staff, and budgets are set to cater to the majority. The following statement perfectly sums up Approach Zero: "We don't have any youth in wheelchairs, so why do something different?" The problem with this approach is that when a visitor who needs additional support arrives, they may feel unwelcome due to the lack of accommodations. Youth often vote with their feet, never walking through the doors. When ministries claim they have no youth on the margins, they create a self-fulfilling prophecy that prevents hospitality and inclusion.

In the One-on-One (1:1) approach, one older youth or adult helper provides 1:1 support during ministry times. Often called the inclusion or buddy model, this approach provides a way for individuals to be integrated into programming with their peers. As appropriate, the buddy can adjust an activity or provide extra support as needed. The idea is that all students are inclusively participating in the programming together with intentional extra support as needed for individuals who require it. A buddy might take a youth for a walk in public areas when they become dysregulated or may suggest a separate activity in another part of the room when a topic becomes too challenging. Then, as soon as the youth has been able to regulate or the curricular focus shifts to a more engaging element, the youth and buddy return to the group.

The Separate Space model involves the creation of a designated classroom for youth with increased functional needs to use, either full-time for ministry activities and learning or periodically to meet their unique needs. Separate space would follow church safety policies for abuse prevention but function apart from the larger group. This type of space can include sensory objects, specialized furnishings, and specialized bathrooms. It can also be a turn-around room for cooling off and refocusing before rejoining the group. Many churches that serve larger communities encompassing a significant number of youth with functional needs beyond the most typical may find an important niche in ministry here.

In the hybrid approach, two or more of the other approaches are used together to support youth in the ministry setting. For example, a youth might be able to engage with peers during the less structured elements of a youth gathering, but during the lesson or teaching time, that youth may benefit from a modified lesson in a separate space. Or a youth may manage well with peers most of the time but occasionally may become emotionally escalated in the presence of a trigger and thus need a buddy to take them to a separate space to calm down and regulate before returning to the group. As always, use of a separate space requires adherence to abuse-prevention policies.

More detailed discussion of each of these four approaches follows.

Approach Zero

Scripture points toward welcome, hospitality, and inclusion. Jesus did not avoid anyone on the margins, whether those margins were due to their geographical background, their physical abilities, their mental health, the consequences of their life choices or those of their parents, or their age. The message of the gospel is clearly one of inclusion, and as coauthors, our hearts grieve for the congregation that did not return the phone call of a family with a child who has special needs and was new to town or the congregation that did not bring care into the halls of a psychiatric unit. These were churches living out an Approach Zero mentality, although families and institutions with marginalized members are the very groups and places that most need the church. The reason why many youth on the margins are absent from our churches is not because they choose to be absent. Youth on the margins often are absent from church because they cannot get in the door, navigate the signage, or scale the stairs necessary to reach a second-floor youth room. Often social prejudices, physical layout, or untrained staff implicitly exclude teens on the margins. Many such youth would participate if they felt the welcome of staff and volunteers willing to accommodate, adjust, and extend extra grace to help them modify aspects of the experience to participate alongside their peers. In short, they would attend if the space were made welcome for them, if they could receive more than Approach Zero.

Sometimes barriers are physical and easy to identify. At other times, barriers are less obvious because they blend into the culture of "We've always done it this way." For someone who has attended the same congregation for many years, fresh eyes may be needed to notice things a new family would notice. Chapters 8 and 9 will address this issue. In using a typical night of youth group as an example, we walk chronologically through the experience of a youth on the margins and identify barriers that might impede their engagement in the ministry, barriers that would categorize a church as using Approach Zero. While churches need not necessarily address every item identified, the hope is that chapters 8 and 9 will help readers look at their spaces of ministry with fresh eyes.

Demographics tell us that youth on the margins exist in every community. Twenty percent of the population has a diagnosable disability.[1] When we also consider additional individuals who bear less visible burdens such as experiences of trauma, family instability, or foster care, and when we add the siblings of youth on the margins, we discover a massive group that research tells us is underserved. This population's rare participation in a church body tells us volumes about the lack of accommodations available in that space. Education researcher Elliot Eisner deems this the "null curriculum."[2] The null curriculum is not what is explicitly taught in a sermon or lesson but rather the unspoken lessons that are taught powerfully through a set of behavioral cues, architectural decisions, and significant silent rules. By offering no accommodations, an Approach Zero youth ministry is communicating that youth on the margins are not welcome. Approach Zero ignores those who need accommodations, adjustments, or extra grace within their environment in order to participate.

In the introduction, I (Laura) described the experience of calling a church to inquire about visiting with my son, who has disabilities, and receiving no

1. "Disability," World Health Organization, March 7, 2023, https://www.who.int/news-room/fact-sheets/detail/disability-and-health.

2. Elliot W. Eisner, *The Educational Imagination: On the Design and Evaluation of School Programs*, 3rd ed. (Macmillan, 1994), 97–107.

return phone call. The lack of a return call exhibits an Approach Zero method. Regardless of the reason behind the lack of a return phone call, the church was implicitly telling me that my family was not welcome to join its members for worship. The business of the church universal, "to go into all the world" (Mark 16:15), did not include my family for that church.

When my (Mike's) foster daughter was hospitalized, also described in the introduction, and the youth pastor did not reach out despite being provided contact information, that church likewise was choosing Approach Zero. One might assume that the pastoral staff felt ill-equipped to minister to a girl in psychiatric care and that rather than invest time to equip themselves, they chose to ignore the situation. But ignoring an individual's need for ministry is quite different from ignoring the need to care for a houseplant. A houseplant simply withers and is tossed in the trash. When we ignore people, God's children, we ignore those God has placed within our scope and influence to nurture.

Approach One—The 1:1

In this approach, one individual on the margins is paired with a "buddy" who helps them navigate the environment, provides extra assistance as needed, and is available for supervised "breaks" while the group continues moving through the lesson as planned. At times, buddies might be needed only for times of transition, and eventually, the youth becomes equipped to navigate the environment independently. At other times, buddies are permanent support. A buddy might be necessary for some teens who have a behavior disorder, anxiety, or autism. Each buddy's role might look different for each person's needs, but their importance is the same.

A new family came to my (Laura's) church with a son who was chronologically fourteen but cognitively about nine. After conversation with his mother, I trained a buddy to attend a multi-age Sunday School class for elementary-aged children with the fourteen-year-old. For the first year, this young man attended regularly with his buddy. He learned the rhythms and routines, and his classmates got to know him. When it was time to set up accommodations for the second year, church staff and volunteers agreed that he no longer needed a buddy. He had adapted well, and his peers had learned to support him when he needed help with a task. His peers had put his buddy out of a job!

A similar situation occurred with Samuel. As a child, Samuel had a buddy, an adult, in each of his Sunday School classes. Without this buddy, Samuel would unsafely leave his classroom. When he entered my (Mike's) middle school Sunday School class, the buddy became less necessary, as Samuel had learned to participate and sit with the group. Samuel's small-group leader became a new kind of buddy, one who was trained and watchful but did not need to stay with him the entire time. Samuel would go to him when he was aggravated or needed to leave the room.

A convenient way to facilitate the 1:1 approach is to train two individuals as buddies for one youth who needs support. The two buddies are provided with each other's contact information and encouraged to work out their own schedule of who will cover each week. This approach provides built-in backup when someone is sick, is traveling, or needs time off. Buddies are trained by church ministry staff using published resources, training materials specific to the needs of the person receiving support, and are trained by the family of that person. Every buddy and volunteer must be trained in and follow the church's child protection policies and be background checked.

Pros of the 1:1 Approach

This approach works well for smaller congregations who have limited resources. The 1:1 approach also affirms that each person in the body of the church matters and is worthy of inclusion in the greater whole.

Sometimes the role of a buddy can be minimal, as for a youth who has a tendency to elope and "disappear," such as Samuel. In this case, the responsibility of the buddy is to keep eyes on the youth. The buddy has minimal additional tasks during meeting time so their attention can remain on the youth who tends to elope. As soon as the youth begins moving outside of the meeting space, the buddy quickly moves to redirect the eloper, allowing the leader to continue teaching the lesson. Once the buddy redirects the youth a number of times, the youth may realize that eloping is not an option, and ideally, the need for the buddy's redirection diminishes as the youth matures.

Many youth on the margins are able to participate at some level with their group but either need support or need to step away at times from the specifics or intensity of an activity. A buddy who has a relationship with such a youth can anticipate the times when they need support or a break and can provide that in a natural flow of interaction without disrupting the gathering. At the church where I (Laura) served, there was a girl with epilepsy. She had frequent seizures that had delayed her development, and it took years before doctors were able to find the right medications to manage her condition. As the years went by, she fell further and further behind her peers. In conversation with her mother, it was decided that a 1:1 would best serve this girl. Her mother wanted her exposed to her peers in the hope that as her condition stabilized, she would do some "catching up," but there were often times when the girl could not engage with the pace or topic of the lesson. At these times, her buddy would take her to a separate area in the room to work on a quiet activity or take her for a walk in a public area while the leader continued teaching her peers. After a short time, the girl and her buddy would rejoin the group.

The Reset

At times, a youth may become escalated from an encounter or a specific trigger, and they may need intentional time to step away as well as encouragement to use appropriate coping skills and "reset" before returning to the group. This type of reset can be especially helpful for individuals with behavior disorders and for some teens on probation or in foster care. Sometimes a reset can be accomplished through a simple walk away from the group and the noise in a safe and public area. The act of walking a repetitive route, mimicking a track or treadmill, helps the body focus away from the issue of concern. Learning to initiate a request for a walk before becoming overly escalated is a mature coping skill, so when a buddy encourages a walk, a healthy pattern is reinforced. At times when my (Laura's) son escalates, I will take him by the hand and initiate a walk until he calms enough to recognize his need. As he begins walking, his body slowly calms, and he no longer needs an adult to guide his steps.

Medications

Some youth with attention issues may struggle to engage with the full length of an activity, especially if the gathering is taking place late in the day. Many youth with ADHD take medication to cover school hours, and by evening, when many youth groups meet, that medication has worn off. In extreme cases, doctors may prescribe an additional late-day dose, but ADHD medications compromise normal appetite and sleep patterns, so the benefits must be weighed alongside the risks. Some families who have youth with attention challenges choose not to medicate for various reasons, some youth reach a point where they refuse to take their medication, and some parents choose to have their children take a "break" from medication on weekends and holidays. If attention issues become a problem beyond what can be managed by a buddy and a break, it is likely time for an honest conversation with parents and then the kids themselves.

Often when a situation can be framed in such a way that the youth can see how it benefits them, they are likely to cooperate. One high school student with ADHD was struggling to remain focused and attentive at track practice after school, even though he wanted to excel in the sport. Once the coach was able to frame the situation in a way that illustrated the benefit for the youth, the student was willing for his parents to have a conversation with his doctor about a late-day dose of his ADHD medications for the duration of track season. The doctor agreed, and the runner excelled, newly equipped to listen carefully to his coach's instructions and focus on practice.

Triggers

Triggers are topics, words, sounds, smells, touch, or any other type of input that reminds an individual of something undesirable from their past and results in a strong emotional response. For someone unfamiliar with triggers, the smell of oatmeal cookies might take you back to your grandmother's kitchen, letting you relive a happy memory. But for those who have experienced trauma and for those with hypersensitivity to outside stimuli, the reaction can be the opposite. For a youth who has experienced physical abuse at home, any time a disagreement occurs, or voices escalate, they may anticipate being physically harmed and react in a strong, and sometimes unusual, way. If a youth experienced a significant loss on the 7th of June, any time the 7th of June comes, the date can trigger the same feelings of loss. A buddy who knows an individual well can sometimes anticipate and help them avoid uncomfortable triggers.

Eliminate Triangulation

Some youth on the margins have learned to play "mom against dad." If they receive an unfavorable response to a question from one adult, they move to another adult in hopes of getting their preferred answer. Triangulation of this kind can be avoided at church by designating a buddy to be their "point person." The teen with a buddy is more likely to get a consistent response to a question: The buddy can intervene to let new adults know about the "playing mom against dad" habit and about what any previously approached adults have already said.

Scaffolding for Success

Before I (Laura) visit a new church with my son, I ask what the flow of the experience will be. How will he be expected to participate, and where will the line be between expectation and accommodation? For example, if the group begins seated in chairs, will my son be expected to stay seated in a chair, or if there is latitude for him to move around, what will that look like? If the group will be having small group breakout sessions, will my son be expected to participate, or is there latitude for him to step away with the supervision of a leader in a public space? These are important questions to explore because there are some things my son can do independently, some things he can do with support, and some things that are beyond his abilities today. Lev Vygotsky offers an understanding of the "zone of proximal development."[3] In brief, this zone represents how far we can stretch our learners when providing support, or "scaffolding." Appropriate support expands capabilities beyond normal developmental norms.

For example, my son does not enjoy sitting in a chair during a lesson, but he is capable of doing so for a short time with the encouragement and support of a leader. And doing so allows him to engage with the lesson as best he can. While he might articulate that he would prefer to wander the room, doing so could create a distraction for the group and cut off his potential learning since he isn't being exposed to the conversation. His zone of proximal development includes being able to sit for a short lesson with support or scaffolding. However, there are types of seating that are better for him than others. There are people he will respond better to if they are in proximity. Those are appropriate kinds of accommodations, or scaffolding, as Vygotsky explains. A type of scaffolding can be temporary until an individual gains enough skill to manage a setting independently, or they might be permanently necessary based on the developmental needs of an individual.

How can you, as a ministry leader, arrive at the appropriate level of accommodation and expectation? First, there will be some trial and error in the process as everyone learns about each other. Second, lean into the guidance offered by parents, as they are usually the experts on their child and have been helping them navigate expectations for years. Third, leverage the buddy: They will often know more current information as changes occur with the child. Keep buddies in contact with parents. Let them help design the plan and also have freedom to adjust it. Finally, the place where you begin offering supports for a teen need not be the place you stay. Each year, my (Laura's) son has gained more skills of independence, so he can navigate more of the church environment independently than he could the year previous. The ways in which a buddy supports him have changed each year, and they will likely continue to evolve alongside his growth and development.

Release People for the Work

Another benefit of the 1:1 approach is that it frees the ministry leader to continue leading most of the time. When the buddy can be trusted to handle

3. Lev Vygotsky, *Mind in Society: The Development of Higher Psychological Processes* (Harvard University Press, 1978), 87.

the needs of the youth they are supporting, a gift of freedom is provided for the teaching staff person. Additionally, and more importantly, the adult buddy is leveraging their gifts and showing love to a teen. The work is shared across the body of Christ. Certainly, there may be times when the ministry staff person needs to step in for support, but the hope is that these times are rare.

Cons of the 1:1 Approach

While a 1:1 relationship can be wonderfully supportive, a 1:1 cannot be in place immediately for a visitor. Establishing a buddy partnership takes time for training and rapport building. There are usually multiple meetings between parents, staff, and volunteers to equip a buddy with best practices, and the time it takes to establish this connection may be a turnoff for a family looking to quickly acclimate or to just occasionally drop in for a holiday service.

Some churches keep a team of buddies "on call" for visitors and emergent needs, although this setup lacks the personal history and relationship to be maximally supportive. Other churches include information on their website, perhaps in a list of FAQs, to explain that a 1:1 buddy can be made available and that a phone call in advance can help facilitate a buddy being available on the day of the visit.

Providing a 1:1 buddy can be a labor-intensive effort. It requires an older youth or adult to consistently give up their participation to be a support for someone else, and for some, that is difficult to sustain. Leaders who want to retain their buddy staff for multiple years need to take care to encourage and support them, regularly reminding them of the significance of their service.

Approach Two—Separate Space

With creativity, money, or both, ministries can provide a separate space for youth on the margins. Most often these spaces operate on Sunday mornings concurrently with adult worship. A youth ministry outside of worship hours that is dedicated to youth with disabilities is largely uncharted territory but could become a powerful reality in a larger community where a critical mass of participants dwell.

Separate space can exist on an "as needed" basis, allowing safe and comfortable space for a child or youth who needs to step away from the mainstream gathering for a time with the supervision of their buddy. This might look like a set apart area within a larger meeting space where an adult could maintain a visual on a teen who is taking a few minutes to calm. It could also be a separate classroom operating for several teens where some stay full time with their trained teachers and others join with their buddy for a portion of the time, much like a special education setting in a local school. This also reflects the public school special education model of providing the "least restrictive environment" to any given youth, mainstreaming as much as possible.

A separate space can include furniture and materials specifically designed for individuals on the margins and can have a high staff-to-participant ratio; additionally, the curriculum can be intentionally geared for the needs represented. Several Christian publishers offer curricula for students of various age levels who require accommodations. Many congregations look to church members with experience in special education and to parents of teens with disabilities for direction in designing intentional space. Many teens can contribute to the conversation with wonderful ideas of how to best support their participation in the local church. Additionally, a consultant can be hired to design the specialized room and bathroom and purchase furniture. While there are many companies that specialize in equipment for dedicated areas that accommodate individuals with disabilities, there are also lower cost and DIY options.

The following paragraphs give a few basic rules of thumb. If this dedicated space is being used for de-escalation, the furnishing and colors should be soft to promote a calming atmosphere. When some young people escalate, they look for objects and furniture they can lift and throw, so organizers would be wise to imagine everything in the room as a potential projectile and use those images as guiding directives.

Tumbling or gym mats that can be easily sanitized can serve as a helpful floor covering for a "safe zone," and they can be stood up on their side to serve as a room divider when needed to separate youth who need space to process emotions or complete work.

Crash pads or large beanbag chairs can offer safe space for de-escalation. While crash pads can be costly to purchase, some handy members in the church who enjoy sewing might create something similar at a lower cost. Beanbags come in many sizes, some large enough for multiple adults. In settings with youth and children, the best rule of thumb is to look for washable covers.

Weighted vests or lap blankets can provide calming pressure, and again, there are patterns available for those who sew. Staff utilizing weighted objects need to be educated in proper use, as they only provide benefits for a short time. The body adjusts to the added weight and pressure, so they ought to be used only for short periods of time to calm and then should be put away.

Fidget toys are now easy to find in stores and online. These kinds of toys provide varied sensory input, as well as something to keep hands busy. Because fidgets are designed to be used in a repetitive fashion, they wear out and need to be replaced often. It is also important to imagine each item as a potential projectile, so choices for purchase and accessibility decisions should be made carefully.

When some youth escalate, having a place to "hide" can help them to feel safe and regain control, so a fabric tent or tunnel may provide a space that feels "separate" while remaining under the watchful eyes of adults and not presenting a danger as a projectile.

Both traditional and saucer-style swings can be a helpful addition, even in an indoor space. Staff should make sure the equipment is rated for and installed in such a way that all can be accommodated by the weight-limit recommendations. Note that teens and other children should *not* be asked about their weight. The repetitive motion of swinging can have a calming effect on many.

Mini exercise trampolines are an easy way to get out excess energy and come with a built-in handle for stability.

Lightweight balls can be a good addition, as a dribbling motion can calm, or a simple game of catch can direct someone's focus when they become dysregulated. Balls with different textures can offer additional sensory input.

Washable stuffed animals with varied textures, kinetic sand, Play-Doh, or a sensory bin with dried beans, construction vehicles, and plastic scoops can be helpful resources to have on hand.

Colored tape on the floor can indicate boundaries or separate spaces. Some individuals with autism have difficulty respecting the personal space of others. Placing colored rectangles around various sections of the room can provide visual cues that show which areas are available for use and which ones need permission to enter. Appropriately sized carpet squares can accomplish a similar goal of indicating space boundaries for people and activities. For example, materials for a particular activity could stay on a carpet, as in a Montessori classroom. Or each participant could have a designated seating area marked out by colored tape if some participants have a tendency to encroach on the space of others. Sometimes, a teacher's desk, stage, or work area can be taped as "off-limits" if participants need a clear boundary.

Rugs with colors or textures can help to add warmth to a space and provide a comfortable spot for conversation. Large pillows with zip-off washable covers can provide just the right comfort for a small-group discussion.

Another trend emerging in many spaces for youth are motor planning pathways. These often take the form of semipermanent sensory path decals on hallway floors in elementary schools. In a space intended to calm, walking the path indicated by the sensory path decals could help children and teens focus on something other than their escalated emotions. Some ministries use prayer labyrinths in a similar way to invite kinesthetic movement to connect to their lessons and focus their participants.

Utilizing the straw of a juice box or applesauce pouch or sugar-free chewing gum can be calming for some, so these might be helpful to have on hand as snacks.

Avoid lamps and hanging pendant lights. Artwork should be painted on the wall so that a framed piece does not become a projectile. Some dedicated spaces offer a wheelchair-accessible table for workspace during times of teaching and learning, but other spaces are geared primarily toward de-escalating, so each ministry will need to clarify its focus before selecting furnishings. Tables that adjust to different heights can be purchased from classroom supply companies; while they are more costly, if a room needs to serve individuals of different sizes or those with mobility devices, they come in handy. If the room is used for de-escalation, classroom supplies like markers and scissors should be stored in a locked cabinet or brought to the room specifically for an activity and then returned.

Another consideration is that autistic youth and youth who have experienced trauma often experience sensory input differently. Typically, they present as either sensory seeking or sensory avoidant. Those who are sensory seeking often enjoy additional sensory input: various textures to touch and manipulate, motions like swinging and spinning, and music. Sensory avoiders may dislike having messy hands, prefer not to be touched, avoid loud noises, and dislike excess motion. When we know the preferences of our youth, we can encourage the activities that are most helpful to them, especially at times of escalation.

Some youth are a blend between seeking and avoidant. My (Laura's) son loves sensory input, as long as his hands don't get messy. He could spin forever, but he does not like loud noises. For him, it is not a straightforward collection of sensory experiences, but adults working with him need to learn his pattern. He also struggles with body awareness, so he doesn't know "hungry," "thirsty," or "full" as accurately as his peers. He needs to be guided on a healthy pace of eating and drinking. He also does not know "hot" and "cold" body temperatures, so he needs coaching on what to wear for a given temperature. A chart that lists temperatures with pictures of appropriate clothes is helping him learn cognitively to support his senses.

Pros of the Separate Space Approach

Churches able to offer a separate space and a specialized curriculum for youth with disabilities are likely to draw individuals with a higher level of need. A program with separate space may give access to church for families who may have never engaged due to their child's needs. For youth with more significant needs, there are likely few extracurriculars available, and the clock is ticking for them to age out of the public school system. While each state determines when students age out of special education, the average age is twenty-one. Past that time, a young adult unable to maintain a simple job has little to keep them meaningfully engaged through the day, and their parents must cover caretaking responsibilities. There is a wonderful opportunity for the church to step into this gap and offer meaningful teaching and experiences to the youth and young adults with disabilities via traditional Sunday School, youth groups, and programming beyond those times.

Churches have been discovering that through social media, families raising children and youth with disabilities gravitate to one another and build online communities to encourage and offer resources to each other. These networks can be powerful forces in word-of-mouth advertising. If a church is offering a meaningful ministry experience beyond simply "babysitting," word spreads quickly. Many communities have few activities and socializing opportunities for children and youth with disabilities, and ministry designed to welcome them and their families communicates value in the *imago Dei* of all God's children. It is also not uncommon for families who have children with disabilities to relocate for access to better supports. A meaningful ministry for youth on the margins may encourage families to move into your community.

Cons of the Separate Space Approach

Creating, staffing, and maintaining a separate space can be labor intensive and costly. Initial training must be extensive to equip staff not only to meet a variety of needs but to appropriately use specialized equipment or facilities and to support the vision of the ministry.

Starting a ministry from scratch is a daunting task in any setting! Once a church's staff or board members have agreed that a specialized ministry is where the Holy Spirit is leading, it is wise to begin with a time of research. Those involved should reach out to the local school district to learn about the special education classrooms and offerings already present in the community. Perhaps a member of the church serves in special education and could act as a helpful liaison. Approaching contacts with the mindset of a learner who is seeking to partner in support for families helps frame the conversation. Learning about the local numbers of children and youth served at each level in the public school system (mainstream, mainstream with paraprofessional support, self-contained, hybrid, therapeutic, and residential schools) provides more contextual information about the community and who might attend a ministry geared toward children and youth with disabilities.

If church staff are not yet familiar with some of the most-used terms and processes in special education, it is important to bring oneself and staff up to speed by learning them, particularly those used in the local school system, which sets a common starting point.

A handful of churches have paved the way and designed wonderful classrooms that meet a variety of special needs. It would be a worthy investment for a church exploring this calling to locate several of these facilities to arrange a tour. Conversation with their ministry leaders might also reveal some helpful tips and best practices learned through experience that can be taken back home and implemented.

Approach Three—Hybrid

Many churches gravitate to a hybrid approach that includes both 1:1 and separate space. In this approach, some youth-centered events, times, and topics are appropriate for youth on the margins and others may not be. Youth on the margins attend the events that are appropriate for them, potentially with a buddy, but use separate space during events or parts of events that are not appropriate, or they simply do not attend. To effectively use this type of hybrid approach, communication between staff and parents or guardians must be ongoing. Together, staff and parents or guardians determine when a youth should participate.

Arrangements might be made for a youth to participate in portions of a ministry gathering but to have a buddy and space to step away to as needed. Perhaps a youth cannot focus for the length of a sermon message but enjoys the music, games, and small-group conversation. A buddy could take the youth on a walk in alignment with church safety policies and engage them in simple activities nearby, and then both could rejoin the group following the message. Or if a youth tends to become escalated because of certain topics or interactions, the buddy could learn to read body language indicating the need to step away and regulate. When the youth becomes escalated during an event, once the pair steps away and the youth is able to regulate, they could be invited to rejoin the group.

Some youth on the margins are comfortable with routine events in the church building, but when an event is off-campus or includes an overnight, a barrier emerges. In these situations, a youth might limit their participation to in-house events, or accommodations could be made for them to participate for the daytime hours or a portion of a retreat with transportation arranged with the help of parents or guardians. Or if transportation is the barrier because a youth is unable to ride in the church vehicle, perhaps a parent or guardian could join the group as a driver and fill remaining seats in their vehicle with additional youth.

At times, a properly trained parent or guardian might join an overnight youth event and be provided with a separate sleeping space so their child can engage during the day with the group but share separate sleeping space with their parent or guardian, allowing appropriate care to be provided at night. Some youth are unable to maintain the rigorous schedule and late hours of a typical youth retreat, so a separate sleeping space would also allow them to step away at a time appropriate for their needs. For other youth, a separate restroom space would allow their personal care needs to be met by their parent or guardian while they participate with the group during most activities.

As my (Laura's) church worked to include a young man with Down syndrome in regular youth group activities, he was left out of camps and retreats for years. Eventually, his parents decided they wanted him to have that experience, so they made arrangements to attend a week of summer camp with their son. They stayed in a small family cabin near the youth group, and they helped the young man to participate during daytime activities to the fullest extent possible. By early evening, the young man was exhausted, so his parents helped him get ready for bed. One of the most memorable scenes from that camp was when the young man hit a bullseye during archery. No accommodation was provided for that activity. He had followed the instructions of the staff, practiced, and participated with the rest of the youth group. He hit the target in fair competition with his neurotypical peers. A picture was taken of him with his bullseye and blown-up to poster size for the youth room wall back home, helping everyone remember that with overnight support from his parents, this young man was able to participate in camp alongside his youth group!

Pros of the Hybrid Approach

This approach communicates the value of everyone as being made in the *imago Dei*. Parents and guardians have frequent contact with staff, and each exchange is an opportunity to affirm the value of the youth as accommodations are worked out. These positive interactions flow naturally out into the church community and in the network of families with kids who have additional functional needs. The testimony of a family well-served communicates far more than any direct mailer. One family invites another, and the group grows organically.

For smaller to midsize churches, this approach allows most youth to participate to some degree without financial or time resources becoming strained. Engagement opportunities can take the form of an à la carte model: a youth and their parents look at the events on the church calendar and determine which elements are the best choices for them based on needs.

Cons of the Hybrid Approach

This hybrid approach can be labor intensive, as staff time is regularly committed toward assessing whether each ministry topic or activity is appropriate and what adjustments need to be made. It also demands that ministry staff plan consistently so that topics and media can be shared with families in advance, allowing decisions about participation to be made ahead of time.

In terms of retreats or off-campus events, this can sometimes mean greater cost for additional sleeping or restroom spaces, and certainly the dynamic of an experience changes when parents are tagging along. A straight cost-benefit analysis would not be effective in assessing benefit here. As the Gospels make clear for us, there is immense value in caring for each sheep (Luke 15). So, while additional cost may be helpful to note, it is not a valid reason for excluding an individual from ministry.

8

Welcoming, Part 1

Preparing the Place

This chapter outlines preparing a physical location and ministry for students on the margins. The chapter after it, *Welcoming, Part 2: Preparing the Program*, discusses thinking through elements of the program itself.

Everything I (Mike) learned about discipleship I learned from Jesus and McDonald's. It is incredible to me that a fast-food chain like McDonald's can serve a hundred billion burgers using part-time adolescents working for low wages. As a bivocational youth pastor, I learned a key lesson from my time as a fast-food manager: "the walk-through." Whenever a manager started a shift, the handoff of the restaurant was not considered complete until that manager had conducted a survey of the store. Knowing the state of the bathrooms, parking lot, lobby, cooking areas, stockroom, office, and break room gave them a full-orbed picture of what needed to be addressed for a safe and effective shift.

In this chapter we invite you to do a literal "walk-through" of your ministry, taking careful note of the areas described below. As you note concerns, keep a list of things to address. The content here will guide you regarding what to "see" and how to evaluate a host of elements. Ultimately, we hope you do not settle for a one-time walk-through or even a set checklist but rather that you develop what is known as "connoisseurship." Connoisseurship is the art of appreciation. Being a connoisseur is more than, but requires, expert knowledge. It is a love of the object of knowing, to be in a relationship with it. An expert with a great deal of knowledge can appreciate an area of life with good discriminating taste and judgment. To do this, the expert draws on multiple sources of knowledge and multiple ways of knowing.

It is not good enough to look; connoisseurship requires the ability to see. A connoisseur does not simply take another's perspective, although this is a vital step. The connoisseur must develop the ability to take all perspectives and appreciate their distinct needs and situations. And just as it is not good enough just to look, it is also not good enough simply to look and see; we must also appreciate, much like a connoisseur appreciates fine food.

A true connoisseur can help others to see, much as a film critic does. Film critics do not simply give their opinions but also help others experience movies more fully or warn them of problems they may need to be aware of. Becoming a connoisseur often requires listening to multiple voices and working with others to discover the truth in experiences, phenomena, and situations. To become a wine connoisseur, one must taste a lot of wine and learn how to pay attention to it, to attend to its qualities, and to recall from memory its taste, smell, and visual characteristics. The qualities of other wines become a backdrop for the wine being tasted, contrasted, and compared. Likewise, only when we acquire a range of experiences in a specific discipline will we develop a sophisticated level of connoisseurship in it. To compare and evaluate clearly, it is necessary to know students with trauma and disabilities and to see good trauma-informed ministries and accessible spaces so we can contrast and grow.

Go on a Visit

Every trauma-informed and accessible ministry begins by knowing what a trauma-informed and accessible ministry looks like. As a McDonald's manager, I (Mike) was trained at a "perfect store" where everything was practiced precisely. While not all stores or ministries operate the same or serve the same clientele, they must have some sort of image or benchmark from which to begin. Being able to "see" your own ministry cannot occur until you "see" other ministries.

It is difficult to get time off from your own work to tour another ministry, but there is nothing more transformative than to see new ideas and spaces in action. Go with your staff, some parents, and teens, and visit three or four other ministries that serve a population you need to "see" better. Seeing more fully leads to serving more fully. Fully functioning disability ministries or trauma-informed youth ministries may be hard to find in some areas. However, there are daycares, schools, hospitals, and other organizations that have been creating, arranging, and coordinating the acquisition of space, architecture, policies, furniture, programs, and staff culture around these topics for years.

Begin your ministry walk-through by learning what a trauma-informed and accessible ministry looks like as a backdrop to your own ministry practice. The goal in visiting other ministries is not to replicate but to appreciate, to see how organizations' views of people are embedded carefully into the ways they implement every aspect of their programs, from parking-lot arrival to departure. Once you have several such pictures, you can better see your own work. Walk-throughs of other organizations' ministries with a checklist are helpful but do not fully create a systemic understanding of how all the insights covered in this chapter work together to form a ministry for those on the margins.

So now, turn to your own ministry. The following is a physical exercise for attempting to see your ministry for the first time from lenses of trauma and disability. We can begin with what a teen would see or experience prior to even coming to your physical location.

Reputation of the Ministry

Before a youth even arrives on the church campus, several factors may have contributed to building an impression of the church or organization and its ministries. Word of mouth, testimonies from friends, street signage, and the church's website or social media presence all contribute toward a first impression. Someone who is considering involvement in a local church looks for positive indicators of these types before they make the drive to campus. Pictures on the church website communicate who attends, and while many churches utilize stock photos due to issues of privacy, it is important that the types of people depicted are the types of people present. Activities pictured and depictions of buildings and meeting spaces shape expectations. Elements as simple as a properly configured ramp leading to the church's front door communicate inclusion. A ramp to the back door surrounded by overgrown bushes communicates "afterthought."

An important first step is to explore what is being communicated about your church in the community. If a ministry does not yet have an online presence, that gap also can communicate unwillingness to speak the language of a technologically savvy culture. A website with outdated activities shows that a church is not focused on timely communication. The church website should also be accessible to people with disabilities by including text for images, including text suitable for screen readers, and using captioning for any videos. The scheduled times of worship services and events also communicate to the audience they seek. A church that only offers worship at 8:00 a.m. or hosts activities well into the evening on school nights is not targeting families for whom those times conflict with a school schedule. Many newcomers rely on online resources to prescreen for suitability and disability awareness, and if no evidence exists that communicates welcome and inclusion, therein is the null curriculum and Approach Zero we discussed in the last chapter.

A welcoming church is intentional about its website offerings, making sure the website follows standard accessibility guidelines and that information is consistently up to date, meeting times and locations are accurate, and inquiries are toward people who are prompt in their responses. If a youth ministry meets outside of business hours, someone needs to be available to check both voice and text messages in the hours prior to each gathering to answer questions from potential visitors. Technology offers many options for message forwarding to an on-call individual, and some churches have made use of an on-call cell phone that is passed between staff members to handle after-hours needs.

A welcoming church is intentional about the reputation it is building in the local community. Do members of the congregation have good things to share regarding their experiences, and are they encouraged to share those stories and invite friends and neighbors? Shirts from ministry events can become walking publicity. Many churches build a relationship with a local screen-printing company and can obtain shirts and other promotional items at a discounted price. Some ministries invite youth or leaders to create a T-shirt design, a special way to celebrate the creativity of group members. Back when printed newspapers were in wide circulation, one of my (Laura's) youth was featured in a full-color, front-page article wearing a T-shirt from a church event.

Churches develop a reputation among their geographic neighbors based on their positive or negative neighborly behaviors. Are the church grounds kept tidy and well-cared for? Regardless of whether a professional lawn-care service or church members keep up the grounds, what is communicated about the values of the congregation through the care of the exterior? And are these outcomes aligned with the values of the congregation? Is the exterior paint peeling and the building in obvious disrepair? Are bushes trimmed and garden beds tended? Do church members park in appropriate places without disrupting traffic to nearby homes and businesses, and how is overflow parking handled for special events? Is the neighborhood welcome to utilize church grounds for recreation, and do they know they are welcome? Do church activities create excessive noise past neighborly hours? All these variables contribute to the reputation of a church.

Several times each year, my (Laura's) youth group used to do a scavenger hunt in the neighborhood adjacent to our church building. I prepared the youth by reminding them of the importance of being a good neighbor, representing their church well in the community, and being respectful by staying on sidewalks. I encouraged youth to keep comments about lawn ornaments to themselves, and I equipped my small groups with a flier on church letterhead about the purpose of the scavenger hunt of that day ("Bigger and Better Scavenger Hunt"; "a scavenger hunt for homeless residents to supply our local shelter"; etc.). I taught the kids to ring the doorbell and introduce themselves as being from the church. Each group of youth was supervised by an adult, and each group was assigned one neighborhood block to ensure that no house was visited, or bothered, multiple times. Through trial and error, I've learned that scavenger hunts in the spring receive a much better response than in the fall. Why? In the fall, during late-afternoon and early-evening youth group hours, the days are getting shorter. Families are less likely to respond to a doorbell when it is dusk or dark.

The ethos of the church grounds also communicates. Is there activity regularly throughout the week that suggests a lively community? Are there places for people to gather outdoors like benches, picnic tables, playground equipment, or basketball hoops? Do neighborhood youth and families know they are welcome to use equipment regardless of whether they are church members? Is the equipment well-maintained and safe? Neighbors often gather in park spaces, so perhaps the church grounds could become that gathering space in some communities. Occasionally, church trustees raise concerns of liability, but umbrella insurance policies should provide ample coverage to allow a church to be neighborly as long as equipment is properly maintained.

The room for a youth group I (Laura) used to be involved with had a large wall of windows overlooking the parking lot, near a busy road. The group intentionally changed out the decor of those windows quarterly to show that there was life and activity in the building. The high school youth were adamant that when they painted the windows, they needed to paint the letters in reverse so people driving by could read their words! Children's and youth ministry can also do regular activities outdoors in good weather with sidewalk chalk. Aside from whether a passerby can identify the drawings of characters in a Bible story, sidewalk chalk communicates life in the community because of its short life between rainy days.

Before a family arrives on the church campus, there exists an opportunity to create an intentional impression in the neighborhood and community. These elements can either help or hinder a family's initial visit. An investment of time and effort in locations visible to the public can create something of a welcome mat.

Parking and Exterior Signage

After considering reputation, we can turn to the actual physical programs at the local campus. When a visitor arrives, parking or access to the building may be unavailable, inadequate, or confusing to someone unfamiliar with the space, creating Approach Zero. Someone who utilizes a wheelchair, walker, or crutches for mobility likely needs access from a nearby parking space, low curbs, and in some cases, wide doors with automatic openers or a curbside usher available for assistance. Churches aiming to be neighborly should teach their staff, leaders, and longtime members to intentionally park in the spots farther away, leaving the first rows for guests and those who need accessible parking. Some churches share parking with neighboring businesses, and without proper signage, visitors can be easily confused as to who should park where and when; thus, churches should take care to ensure signage is clear and is posted in obvious locations.

Many churches have more than one entrance, and it often is not clear which one is to be used for a given worship time or gathering. Some churches remedy this by modeling signage after the school district's and labeling doors with large letters or numbers. Then when a ministry is advertised, the door to use is always included within the information. Winter weather may become a barrier if sidewalks and parking lots are not kept clear during meeting times. Parking areas that are poorly lit can create situations of anxiety. Intentionality in outdoor spaces and signage is an important component of welcoming individuals into our buildings.

A good test of your space and signage is to invite a guest to attend your gathering willing to evaluate the welcome of your space. While in graduate school, I (Laura) had a professor visit my children's ministry on a busy Sunday morning. Rather than provide specific directions, I asked if my professor would be willing to test the welcome of the people and the signage of their space. My professor agreed. Thankfully, the professor easily found parking near the building, was warmly greeted by an usher, and was walked down to the children's area by a welcome team member to find me. This kind of encounter could be replicated by hiring someone with a physical disability to see if they are able to comfortably navigate your church space.

Many churches post ushers at the door or outdoors to help anyone who might need assistance exiting their car or with directions to a specific space. Youth and adults could be trained to serve in this capacity, working as a team.

Doorway greeters can also serve a role at youth group, engaging with parents dropping off and picking up, keeping an eye on young drivers, making sure youth are being picked up by the custodial parent, and remaining available to help should a problem occur. One afternoon, a grandmother picking up her grandson after youth group backed into a light pole. Because an adult leader was stationed at the door, he saw the incident happen and could respond immediately. While nobody was injured, the grandmother was shaken, and the leader was able to offer a calming presence to help her think through next steps. A youth living in a joint custody situation or in foster care may have court-ordered rules about which adult(s) can pick them up. A youth leader who is familiar with the situation can assure that pickup goes smoothly and will know what course of action to take should the wrong adult show up, whether that be a simple calendar reminder or a call to 911.

Navigating the Space

For some people, finding a specific meeting room in a large building might be overwhelming. Ministry to youth is often relegated to a space off the beaten path. The idea is often to separate the boisterous behaviors of teens from the solemn worship of adults, but unintentionally, this can create a floor plan that is difficult to navigate. Many churches boast multiple additions, creating spaces that are not laid out in logical ways. Good signage is imperative to guide everyone around a space; this signage should use clear language for a visitor who would not necessarily know the church-given names of various groups. When a church has a specific name for the youth gathering space, it is appropriate to list the logical name beside it so a visitor can identify and locate the space. For example, a sign might read, "The Hive: High School Youth Room."

Additionally, restrooms need to be easy to locate and accessible to those with various functional needs. Many churches were initially built before the Americans with Disabilities Act was passed in 1990. Churches built before that time are "grandfathered in," meaning they are not required to adhere to current ADA building design standards until they undergo significant renovations. This means that older buildings without a wheelchair-accessible entrance, lacking an elevator for multiple floors, possessing restrooms with small stalls and high sinks, and even having doorways constructed narrowly with round doorknobs are allowed to remain as they are. The idea of "grandfathering in" these older buildings came because of the cost implicit in making changes. But also because of the cost, many churches avoid significant renovations that would necessitate the updates, leaving their facilities outdated and inaccessible.

Additionally, some churches add new spaces for adults that meet ADA requirements while relegating older spaces to children or youth, which in theory might sound good, but our children and youth then have spaces inaccessible to those with physical disabilities or injuries.

At times, grant money is available to make ADA-compliant renovations, and that can help offset the cost. Some churches have made creative adjustments to spaces that, while not fully meeting ADA requirements, have improved accessibility, such as by merging two narrow bathroom stalls into one larger one. Churches have installed lifts along a staircase that don't help everyone needing assistance but nevertheless welcome many more than the staircase alone does. Including various types of seating in a gathering space for youth allows for more creative adaptations for including wheelchair-using youth in a discussion circle or allowing an injured youth to elevate their knee while recovering from surgery.

My (Mike's) second youth pastorate was a small congregation with a large, 140-year-old building. It had numerous floors and additions but the perennial curse of an old building's lack of access. It did have a very nice hospital-grade elevator, surprisingly shiny and accessible. The church had also added an entirely new building entrance to facilitate the new elevator's easy street access to handicapped parking. Interestingly, the sanctuary doors were still too narrow for wheelchairs. The church had contrived a special transfer system involving specially designed wheelchairs so that individuals could enter the sanctuary. Unfortunately, it made people literally enter from behind the pulpit, immediately adjacent to the stage, and they had to leave behind their own conveyance for the duration of the service. Someone with multiple sclerosis, for example, would have had to be carried in, which is not safe for untrained individuals or an appropriate way to welcome someone into the community.

This was unacceptable as a space in which to conduct youth ministry. I abandoned the typical spaces, stairs, and narrow doors in favor of the fellowship hall, which was on the same level as the entrance and had modern double doors. Each week, a crew would transform the space using hangings and pulleys and bringing out lighting and sound equipment. Donated fabrics and lights made a youth-friendly space that was also ADA compliant in ways the youth room or sanctuary could never be made available. Creativity and regular setup and breakdown work were required, but the transformation enabled everyone to participate, all for a few hundred dollars.

Sensory Sensitivities

Once someone has arrived in the designated meeting space, there might continue to be barriers to meaningful participation. We can begin by exploring the sensory experience. While this list may read as overwhelming, please know that it is compiled in an effort to be nearly exhaustive as a source of reference. It is unlikely that a ministry would need to address every item on the list. Rather, the following are offered as points for consideration, encouraging ministry leaders to look with fresh eyes at their context and the youth they serve. While there is no perfect formula to include the needs of all individuals with sensory sensitivities, there are certainly some categories to keep in mind.

Acoustics

For some, acoustics are a critical factor. Sound-system volume levels common for teenagers or sound bouncing off concrete walls can be overwhelming to someone with autism or with a sensory processing disorder. Conversely, some who have hearing loss benefit from the clarity produced by a sound system, closed captioning, or both when possible. Once a youth group moves past about a dozen, it is time to invest in a sound system. This not only saves the voice of the youth pastor, but it communicates professionalism and value to those who participate. Sound systems should be installed by experienced individuals who can maximize effectiveness. If the meeting space has concrete walls or floors, adding fabric panels, rugs or carpet, and furniture can soften the room and absorb sound.

Making noise-canceling headphones available can be helpful, along with alcohol wipes to clean them between uses. Noise-canceling headphones are available with various levels of noise blocking. While some, often marketed to parents of newborns, claim to eliminate all sound, others allow a low level of sound to come through. Allowing some sound to come through makes it possible for a youth to continue participating without being overwhelmed, but there are also times when blocking all sound may be beneficial.

Individuals who are sensitive to sound can sometimes be difficult to predict. One week, they may feel uncomfortable, move to the back of the room, and request headphones. Another week, they may participate fully in activities with comparable volumes. While several variables are likely at play, one to note is called "trigger stacking." Triggers in this case are anything that prompts an unfavorable response. If an individual has had a good day including a restful night of sleep and a favorite breakfast, and they are wearing comfortable clothes, the triggers have not "stacked up" through the day, allowing their tolerance for loud noises to be higher. Conversely, if they came from school where they had a conflict with a classmate, a pep rally required a modified schedule, and their water bottle leaked—each a trigger with the potential to cause escalated behavior—then triggers have been "stacking up." For someone with sensory sensitivities, navigating their environment requires extra energy, and if they have faced difficult triggers all day, their energy for dealing with their environment may be depleted. Thus, when they arrive for youth group, the first loud worship song may send them running to the back of the room. So rather than predicting that a student will always need noise-canceling headphones, it may be sufficient to have the headphones available but let the individual tell you if they are needed on a given day.

Generally, any time closed captioning is available, it should be turned on. This communicates inclusiveness as the norm rather than the exception, and the group is then equipped to welcome a visitor who has hearing loss while supporting visual learners.

Lighting

Lighting can be tricky, as youth typically inherit a hand-me-down building space with dated fixtures. Thankfully, lamps and, if permitted by the church's policy, unscented candles can be added to adjust the mood of the space even for different activities in the same room. For someone with sensory sensitivities, this might mean fluorescent lights are perceived as physically uncomfortable. And while strobe lights or flashing lights can enhance an atmosphere for teenagers, for those with neurological concerns, they can be a trigger for seizures. Dimmer switches are a wonderful option, if available. My (Laura's) youth group would set up an altar space each month for a time of worship. Youth would take turns creatively arranging the space with glass blocks and candles to create a special atmosphere.

Temperature

We have all had experiences in spaces where the temperature was so uncomfortable it was a distraction. It is important for ministry leaders to adjust their meeting space temperature appropriately. In older buildings, this might mean turning equipment on several hours before a meeting or using quick thinking to open windows during a game before the middle schoolers break a sweat! I (Laura) worked with my church custodian to learn "tricks" to get the old boiler going on cold days when I was the only one using the building.

Smells

Individuals with sensory sensitivities can struggle with strong scents, and for some, particular scents can cause allergic or asthmatic reactions. It is best to make sure meeting spaces are free from scents and have good ventilation, especially after those active middle school games! Avoid using air fresheners, plug-in devices, scented candles, or incense, as these can all cause allergic or asthmatic reactions. If care is taken but unpleasant scents remain, explore the cleaning products being used, what might be living in the couch that was donated, and how often HVAC filters are being changed. Some facilities may need to be checked and treated for mold if maintenance has not been diligent.

Some churches bring in fresh flowers to enhance the worship setting, which can cause allergic reactions. While the cross made of Easter lilies at my (Laura's) church was a lovely tradition, I couldn't make it through Easter Sunday without multiple allergy tablets. When allergies and asthma flare, individuals also become more susceptible to illness. I (Laura) was grateful when the church decided to switch to plastic Easter lily plants!

Seating

Textures and colors within a space may become a barrier as the particular carpet or furniture feels "uncomfortable" to an individual with sensory sensitivities. As suggested, having various options for seating can provide flexibility for needs and situations. At times, sitting in open floor space can be conducive to a relaxed conversation. When parents join for a meeting, they typically prefer chairs, so my (Laura's) youth room had chairs that could be easily pulled out and then stacked and slid into a corner. Couches encourage comfortable conversation, but sometimes youth become too comfortable and fail to engage. At times, couches promote too much friendly contact. Youth room couches can often be sourced as donations from parishioners' basements, but I (Laura) would always explore the donation ahead of time to make sure it was coming from a clean home that would not bring any contaminants into the church. I could accomplish this by asking to stop by and see the couch to determine if it would meet the need, if I had any question about whether it would. We would also routinely decline pull-out couches because they are very heavy and difficult to move. Couches with washable slipcovers are a blessing after a snack of cheese balls!

My (Laura's) son, who is autistic, can be particular about seating choices. At church, he finds the blue chairs uncomfortable, so when the children move into small groups, his group uses the black chairs to help him stay relaxed. Whether such a preference is due to the color or a construction that causes physical discomfort, this is a small accommodation that can be made to keep an individual comfortable and engaged with the topic.

While few youth groups meet in the sanctuary worship space, for those that do, traditional pews can be a natural barrier. One man who uses a wheelchair shared how he did not feel included in the congregation because his chair hung out in the aisle. He felt he was an inconvenience as people stepped around him to move to the altar for prayer or Communion. When a team began exploring a loving response in conversation with the man who used a wheelchair, the decision was made to cut one pew on each side of the sanctuary to half its size. This would allow space for two wheelchairs each on either side of the shortened pew without impeding the aisle. Because two pews were cut short, space was created to easily park eight wheelchairs beside regular pew seating for the wheelchair users' families. It was also important to the team that the modified pews not be in the back because that could communicate that the needs of wheelchair users were an afterthought. Rather, the center pew on either side of the church was modified. Several woodworkers from the congregation took on the project. They removed the pews, removed the endcaps, cut the benches shorter, reinstalled the endcaps, and returned the shortened pews to the sanctuary. The carpet was then patched. Inclusive space was thus created in the center of the congregational seating.

If a ministry provides bus transportation, as do many after-school programs and ministry day camps, it is necessary for the transportation to be accessible and comfortable. I (Mike) once ran a youth group of 120 kids on a $500 yearly budget. Everything was donated or salvaged to let us run a zero-budget program. Yellow school buses with volunteer drivers were the cheapest form of mass transportation. Suffering together in a school bus surely built community and stories while being budget friendly. However, the buses' lack of wheelchair lifts meant that they were inaccessible for wheelchair users, and their lack of bathrooms meant that, for longer trips, they were inaccessible to students who needed frequent or unscheduled bathroom breaks.

Wall Coverings

Research affirms that color influences mood and experience. Left alone, many youth in our churches would choose neon-graffitied walls, which may not be a calming choice. Just prior to my (Mike) being hired at a church, the youth had been allowed to paint the youth room black, and one wall boasted a giant, blood-red Chicago Bulls logo. The room received a second remodel that year. Consulting with an interior designer can be helpful when considering lighting, flooring, and paint-color options. When it was time to renovate my (Laura's) youth room, a member of the church who did interior design was helpful in steering the youth toward a color palette that was fun but appropriate for other groups who met in the space. The designer was also helpful in suggesting a carpet that was durable and by securing a discount from her sources.

Now that we have considered physical buildings and spaces of ministry, the following chapter turns to programming considerations that allow for access and welcome.

9

Welcoming, Part 2

Preparing the Program

This chapter continues where the last leaves off. In chapter 8, we considered the ministry location and preparation work necessary to welcome students on the margins. Here we turn to the program and its elements. We describe how to create a welcoming program, starting with front-loading information and arrival all the way through departure.

Front-Loading

Ministries that exist by the "guidance of the Holy Spirit" tend to avoid a preplanned schedule or itinerary. While there is unparalleled benefit to following the guidance of the Holy Spirit, it is also possible for the Holy Spirit to move through a planning meeting several weeks prior to an activity or sermon. Many individuals on the autism spectrum and kids living in changing or unstable family situations, like foster care, benefit from knowing up front what to expect in a ministry gathering. Called "front-loading," the process of providing information ahead of time helps individuals prepare for an experience. For some, receiving a timeline along with the front-loading information is also helpful, as it allows them to pace their expectations for the gathering time. In response to front-loading, a youth could bring and utilize noise-canceling headphones during worship, or a 1:1 volunteer could take their buddy for a walk during a longer time of teaching. Another individual might not enjoy small-group discussions, but knowing that a discussion will end in fifteen minutes could allow them to pace their feelings of discomfort and focus on the game that will follow.

For some youth, using timers is helpful. However, some youth, especially some on the autism spectrum, can be very sensitive if a gathering does not end precisely on time, or if different clocks in the same meeting space do not read the same number. Clocks can also be perceived as limiting the movement of the Holy Spirit. In most ministry settings, a rough timeline with a firm ending time is enough to equip a youth to navigate well. As an aside, parents and volunteers also appreciate events that end on time!

Sometimes front-loading can be accomplished through a printed schedule or one posted on a wall to be viewed in real time. Other individuals may need several days to prepare for their participation. Posting a youth calendar in an easily accessible location both online and in the church building can be a help for individuals and families who might make their choice to participate based on the content of the day. If a given topic is not appropriate for an individual, a family then has time to make alternative plans for that time in a way that does not draw attention to the absence.

One example from my (Laura's) youth group involved a young man with Down syndrome who participated in the group. Although past the traditional youth group age, this young man had been allowed to continue attending because he enjoyed his time so much and was a delightful member of the group. Most of the time he would sit quietly and observe, just glad to be included. Some topics, however, were beyond his cognitive abilities. Because I posted online and mailed a youth group calendar a month ahead of time, this young man's parents could scan through the topics to make sure they were appropriate for his level of understanding. Every February when the group would take time for more mature topics, this young man would approach me on Sunday morning after service to report, "I can't come to youth group tonight because my mom planned a family bowling trip!" The young man loved bowling and family activities, so his parents chose to exercise their love and guidance this way. I would express my disappointment that he would not be at youth group, all while knowing the intent for the arrangements. Because of the relationship we had built with his parents, they always felt comfortable asking for clarity on a scheduled topic and scheduled family outings as needed.

A student who uses crutches to walk due to cerebral palsy could read a calendar provided ahead of time and see a field trip posted. Knowing that a lot of walking would be required by the field trip, the student could plan ahead and arrive with their wheelchair. Related to that, it would be important for the leader to provide appropriate transportation, knowing that a wheelchair would need to be transported.

For youth who have experienced trauma, particular topics may exist as triggers of past experiences. As an example, the topic of sex and dating may bring up difficult memories for someone who has experienced sexual abuse. Depending on where that teen is in their process of healing, they may be able to participate with support, or it may be a good time for a family outing instead. Youth leaders, and even foster parents, will not be aware of all the prior traumatic experiences of the kids they serve, so one way to be proactive is to publish topics ahead of time, as well as announce them in preceding weeks. This gives youth a measure of agency over their participation, knowing, at least in broad strokes, what to expect.

Two of my (Laura's) children are sensitive to noise and become overwhelmed in noisy, crowded situations. Knowing what to expect allows our family to prepare and make efforts to avoid dysregulation or disruptive behaviors. Sometimes they pack noise-canceling headphones or choose a seat intentionally in the back of a gathering or away from speakers. When I bring my children to the main service, they intentionally choose the last row of the balcony. This allows me to provide frequent redirection and support as they navigate the experience, with minimal distraction to others. It also allows for a quick escape if needed.

At both church and school, my son, who is thirteen, has a designated area where he can go when he becomes overwhelmed by the noise of large-group worship or the exuberance of a school pep rally. Knowing that these options exist gives him an "out" before he becomes dysregulated. My daughter is younger, so her diagnoses are still presenting themselves. During kindergarten lunch in a crowded cafeteria, she struggles to eat her food, often defaulting to disruptive behavior. These choices lead to disciplinary consequences and an empty tummy for the afternoon. Conversation with her teacher is ongoing as we refine a 504 plan to include appropriate accommodations, including the possibility of a separate dining area alongside equipping her with helpful coping skills.

In terms of schedule within a youth group gathering, some churches are very consistent with the same three or four elements: perhaps a game, worship, a lesson, and small-group conversation. If the schedule is the same each week, it is easy for a teen to become familiar with the routine and pace their anticipation.

Other churches flip elements of the schedule regularly to support each day's teaching focus. In situations of this nature, having a printed schedule or a poster with Velcro cards that can be moved around as the day dictates can help a teen sensitive to schedule changes know what to anticipate. Most elementary school and special education classrooms include some type of visual schedule, so a simple internet search would provide many ideas. Visual schedules can also exist with pictures for emerging readers.

Welcoming

The vibe and language present when a guest enters a space can influence their experience. When participants, both leaders and peers, are not equipped to welcome newcomers, a guest may awkwardly stand in a corner, unsure of who to talk to, how to engage, what behaviors are acceptable, and where to sit or gather when the meeting time begins.

Preparing regular youth and leaders to be welcoming and to notice visitors can go a long way toward creating an environment of hospitality. A larger group can allow for rotation of this role at the door. Once a guest arrives and simple introductions are exchanged, it is important to help that visitor know how to engage. For a visitor at youth group, I (Laura) would often look for a school connection or an extracurricular interest. As an example, if a visitor arrived who attended "school A," I would scan the room and look for others who attended "school A." I would point out several students and ask if the visitor knew any of them. Often, this was enough for a connection to be made. The visitor might indicate that they knew the students at the ping-pong table from math class. I would invite the visitor to walk with me to the familiar students, help them make a connection, and ask the regular attenders to include the guest in their activity. Ninety percent of the time, this was enough to help a guest find their way into the space. For those who did not have a natural connection, I might look for a leader to pair up with them as a "buddy" for that day. Well-trained greeters or volunteers can facilitate this process. If regular attenders are taught and encouraged to be hospitable to visitors, the transition into the group can happen easily.

Language is another thing that can exclude when "insiders" talk with words and terms unfamiliar to someone outside the culture of the ministry. For example, many youth groups have a name that is not simply "Youth Group." They might call themselves "The Edge" or "SALT." Those names are wonderful and fun, but they speak to the insider. An outsider doesn't know what these terms mean in this context. So, while a youth group may continue identifying as "SALT," it is important to include with that a tag line that explains what it means: for instance, "SALT (Seeking Awesome Light Together), a gathering of high school youth on Sunday evenings." Now, a visitor is equipped to make meaning of the group's name. Even special events in the church like "Car Hop" and "Dinner Theater" have specific meaning to insiders but may immediately place a visitor on the outside. Making a habit of offering a tagline definition in printed materials and in the verbiage of announcements can go a long way toward helping people feel welcome with the terminology they hear: for example, "Car Hop: A 1950s-Themed Cookout with Hot Dogs, Burgers, and Root Beer Floats," or "Dinner Theater: A Dinner Prepared and Served by Youth Followed by Entertainment Showcasing the Talents of the Congregation."

Name badges may also play a role, as they bridge a gap in personal communication for a newcomer who is acclimating. Name badges may not be perceived as cool by teens and preteens, but there are times when intentional name games and name badges can go a long way in building community. Including name games at the beginning of a season and periodically throughout the year can reinforce names and build personal connection. During camps and retreats, it can be worth the investment in name tag buttons or lanyards more durable for the length of the experience. Many camps and conferences have implemented lanyards for safety, clarifying who belongs at the event and drawing attention to someone who might not. Holding periodic "drawings" at camp for treats and other desirable items that can only be won if a camper is wearing their name badge could serve as a motivator. And if your group is engaging the local community, as on a mission or outreach trip, name badges are about appropriate hospitality and can be framed that way. Encourage your group to see name badges as a tool in building a meaningful connection with those you are serving.

Expectations of Participation

Once a meeting has begun, certain behaviors are expected of its participants, including behaviors related to listening, speaking, sitting, and standing at specific times. For regular attendees, the behaviors are familiar and natural responses, but for someone new, especially if they have certain disabilities or challenges, some of the behavioral expectations in an environment may put that experience out of reach unless some adjustments can be made.

If musical worship is included, participants are expected to process a variety of sounds at different volumes with postures that might include standing, kneeling, clapping, or raising hands, and possibly hand motions and gestures that may be unique to the group. Game times may include the need for coordination and mobility, as well as a willingness to play by an agreed upon set of rules. Snacks or meals might pose difficulty for those who have allergies or sensitivities. During social times, skills are needed to navigate the environment, even more so during special events, field trips, camps, or retreats that stretch across additional hours. While no ministry could anticipate every potential barrier, building tools of awareness can help us anticipate as best we can and respond with grace when an issue arises.

Another consideration is the range of postures that are expected for a youth to engage in during a typical meeting: sitting, standing, kneeling, praying, running, and so on. Are there students who are physically incapable of participating in some of these postures either permanently or for a time as they heal from injury? How can those limitations best be accommodated? For example, a youth using crutches while healing from an injury could navigate game time by being a referee or keeping score. While one of my (Laura's) leaders was pregnant, she became the "human scoreboard." This became such a fun role for her while engaging with the group that she continued even after her baby was born. During worship, if the group is standing, could a buddy, or several buddies, sit with a youth who cannot? During song worship, if motions are included, leaders can remain sensitive to newcomers and practice the motions before singing the song.

Meals and Snacks

Including food in youth ministry is a wonderful way to nurture social connection. Some youth groups include a full dinner for kids who might not have the experience of family dinner time. Unfortunately, food can also present barriers. More and more of our teens are recognizing food allergies and sensitivities. It is important for leaders to know what their kids are allergic to and what type of reactions to expect. Will a youth need an inhaler, or should the leader be calling 911? Different from a true allergy, a food sensitivity is an issue in which something unfavorable happens when a food is consumed, but perhaps in small amounts, that food is acceptable. A youth with a sensitivity to dairy may be allowed to have one scoop of ice cream but not the triple cone because in larger amounts a migraine headache will result. At times, kids may try to minimize their food allergies to better fit in with peers, potentially allowing a reaction to occur, so seeking clarity from parents is helpful.

A common side effect from many ADHD medications is appetite suppression. For individuals who take a typical morning dose of ADHD medication, appetite is typically reduced until midafternoon, when the medications begin wearing off. Many children on these medications will eat very small amounts of food for breakfast and lunch but will make up their calories with a large after-school snack and dinner. Church staff who are aware of these patterns will learn not to become alarmed if a youth picks at their lunch during camp, as long as a good dinner follows. Children and youth taking these medications are monitored closely by their physicians to make sure they continue to gain weight at a healthy pace.

Some foods should be on the radar of all ministries, like sugar, caffeine, and for some children, food dye, particularly red. Our American diet boasts an exceptional amount of sugar, and for many, sugar impacts health as well as behavior. Caffeine in the late afternoon or evening can impact behavior and sleep. More families are experiencing that food dye, especially red, can have a negative impact on the behavior of some youth for several hours following consumption. For a youth group seeking to work through a meaningful lesson, a snack of red candy and caffeinated beverages will not support calm behaviors, and a snack of red caffeinated soda might ensure six hours of chaos! If a youth is sensitive to red food dye, avoiding it can be particularly tricky, as it is present in things that are orange, blue, and purple at times, so candies, juices, popsicles, frosting, fruit snacks, and even some chips contain red food dye.

When taking our youth off-site for a field trip or retreat, it can be helpful to note ahead of time what snacks and vending machines are available and to place limits if needed. One camp where I (Laura) would take youth offered an evening snack for an additional charge, but it typically served sugary juices and snacks shortly before bed. I saved money and helped support a smooth bedtime by bringing bottles of water, also easy to refill, and bedtime snacks that were healthy. It can also be helpful to think about offering snacks with protein that tend to keep kids full longer and curb the crash that comes with eating carbs.

My (Laura's) son is picky about food and can react negatively if the menu is not to his liking. Having the menu posted ahead of time in situations when food is served matters, and for my son and some other teens, knowing the brand of an item also matters. My son loves pizza from a restaurant but will balk at homemade pizza. He likes the store brand of chicken nuggets I buy, but most others are unacceptable. And because his body doesn't appropriately cue "hungry" or "full," he will just not eat and will fail to make a connection between being hungry and the deterioration of his behavior. When he attends youth group where dinner is included, I need to either serve him a small meal ahead of time or know the menu and potentially send a supplemental item to prevent concerns when he does not care for the meal.

Offering options is another helpful way to serve the needs of individuals. While soda might be assumed to be the drink of choice among teens and preteens, a leader who offers water, sports drinks, unsweetened iced tea, and even some juice might be surprised at the response. And while knowing the number to the local pizza place can be a rite of passage for youth pastors, offering fruit or a veggie tray alongside the pizza can teach balance. When traveling, it can be helpful to stop for lunch in an area with multiple choices so teens can decide between multiple fast-food locations. In this way, teens and preteens are learning to accommodate their needs and gaining independence. And of course, leaders fan out and eat at each of the locations.

Sadly, food is also linked to eating disorders, so leaders need to be aware of youth who may have unusual tendencies like picking at portions and throwing food away or eating and then disappearing into the restroom. Certainly there are menu items that will not appeal to everyone, but if there is a pattern of concerning behaviors, it is worth exploring with the youth and their parents.

Conversation, Social Skills, and Games

In any group setting, appropriate social skills are necessary to navigate well. Many of our teens and preteens lack social skills for a variety of reasons, including the effects of extended lockdown during COVID, anxiety, and autism, among other reasons. So while a youth pastor may assume that giving kids time to "hang out" would be a welcome option, for some it can magnify differences and even cause anxiety.

Knowing how to begin and maintain an appropriate conversation can be difficult for some youth, so activities that offer topics to talk about in small groups, guided by adults, can nurture social skills. Some youth have difficulty understanding a joke, sarcasm, or nonverbal cues, so comments and gestures can be misunderstood, creating tension in relationships. For others, not knowing or respecting appropriate boundaries in touch and physical space can cause peers to distance themselves.

A teen I (Laura) worked with has difficulty in social situations for all these reasons. To navigate, he needs clearly spelled-out boundaries and expectations. Recently, our pastor asked him to stop hugging peers because of the uncomfortable situations it has created. He is now only allowed to hug adults, and only if he asks and receives permission. At school, his special education curriculum works on appropriate conversation tactics, but it remains a work in progress. He misses most nonverbal cues and does not understand the jokes of his peers. He interrupts when others are talking because his focus is on his agenda, and people are put off by the lack of attention he gives to their words. While others might be frustrated, it is very important for peers to be clear with him. He does not understand the general playful roughhousing of boys his age, so regularly, a playful shove from a peer will cause him to respond with a punch. If he sees a friend from church in public and they offer him a kind greeting, he immediately assumes they are interested in more extensive socializing because he does not understand the social norm that calls us to greet others in a friendly way. Peers also need to be empowered to ask for space from him or to stop behavior that is not appropriate. Otherwise, he is confused when adults impose a guideline, like no hugging peers, but his peers are not reinforcing it because they want to avoid hurting his feelings. This scenario also highlights the need for times when the larger group needs to be equipped to engage well with one youth who has certain disabilities or functional needs. When this teen initially transitioned to the youth group, I asked to meet with youth and leaders to talk about how they could help him integrate into the group in healthy ways. I emphasized the importance of being clear with him, even at the risk of hurting his feelings.

Games can bring a different set of social expectations, as participants are required to follow rules. For those who struggle with social norms and with people in positions of authority, the unfavorable call of a referee can trigger negative behaviors. Games carry the expectation that participants can and will follow rules and that they will accept defeat with good sportsmanship. For some, these expectations can be unrealistic. A good question for parents is how their child navigates gym class at school. If gym class causes no concerns, game time should go well at youth group. Conversely, if a youth has issues in gym classes related to fair and respectful play, it would be wise to plan with parents regarding how game time in a church setting should be handled. A plan might include identifying two or three coping skills that could be used in the game setting if the youth becomes frustrated, such as getting a drink of water, taking a walk in a designated area, or using the restroom as a place to practice breathing techniques. This way, when the youth escalates due to frustration during a game, leaders immediately know how to redirect the youth.

While building tools to look at our ministries with fresh eyes can be daunting, it is important to frame it as a means of loving the people God has entrusted to our care. When a ministry's leaders give attention to the concerns of their people, trust is forged. Years ago, another leader and I (Laura) were taking a group of middle schoolers to a daylong district event in another town. I was new to the church and still establishing relationships with its families. The day before the trip, a mom called to explain that her seventh-grade son had just gotten contacts and was still adjusting, so he was allowed to wear them for only a portion of the day. The mom was concerned because her son would need to remove his contacts early in the afternoon of the event. I assured the mother that I would make sure her son would have access to the restroom at the appointed time to remove his contacts, but the mother pushed further. She did not feel her son would be capable of removing his contacts independently, so she was asking me to go into the men's restroom with her seventh-grade son and physically remove the contacts from his eyes at the appointed time. While several layers of the request were concerning, I was able to see the root of the issue. I was young and new to the church. I was driving a large group of middle schoolers in a van about ninety minutes away for a long day. The mother was not sure she could trust me with her son. Many times thereafter before retreats, trips, and camps, I received parent phone calls with unusual requests while underneath was the question of whether I could be trusted to care for the caller's child. In this case, I assured the mom of the child with new contacts that I would ensure her son had access to the restroom and that I would be available nearby if he had trouble, but that it wouldn't be appropriate for me to walk into the men's restroom at a large gathering. I affirmed how much I enjoyed this young man and how I believed he could manage the responsibility of removing his contacts. Eventually the mother agreed, and the plan was executed. I waited near the restroom, and the middle school boy removed his contacts right at the appointed time, independently. After returning to the church parking lot that night, I went right up to the mom to report on how well her son had done at the event and with his contacts. From that point on, I had the full support of that mother. In whatever the youth group was planning, whatever resource we needed, that mother was available because I had been available to respond to the seemingly unusual need of her son, which was simply a cover for the real need of trust.

Cues from the Public School System

While each state includes unique policies and processes, the following is a description of general practices. Some districts screen children before they begin public school to identify who may have a disability that makes them eligible for special education services. For eligible students, special education services are often set up immediately, prior to their first day of preschool or kindergarten. Many communities invest heavily in early intervention in hopes of identifying children with concerns and starting therapeutic measures as early as possible. For some children, however, disabilities that affect schoolwork are not apparent during screening, and their needs emerge later as the gap widens between them and their peers or when they experience a traumatic event. For others, assessments are done later and their needs become apparent then. Some challenges emerge at developmental milestones, as some mental health conditions escalate at certain stages of puberty. In addition, some suspected disabilities may seem as though they require no intervention, such as autism with low support needs, so parents may delay seeking a diagnosis, choosing to wait and watch symptoms to see if the child "grows out of them" or simply never needs or desires formal school-based support.

Importantly, private and Christian schools are typically limited in their special education support. They receive no tax dollars toward support staff or specialized equipment or curricula. As a result, for most families whose children have functional needs that require support in school, private schools are not an option. When such families would prefer their children to have a Christian education, it can be frustrating for them that their local Christian schools cannot accommodate their children's needs, so it is helpful for ministry leaders to be aware of these limitations and remain sensitive to the parents.

Once a child or youth is assessed, and it is determined that supportive services would be beneficial, a 504 plan or an Individualized Education Plan (IEP) is developed for that student. A 504 plan is a plan for supportive measures while the curriculum remains the same as that of their peers. A student with a 504 plan is on pace with peers academically but would benefit from adjustments to the classroom and school environment, like preferential seating or extra breaks during standardized testing. An IEP includes accommodation in the classroom and school environment, but it also means that adjustments to academic work are included. A student with an IEP either cannot complete a volume of work comparable to that of their peers, or they need modified assignments as they are not functioning at grade level. Some students with an IEP might spend their full school day in a special education classroom, while others will split their time between a special education classroom and a mainstreamed classroom based on their specific needs.

To formalize a 504 plan or IEP, a meeting is held by the stakeholders: the classroom teacher or teachers; the principal; the parents or guardians; any relevant support providers, such as physical therapists, occupational therapists, or speech therapists; and sometimes doctors or church leaders. Parents or guardians are welcome to invite anyone they feel would be important to support the needs of their child or youth. This meeting offers a way for a church leader to enter in, offering their perspective on how the child or youth is accommodated or functions in the church setting. An IEP or 504 plan meeting is generally cordial and functions as a brainstorming session among parents, teachers, and other service providers to determine the best way to support the child or youth.

The list of possible classroom accommodations that emerges from a 504 or IEP meeting can be quite long, but it can give the church ideas for adjustments that can also be made in a ministry setting to help the child or youth to be successful. One example is specific seating in the classroom, in the cafeteria, or on the bus. For someone who is easily distracted or struggles with impulse control, it can be helpful to be seated near the teacher or with a bit of distance from peers. Another example is frequent breaks. For someone who struggles with attention or the ability to stay regulated through a challenge, it can be difficult to focus for the same length of time as peers. Offering such a student more frequent breaks than is typical can provide space for them to pace themselves in a way that helps them be successful.

Some students need more or more frequent reinforcements or positive feedback than their peers to stay on track. Teachers with years of experience can be very creative and resourceful, and once they know a student's preferred "commodity," they can leverage it to promote motivation. Most special education classrooms use a point or level system according to which positive behaviors are rewarded with high frequency, and students can work toward higher levels of privilege or reward by making good choices. While there is disagreement in the educational community about nurturing intrinsic versus extrinsic motivation, educators who serve students with high support needs generally agree that intrinsic motivation can be slower to evolve in these students. As a result, their teachers may lean into extrinsic rewards longer until the youth can see the benefit of cooperation as they prepare for their future. Rewards need not be tangible items. They could include privileges such as being entrusted with a particular classroom task, being allowed to bring a stuffie from home, or even being permitted to walk barefoot in the classroom (if district policy allows it), which could heighten sensory input for sensory seekers. My (Laura's) daughter in kindergarten loved the reward of a piece of "the teacher's gum," which she perceives as quite special! The additional sensory input helps her to regulate and manage her day better.

Accommodations can be made at any level of the public school educational system, from support in a mainstream classroom to support at a therapeutic school. While 504 and IEP meetings are typically held annually to update changes, one can be called earlier should the parent or school feel the need to change the level or type of support a student is receiving. Students can also be moved to a different public school setting midyear should it be determined that a different support is needed. Both 504 and IEPs go with a student as they are promoted to the next level of education, as in from middle school to high school. Special education is very fluid and always adjusting to the emerging needs of the learner.

Reactive Attachment Disorder

Children and youth who have experienced a disruption in their relationship with a primary caregiver often develop RAD, or reactive attachment disorder.

While the root of RAD often occurs in infancy, the symptoms can persist for a lifetime. Infants are wired to connect with a primary caregiver who meets their needs on a consistent basis. Researchers believe this initial bond becomes the blueprint for building relationships throughout life. If the bond with the primary caregiver is disrupted at a young age, something is lost that cannot be replaced. A toddler who is removed from their home because of their parents' serious substance use disorder might be placed in a foster home. Despite the loving care of the foster parents, this toddler's bond to their primary caregiver was disrupted when they were removed from their home, and likely even more so when their parents failed to provide adequate care due to their untreated substance misuse. The blueprint was lost, and for many, it cannot be replicated.

Imagine a preschooler at work in their classroom. They carefully color their picture because they know their parent will pick them up, and they want to see their parent's smile and experience the warmth of their hug when they display their work. That preschooler has a desire to please the parent or parents who care for them. But for those who have experienced disruption in that relationship because of trauma, abuse, neglect, or death, that natural process does not function as effectively.

From a therapeutic perspective, RAD is difficult to improve, even with therapy. Children and youth with RAD often work to sabotage relationships with caregivers, sometimes unintentionally, before they can be disappointed by the loss of another relationship. Working with children and youth who have RAD requires consistency and commitment, and willingness to persist whether or not a child or youth makes any meaningful gains. At times, RAD can be more targeted, perhaps only at caregivers of the same gender as the one with whom the child's relationship was disrupted. One boy placed in an orphanage in China because of heart problems that were later surgically corrected was adopted by a family in the United States when he was four. He bonded moderately well to his adoptive father, but for years, he refused touch or care from his adoptive mom because even subconsciously, losing his birth mother was his greatest wound. In a ministry setting, choosing a consistent and committed leader, likely of the same gender as the child or youth, is the best way we can serve a child or youth with RAD.

Departure

Youth who have experienced trauma or have certain disabilities often have difficulty with transitions. Whether these youth are moving from music to games or from youth group to home, transitions impose a new environment and expectations, as well as requiring a new set of behaviors and prompting different emotions. If a church has done its job well, leaving an engaging setting can be difficult for all kids!

Consistency is the most important tool churches have to ease the transition of departure. If youth group ends at 8:00 p.m., the goal of the church should be to always end within five minutes of the published time. This helps everyone know what to expect and how to prepare. Ending on time also builds trust with parents waiting outside in their minivans, communicating that their time is also valuable.

Some youth do well with time reminders, another facet of front-loading. When I (Laura) take my children somewhere like the park, I usually give them ten-minute, five-minute, and two-minute warnings as time is winding down. At two minutes, I encourage my children to find one last favorite thing to do—perhaps one more trip down the slide. This system allows my children to pace their time and prepare for a transition without it coming as a surprise. Even for youth who are able to tell time, reminders can be helpful as everyone loses track of time during an enjoyable activity. Some ministries provide a countdown clock on a large screen during the last round of a game or as a quiet reminder during a small-group discussion time. Just as a time clock counts down at a basketball game, the countdown clock helps everyone to pace themselves for transition.

Some youth ministries close with the same routine each week, providing a meaningful experience of tradition alongside a cue regarding time. My (Laura's) youth group would close each night by trekking across the church to the empty sanctuary. The space was beautiful with the darkness of evening and the streetlights shining through the stained-glass windows. The space felt like holy ground. A few candles were the only light source, and youth would kneel around the altar, sharing joys and concerns and praying for one another. The time served as a wonderful transition between youth group time together and the return to home and family.

Leaving a camp or retreat can also come with the challenge of transition, sometimes escalated from the emotions and lack of sleep woven into a meaningful experience. For a youth who comes from a difficult background or who experiences acceptance at camp in contrast to their experiences in their school's hallways, camp can feel like a safe haven. Leaving safe space is painful, so church staff can walk through the transition in an intentional way. Building traditions into the last night or chapel of camp provides youth an anchor to depend on and tools with which to make meaning of the time they have spent together. Adding something for the drive home can also help. My (Laura's) youth group would spend some time at camp writing "care cards" for one another: positive notes with affirming words. No peeking was allowed, and the envelopes were delivered after our meal stop while boarding the bus for the last leg of the journey before arriving at home. Following some mission trips, groups can regather the following Sunday to share their stories with the congregation in morning worship. Timing a mission trip to return on Saturday with the responsibility to lead and share the next morning can provide something for youth to look forward to amid their transition home.

Whatever the choice for closing routine, elements should be meaningful to the group and serve to send participants off on a note of intentionality. Much like a worship service closes with a benediction or a blessing, sending our youth off with good words sets the tone for how we hope they will leave the church space and engage their world.

PART 3

Pearls of Wisdom—Topics and Tactics

In the previous chapters of this book, we took time to explore the "why." Why should churches, ministries, and youth pastors invest intentionally to make sure their building and group ethos are welcoming to youth on the margins? We dug deep into theology to consider the power of the *imago Dei* and examples of hospitality throughout Scripture.

In this section of the book, we aim to explore the "how" question. Here we speak to the practical aspects and practitioners of ministry on the margins. These are stand-alone topics that can be used as a quick-reference guide. While there is no magic formula or one-size-fits-all approach, our hope is for the following pages to serve as tools for your toolbox. The topics and ideas come from our experience in the trenches of youth ministry, both with our own teens and with those we served as youth pastors. Many of these ideas were birthed out of "building the plane while you fly it" types of experiences. A teen walked through our doors, and we were suddenly tasked with meeting both their immediate needs, however varied they may be, and their ultimate need of Jesus. Other ideas and best practices grew out of thoughtful peer-reviewed research.

Walking into the church youth room can feel like strapping on fishing waders, the giant rubber pants with boots attached, aimed at protecting an individual from whatever surprises the water holds. Youth ministry can be full of surprises, but rather than giant rubber pants, we who serve the church are compelled forward into the unknown by the grace of God and the call on our lives. We wade in, often not knowing fully how we will accomplish the task before us but trusting in God's sufficiency. May the following pages become tools for your toolbox, so the waters ahead feel less murky.

10

Welcoming a Teen on the Margins into Your Ministry

Immediate Ideas for Day 1

While the previous chapters look at the big picture and philosophical approach to welcoming teens, this chapter will give practical ideas that can be put into practice on day one.

Many teens on the margins find themselves always feeling as though they are wearing shoes a size too big or a size too small. The world does not always feel comfortable. Because ministry is the business of making sure all find their place at Jesus's table, intentionality in our welcome matters! Taking a few steps to be mindful of the way we welcome can go a long way in helping a visitor from the margins become comfortable in our churches.

Sometimes our church and youth group routines can become overly familiar. We do not notice the volume of the music, because it is always loud. We do not notice the way kids gather in groups, because we are always in one of those groups. We do not notice the smell of the space because we are simply there too often. It can be helpful to invite a friend outside of our ministry to visit and share the experience as one with fresh eyes. What do they notice, and how might that translate to sensitivity in welcoming a guest?

In some of our churches, teens equal intensity. Whether that intensity occurs through literal noise or through the energy they carry, it can cause a visitor to feel overwhelmed. Some youth groups exist as tight-knit social groups, which can be a great benefit for those on the inside but present as an impossibility for those on the outside. And some youth groups present as disengaged, which is not inviting to anyone.

Assuming the parking and signage of the church are done well, and the guest is able to easily find the gathering space, we can begin our welcome at the door. Youth ministries need to staff the door intentionally with youth or adults who have the gift of hospitality and warmth. This could be a regular post for someone or a shared responsibility between several youth and adults. Many youth groups begin with a hangout time where teens can play games and catch up with one another: ping-pong, table games, foosball, video games, pool, carpet ball, and a circle of comfy couches. Games are to kids and teens as coffee is to adults. Games are a way through which kids and teens socialize, so they can offer a helpful place of entry. However, entering as a newcomer can be intimidating for anyone, so we need to be thoughtful in the way we ease the fears of our guests and visitors.

Greeting and Connecting

We can all share stories of making connections with others over shared experiences or common interests. For some, making connections comes easily. For many, it can be a hurdle. Sometimes during introductions with a guest at church, we can intentionally gather information to facilitate connections. For example, "You're wearing a Pokémon/Packers/Disney hoodie—are you a fan?" can generate conversation and let you point out others in the group are also football fans. Sometimes those natural opening questions can begin building a bridge. "Oh, you go to West High School—do you know Jenna or Roberto? Both of them attend West." Maybe the youth you are talking to recognizes Jenna from math class, so you invite the visitor to join Jenna in the game she is playing. Jenna recognizes the visitor from school, and because your church has been intentional about training everyone to be welcoming, she invites the visitor to join her game without prompting. Jenna then takes the lead in helping the visitor acclimate in a peer-to-peer manner. Just make sure you have accessible games and some noncompetitive options. Wheelchair-accessible foosball, table tennis, and carpet ball are easily available.

At other times, a guest may not have natural connections to work with; this can be a time for a leader to step in and become "buddies" with the guest for the day. The leader can invite the guest to play table tennis or a cooperative card game or show them around the space to help build comfort.

Predictability and Routine

Visiting a new group takes a great deal of courage. Beyond engaging with unfamiliar people in a new space, it also requires a teen to submit to an unfamiliar routine. A surrendering of control must occur, and for many kids on the margins, for many reasons, surrender can be scary. One way we can offer back a measure of control is to explain the routine for youth group. This could be accomplished verbally or by use of a fun poster highlighting the order of worship in words or pictures. If your group tends to switch up the order, the poster might have titles with Velcro strips that could be rearranged according to the plan for the day. Beyond making the daily schedule available, it is helpful to give everyone printed calendars for the upcoming months, highlighting special events and activities. This information gives teens a sense of agency over their experience. They know what will happen next during gathering time, and they know what will happen next week.

Calendaring

As an aside, calendaring ahead creates a partnership with parents and families, as parents can count on the intentionality and thoughtful planning of the church staff. While each ministry functions a bit differently, my (Laura's) commitment to my families was to publish the summer calendar, which included the biggest events and the most significant travel, by October 1, literally eight months before the start of summer. This was important because families were booking vacations that far ahead; receiving the summer church calendar early let those families plan their vacation time around significant church events. The church shared the dates of other camps and larger events three to six months in advance on the website and printed calendars, but their dates fell in a predictable pattern. Middle school always did their fall retreat on Columbus Day weekend. High school always did their winter retreat over Martin Luther King Jr.'s long birthday weekend. But sometimes the nature of summer camps and mission projects necessitated date changes from year to year, hence the October 1 commitment.

Fidgets, Noise, Texture, and Buddies

Sometimes our teens on the margins can be supported by having a few helpful items on hand. Noise-canceling headphones can be made available, along with alcohol wipes to sanitize them after use. A teen unfamiliar with the volume of the youth group might be able to participate with the support of the headphones. It can be helpful to have a box of fidget toys available to keep hands busy during times of conversation or listening. Be mindful of what fidgets are offered, as many make noise and could be distracting to others. Also create a cleaning schedule for sensory items. Several seating options can provide a teen a measure of control over their experience. Sometimes a color, texture, or design element can make the difference in the experience of a teen with sensory sensitivities. Along with seating options, it can be helpful to offer a guest the opportunity to be an observer rather than participant, especially at first, always with a peer or adult buddy. Each aspect of youth group might present different layers of comfort and challenge, so offering a back-row seat during worship if the teen prefers it allows extra space for them to encounter an intense element. For some, games are intimidating, so a spectator box with an engaging adult provides an out from participation while the youth is still included in the experience. During times of teaching or conversation, a topic may be out of reach, so it can be helpful to make it a practice to enter in cautiously and to provide options for levels of conversation depth. A leader might be available to take a walk with those who need a moment away, or in some situations, a designated area can be made available where they can excuse themselves to take a short walk. Make sure to design these interventions and spaces with your organization's child-protection policy in mind.

Escalation and Regulation

At times, teens on the margins might become escalated, more easily so than peers, following an encounter with a person or in response to a topic being explored. It is important for ministry leaders to have conversations with parents and caregivers to anticipate triggers when we can and to have a collection of strategies available to help a teen calm down and regulate. I (Laura) communicate to let ministry leaders know my son responds well to taking a walk, bouncing or dribbling a ball, or engaging in some other repetitive task. Sometimes sipping water through a straw, blowing hot chocolate to cool it down, or handling an ice cube can help a teen regulate. A teen can be encouraged to use their five fingers to connect with their five senses and name one thing they can see, one thing they can hear, and so on. These types of practices require the teen to be present in the moment and grounded with their immediate environment, which draws them back from a place of emotional escalation.

Trigger Events

We can never anticipate every triggering event, but if we know some of the things that are likely to cause trouble, we can enter our ministry spaces prepared.[1] There may be times when we call families ahead, knowing a sensitive or triggering topic is on our calendar, and ask whether the youth will be comfortable attending or if alternative plans could be made for that evening. To reach out ahead of time also communicates care and knowledge about the unique needs of the teen you are serving. As an example, if you have a teen in your group who was adopted, knowing they experienced domestic violence in their birth home, and you are planning a trip to do laser tag, a call to the adoptive parents might be wise. Would the dark space, flashing lights, and feeling of being chased by someone with a weapon potentially be a triggering event for their teen who experienced early trauma? Should the event be skipped, or is there support that could be offered to allow the teen to still participate? Perhaps the teen could be paired with a trusted adult leader or tag along for the event but sit out of laser tag?

Physical Contact

Youth group can often be a place where hugs are regularly exchanged, but for kids on the margins, hugs and physical touch may be less comfortable than for their peers. It is good to teach everyone in our ministries to ask permission—"May I give you a hug?"—to check on the other person's comfort level. Adult leaders can easily model this with each other to show that both declining and agreeing are OK. Greetings or goodbyes can include options of a wave, high five, handshake, or hug, which also gives a teen permission to be in control of whether to engage in physical contact and the type of physical contact they experience. While youth groups often play games involving physical contact, like the human knot game, a team's course challenge, or a ropes course, giving each youth the ability to choose their level of participation or to opt out can be quite helpful. The motto for many adventure course instructors is "challenge by choice," affirming the opportunity for agency within each participant. For one who has experienced physical or sexual abuse, the opportunity to maintain control over whether and how they are touched can be an empowering and important part of the healing process.

Partnering with Parents

For all teens served by our churches, it is important for ministry staff to invest in healthy relationships with their parents or guardians. Except in situations

1. Eve Riachi, Juha Holma, and Aarno Laitila, "Psychotherapists' Views on Triggering Factors for Psychological Disorders," *Discover Psychology* 2, no. 44 (2022): 8.

of abuse or neglect, church staff and volunteers are on the same team as parents, seeking to nurture healthy emerging adults. And even when we disagree with decisions parents make, there is still a responsibility to teach our teens to honor and respect their parents. We can personally disagree with parents and still support a teen by saying, "I can understand how you are frustrated with the consequence your parents gave you, but remember we are still called to respond in love and respect. Let's think together about what that might look like for you."

Parents and caregivers can be important resources for all our teens in knowing more about their background, home situation, strengths, and growing edges. A registration document for parents to complete can include questions that explore the ways ministry staff can be aware of and support the unique needs of their teens. Providing the form both on paper and electronically allows parents to choose the most private manner of communication in case they wish to disclose sensitive issues. Contact information should be requested on this form to allow ministry staff to follow up with parents for more information or clarification on something shared.

Another helpful practice is to host regular gatherings to build relationships with the parents of our teens. This might include regular parent-teen events for everyone in the group. It could instead or additionally take the form of small dinner gatherings, usually two to three families at a time based on seating availability: Over the course of a year, each family in the youth ministry would receive a no-strings-attached dinner invite to the home of the ministry leader. Food might be catered, but attached to genuine hospitality, such a meal can be quite meaningful. I (Laura) practiced these dinner invitations for a season of ministry, and families were always surprised to learn there was no agenda. Over a meal, families shared in conversation easily, and families that were once strangers became friends.

Quick Responses

Once parents or guardians share significant information about a teen, or the teen has done so themself, provided the family or teen has given permission to share, it is important to be quick to communicate with the leadership team. One Sunday morning I (Laura) was introduced to a middle schooler with reactive attachment disorder (RAD) who would be attending youth group that afternoon. I obtained permission to share that information with relevant leadership, and I went home quickly to look up more information on RAD and to read several articles. Following up, I intentionally chose a small-group leader to assign to this youth and reached out to the leader to equip him with some basic information before the middle schooler's first visit. In the weeks that followed, both of us read more articles and asked more questions of the teen's adoptive parents in order to best equip ourselves to serve our new friend. Sometimes a ministry team can read a book together or host an expert for a training session to better equip them to meet the needs of a particular teen. Taking these extra, intentional steps helps make the gathering time more effective and communicates to the teen and their family that they matter, whatever uniqueness they bring.

Social science tells us that so much is determined in the first moments we spend with another, and Scripture calls us to love and welcome our neighbors. The call is clear, and with a few intentional steps, we can make sure the welcome of a visitor is just the first day of a long relationship.

11

My Building Is Inaccessible! How Do We Adjust Our Building?

In 1990, the Americans with Disabilities Act (ADA) was signed into law by President George H. W. Bush, requiring public places to be designed in ways that make building space accessible to individuals with disabilities. While the ADA was an important step in assuring all can access a space, this law does not force change in churches built prior to 1990. The law exempted older buildings and allowed such structures to remain as they were initially built until any significant renovations began. When a facility is renovated, it must be brought up to the current ADA building code and, in many settings, the current commercial fire code, thus requiring a sprinkler system. In concept, this exemption bought churches time to set aside money and did not immediately force costly changes. However, many churches have instead simply remained frozen in time, inaccessible and unable to afford accessibility changes.

In the early 2000s, the church I (Laura) served hired a contractor to determine whether it would be cheaper to bring its older wing, circa 1950, up to the current ADA code or tear it down and start over. The results of the study affirmed the challenge thousands of churches are faced with. Tearing down and starting over, while incredibly costly, would be cheaper than bringing an old building up to ADA building code. This reality leaves many church leadership groups in a difficult place, as they do not have the funds to tear down and start over, but they also recognize how their outdated building limits their ability to inclusively welcome their neighbors. As this is a widespread concern, consulting companies that specialize in church renovation have been established, and an online search might produce the name of a company local to your area.

I (Laura) had an eye-opening experience following knee surgery. My youth program used a room accessible only by stairs. For several weeks, this necessitated that I carry materials in a backpack and hop up and down the stairs with crutches, a practice that would have likely made my physician cringe! This firsthand experience was an epiphany. Any church staff member could choose to spend a day, or even an hour, using crutches or a wheelchair to navigate their church building to notice the challenges present.

The limbo of living with an old building and still seeking to be welcoming can be overcome. Modifications can be made that are not fully up to ADA standards but are nevertheless better and offer more access to more individuals. The key is increasing accessibility as much as possible with the confines of the context. Sometimes grants are available to help with funding for making smaller changes for those willing to do the homework. Churches can also request help from working and retired tradespeople in the congregation to help offset the cost of some of the proposed changes. Always make sure efforts to increase access are done safely.

Some church leaders might push back at the idea of making a building accessible, saying, "But we don't have anyone in our congregation who uses a wheelchair." And in that response, an important message is communicated: People who use wheelchairs have likely not felt welcome to attend, and people who use walkers, canes, or crutches have likely felt that their needs have been disregarded. Curbs without curb cuts and an entrance at the top of a flight of stairs communicate before a wheelchair-using individual has attempted to enter the building. Educational theorist Elliot Eisner wrote about the explicit curriculum, the implicit curriculum, and the null curriculum.[1] The null curriculum is what we communicate without saying a word. A building that has not been made accessible communicates without speaking that anyone with a physical disability is not welcome. Ultimately, the church leaders in this situation are right: No one using a wheelchair attends—because the congregation has already communicated they are unwelcome through the building.

As such, the exterior of the building is just as important as the interior is to welcoming and safety. Adequate lighting in the parking lot, and throughout the interior of the building, is important for general safety and especially for those with visual impairments. Accessible parking spaces should be clearly

1. Elliot W. Eisner, *The Educational Imagination: On the Design and Evaluation of School Programs*, 3rd ed. (Macmillan, 1994), 97–107.

marked and adequately wide to allow a wheelchair van to unload. These spaces should be present at each of the building entrances regularly utilized. Curb cuts should be present near each of these spaces and should be clearly marked to indicate where a wheelchair may access. It can also be helpful to check up and down the sidewalk around the church to look for raised sections that may pose a tripping hazard for someone using crutches or a cane. Any section of sidewalk raised more than an inch should be replaced or grinded level. During winter weather, it is important to make sure that parking lots and sidewalks are cleared immediately prior to services and gathering times, including Sunday-night youth group. If snow falls during an event, access needs to be maintained for people exiting the building as well. Many churches recruit outdoor ushers to assist people as they exit cars and transition into buildings, or the reverse, and this role is particularly important on days with poor weather. Related to exterior spaces, ministry leaders can teach their staff and volunteers to park farthest away from the building entrances, making sure to leave the closest spots available for guests and those with physical challenges.

Stairs and Elevators

Stairs are one of the immediate challenges a congregation faces in creating access to their church building. Elevators are expensive, particularly to add post-construction, and sometimes there is not space to add a safe ramp. So then, how do we help people access our buildings? Stairway chair lifts, like those in some two-story homes, are one option that can be added to offer a solution for many individuals with limited mobility. A platform lift is a scaled-back version of an elevator requiring less space, usually capable of holding one wheelchair.

In the church where I (Mike) served, access to the sanctuary built in 1880 was quite limited. Although the church had added a massively expensive elevator with special parking near a new accessible entrance, a person using a wheelchair could access the sanctuary only via a backdoor entrance that brought them in behind the pulpit. Then the individual had to be capable of transferring to a specially designed narrow wheelchair to fit through the entrance to the sanctuary and then reach the congregation. It is important to think through the entire experience from parking lot to pew.

At times, landscaping changes can change the grade of an entrance, making the installation of a ramp possible. Often the most accessible entrance is not the main entrance. In some cases, a congregation might choose to leave their traditional worship space that is reachable only by stairs in order to instead gather in a fellowship or common area accessible at ground level. Some might consider it a sacrifice to leave the stained glass and historic wooden pews, but in such a place, the congregation must assess their priorities. Many youth groups inherit unusual spaces: the original sanctuary, the old parsonage, the church basement. While church leadership certainly means well in "gifting" these spaces, youth group leadership needs to consider accessibility. It sounds cool to have a whole house dedicated to youth. However, if that house is an older two-story with small rooms, a tight staircase, and a front door at the top of seven stairs, many youth are unable to attend gatherings in that space. Housed in an older building, my (Mike's) former youth group opted to move meetings to the accessible floor of the building, devising a way to temporarily curtain off a fellowship area each week to make a cozy gathering space for youth. A youth group may even make arrangements to meet in a local school or YMCA if it offers better access than other possibilities.

Restrooms

According to ADA code, restrooms are required to be spacious enough to navigate using a wheelchair or walker. In many cases, merging two stalls into one creates more space. While it might not meet ADA standards, it is better and makes the space usable for more individuals. Adding a lower vanity in a bathroom or modifying the toe kick of a cabinet that extends to the floor can make it wheelchair accessible without being a costly project; these modifications make the space usable for more people.

Pews

Churches that utilize pews or other seating that is permanently installed into the floor can opt to remove a portion of a pew or two seats at the end of a row. This space allows a wheelchair user to sit next to family in the pew or standard seats without sticking out obtrusively in the aisle. A handy carpenter in the church can help make sure these adjustments are made well and look natural in the space.

Hardware

Simple changes in hardware can also make a significant difference in building accessibility. Changing outdated round doorknobs for the lever type allows many more individuals access. Installing grab bars in the restrooms or railings down a hallway again helps make the space usable for more people, young or old.

Assistive Technology

Technology can also help make our buildings more welcoming. Some churches install motion-activated or push-button entrance doors. Amplifying devices for congregants who are hard of hearing can help ensure that everyone can hear the sermon. Some congregations hire one or more sign-language interpreters to be present for all major events, and large venues are even adding open captioning in real time to allow everyone who can read the captioned language or languages access to the teaching. AI services can cheaply provide captions in real time. PDF documents and PowerPoint teaching slides can be checked for accessibility using their own built-in software suite. Signs with large-print letters and braille type support congregants who have low vision or are blind.

Doorways

Congregations should also assess the width of key doorways in the building and particularly to the restrooms. To accommodate a typical wheelchair, a door must have a width of thirty-two inches, but a bariatric wheelchair requires additional space. In homes built after 1990, thirty-two inches is the size of a standard door, but spaces built prior to that time use many smaller custom door sizes intended to work within the building's architecture.

Flooring

Flooring is another consideration. The shag carpet from the 1970s lingering in a church classroom can be a tripping hazard or mobility challenge. Rugs can particularly pose a risk for tripping and should be replaced with rubber-backed mats. Low-pile carpets, hardwood, laminate flooring, and tile are much easier for all to navigate. Transition strips should be used for gaps or uneven flooring. Churches should regularly inspect and remove excess items from hallways to maintain clear paths for traffic. While lovely, a potted plant or a decorative side table can present a barrier. It is especially important to follow safety procedures for wires, cables, and sound equipment on the floor.

Engagement

Ministries can also consider the way people are expected to physically engage during a service or event. If Communion is served, is everyone expected to go forward? What about people with mobility challenges? Are they able to navigate the established traffic pattern, and what other options are available?

During times of worship, does everyone stand? If an individual cannot stand, how is their sightline impacted? In the context of an activity or game, are there ways for those with physical challenges to still engage by acting as a referee, by keeping score, or by modification to the rules?

Seating

Churches might also consider nurturing settings for conversation by offering seating options in gathering spaces, whether that be bistro tables along the edges of a fellowship area or comfy couches in a youth room. This invites those unable to stand for lengthy periods to still stay and visit. Renovations around the sanctuary pipe organ at the church where I (Laura) served required that a pew be removed. As the church leadership considered what to do with the extra pew, it was set aside in the fellowship area. Immediately, seniors in the congregation began sitting on the pew during coffee hour, glad to have a place to rest and visit with friends. Very quickly, the church leadership realized the extra pew had found its new home, all on its own. Likewise, my (Mike's) comfy accommodations of accessible tables and chairs for youth group became a favorite during the fellowship hour for attendees of all ages.

Individuals with disabilities network with one another through social media. If one family discovers a resource locally, it is quickly shared with other families. If a church is intentional in its efforts to make changes, while maybe not meeting full ADA standards but making their space accessible for many more, word gets out. One wheelchair-using visitor who is warmly welcomed will want to share that experience with others. Suddenly a church with "no wheelchair users" becomes a place with many members who utilize a wheelchair!

Building Accessibility Checklist

- ☐ Well-lit parking lot
- ☐ Well-marked accessible parking places at each entrance with ample space for unloading
- ☐ Curb cuts near each building entrance
- ☐ Sidewalks kept clear in winter weather
- ☐ Entrance doors accessible to people using wheelchairs, walkers, or crutches
- ☐ Access to the building available on the same level as parking or via a ramp, lift, or elevator

- ☐ Restrooms available on the same level as parking with adequate number of stalls large enough to accommodate a wheelchair and a sink mounted at wheelchair height
- ☐ Pew or seat cutouts in sanctuary to accommodate wheelchairs
- ☐ Accessible doorknobs and light switches
- ☐ Assistive technology for deaf and hard-of-hearing individuals as well as for those with low vision
- ☐ Doorways at least thirty-two inches in width
- ☐ Flooring choices and transition strips allow individuals using wheelchairs, crutches, canes, or walkers to navigate with ease
- ☐ Multiple ways for those of differing levels of ability to participate in worship, youth group, and church events

12

Low-Budget, Sensory-Friendly Spaces

Many congregations genuinely want to offer welcoming spaces to youth on the margins who come through their doors, but budget limitations make the task feel insurmountable. Thankfully, there are many DIY projects that work on a low budget. Following is a list of simple ideas that can transform a space or the way a space is used to accommodate youth on the margins. Many of these items can be sourced from the basements and homes of congregation members, garage sales, dollar stores, and online stores that offer sensory-friendly furnishings.

- Swings: Both saucer swings and traditional seated swings can be mounted indoors and outdoors. Many people find the rocking and repetitive movement of a swing to be calming, particularly when an individual becomes escalated. My (Laura's) church has a children's playground outside, and at times, I take my middle-school-aged son there to swing in between services or for a break during an activity. My son finds the motion soothing, and it helps him to stay regulated. Hammock-type swings are also popular and can provide the opportunity to "hide" and feel cocooned in the fabric but are more costly options. While some swings are made to hang from a stand, I can speak from experience that even small children can knock them over, and the frame of the swing can easily put a hole in drywall.

- Fidget toys: Fidget toys are now widely popular and easily sourced with an internet search or a trip to the dollar store. Offering the choice of a fidget toy during a quiet portion of a lesson offers an outlet for a youth who needs to be releasing energy to listen well. Be mindful to choose fidgets that do not make noise!
- A separate space: Many church buildings have a spare room . . . somewhere . . . that could be repurposed! For some, this separate space is a quiet space to retreat to when the sensory input from the group activity becomes overwhelming. A time away from the noise in a space with simple furnishings and calm colors can help soothe. This separate space is a room where teens can calm and regulate while a buddy remains in the doorway offering support and/or supervision. Gym mats on the floors and walls provide a safe environment to release emotions. Use crash pads, foam blocks, or beanbag chairs for regulating. Regularly check that nothing is hung on the walls and no potential projectiles are near this space. If some users need specific objects that could be used as projectiles by others experiencing significant dysregulation, those objects should be stored nearby but should not be accessible by other users.
- Balls to bounce: Repetitive motions that require an individual to be consciously present with their environment help ground an individual who has become dysregulated or overwhelmed. Providing opportunity to bounce a ball, dribble, or play catch for five minutes in the hallways while the door to the meeting area remains open nearby can help settle emotions. While balls can be purchased in stores, sometimes garage sales can be a jackpot for finding playground balls of various sizes and textures.
- Texture: Sometimes spaces can include places of texture. My (Laura's) son was given Velcro strips to stick under his desk at school. Running his fingers back and forth across either the soft or rough texture of the Velcro provided the additional sensory input he sought while serving as a calming mechanism. Some churches build a board with various textured items and mount the board to the wall in a separate space. At other times, texture can be added intentionally to a bin of fidget toys: Play-Doh, silly putty, squishy toys. Sensory-seeking youth usually have a favorite type of input and gravitate toward those items.
- Seating: We can offer various seating options in our ministry spaces, like what many elementary schools are now doing. Providing choices between various colors and soft and firm seating gives options for individuals who are sensitive to one or the other. Many times, the seating for

a youth room comes from the basements of church members anyway, so there can be a measure of intentionality in what selections are welcomed.

- Walking path: The repetition of walking can be calming to an escalated youth, but church leaders need to designate the parameters of these spaces to avoid elopement. Sometimes, churches have a natural loop in the design of their hallways that can become a designated path. Sensory floor stickers have become popular in elementary schools, providing an intentional path of hopping, jumping, and sequencing, all with the intention to focus attention and regulate the user. A dysregulated teen would also still enjoy these, perhaps with some adaptations. Outdoors, a path could be created around the church property, marked out in some way. Again, many elementary schools are including a paved path around their playground and offering incentives to kids who complete laps at recess, recognizing the benefit of walking and running in keeping kids regulated. A paved path around the church property might also attract seniors in the congregation to meet up for walks. Some public schools include a treadmill accessible to youth when breaks are necessary for regulating. Many times, a church member would be willing to donate an item like a treadmill, but there are often costs associated with maintenance.
- Weighted blankets or vests: Research has found that for many individuals who find themselves dysregulated, pressure produces a calming effect.[1] This can happen through some means of applying pressure to the body. Some youth may be comfortable under a beanbag chair or heavy blanket. Weighted blankets have grown in popularity, and you can now find them online for a reasonable cost. Most are machine washable, and patterns are available if you have someone crafty in your congregation. Blankets can be made full size to fit a bed, or they can be smaller, just to fit on a lap. Weighted vests are more costly, and they must fit the user's size and follow the appropriate formula to determine the garment's weight. The body also does adjust to a vest, so a vest is best used only for short amounts of time: no more than twenty minutes. Somewhat similar to a weighted blanket, a "fishtail blanket" was popularized in infomercial advertising. This type of blanket, sewn to resemble a fish or mermaid tail, provides a soft, restricted space in which the user feels comfortingly cocooned. Patterns exist for a homemade version that would likely be

1. Lana Bestbier and Tim I. Williams, "The Immediate Effects of Deep Pressure on Young People with Autism and Severe Intellectual Difficulties: Demonstrating Individual Differences," *Occupational Therapy International* (January 9, 2017): 1.

more durable. You might accomplish a similar goal with a mummy sleeping bag: perhaps something available from a parishioner. Weighted items and cocooning blankets could be made available in a set-apart space for youth who become particularly dysregulated.

- Heavy work: For many kids, doing "heavy work" has a calming effect on the nervous system. Heavy work, also known as proprioceptive activities, helps teens with sensory processing difficulties by putting pressure on joints and stimulating muscles and receptors. Pushing, pulling, climbing, and moving are all part of heavy work. If the church has taken a delivery of supplies that need to be moved or unloaded and you see a teen beginning to escalate, you might invite them to help you move and unload the boxes. Sometimes making up a task can be helpful in a pinch: "Could you help me move that couch over to that wall?" Working as a team and engaging a teen's balance, muscles, or sensory system helps the teen stay grounded in the moment.
- Timers: Timers are an important tool for two reasons. Timers are inanimate objects, and many individuals find it easier to respond to an inanimate ding than to a person's voice. Timers also serve as a natural boundary. If an individual needs a time-out to regulate themself, it shouldn't become a pass to let them hide from the group situation indefinitely. It should be a break with a defined ending. While some trial and error may initially be required to determine what break length best serves a person, generally five to fifteen minutes should provide enough time. At school, my (Laura's) middle-school-aged son is allowed breaks that are monitored to last no more than ten minutes. Otherwise, he uses them as an escape mechanism to avoid doing classroom work. Generally, younger kids regulate with less time than older teens do.
- Lamps or Christmas lights: Fluorescent lighting can sometimes be a trigger for those who experience sensory sensitivities. Creating a space without fluorescent lighting can be helpful. Lamps might be a natural solution, and something like a lava or bubble lamp might have a calming effect, but they can also easily be knocked over and broken if a youth is particularly dysregulated. Christmas lights affixed to the ceiling might be a better option, and post-Christmas sales usually make these a cost-effective solution.
- White noise: A sound machine or box fan can be a simple investment that supports a person in tuning out an upsetting noise. This can be helpful when a separate space is not available but a corner with a curtain is an option. A curtained-off area with a sound machine and a beanbag chair could be the separate space a teen needs.

- Trampoline: Teens who seek additional sensory input often enjoy bouncing on a trampoline. While the youth group may advocate for a full-size trampoline park inside the church, a mini-trampoline or exercise trampoline made for adult exercise classes will work just as well.

When working with a youth on the margins, it is important to pay attention to patterns involving triggers, dysregulation, and what helps the teen regulate. Once you have some history and can anticipate the teen's needs, you can make sure your youth room and church have appropriate items and activity ideas in place to help the teen regulate.

13

Preparing the Group for Successful Integration

While having a prepared greeter is a great way to begin with a visitor, it can also be helpful to equip the group to be welcoming to newcomers. This preparation can be intentional and straightforward, and some will happen naturally through the undercurrent of biblical teaching.

While teaching the stories of Jesus reaching out to individuals on the margins, emphasize the kindness and the grace he offers. Grace, kindness, and hospitality are often counter to the culture in which we live. Hold up a story from Scripture as a model and discuss following that story's lead in our lives today. When the theme of welcome and kindness resonate throughout our curriculum, we build an ethos that behavior naturally follows.

Adult leaders can be trained to welcome and extend kindness to everyone coming through the door. I (Laura) had a husband-and-wife team of volunteer leaders who loved to greet at the door of the youth room each week. They celebrated each person, calling them by their name or youth group nickname, offering high fives and brief hugs, checking up on their week, and setting a tone of joy for the time together. The greeting from the couple came with the same level of energy whether they had known a teen for five years or five minutes. Everyone was celebrated. Often, the youth in a ministry mirror their leaders, so if a church has joyful and kind leaders, the youth pick up on those behaviors and reflect them to one another. If a guest arrives with visible challenges, the youth will often look to the leaders to set a tone of response. How should they engage this new friend? If the leaders model warmth and welcome, the youth follow. If a leader asks permission to push a newcomer's wheelchair to the meeting space, the other youth learn that asking permission to push the wheelchair is an appropriate way to engage. Regular training should occur to familiarize adult leaders with trauma and physical disabilities just as much as with how to lead a small group or game.

Introducing guests to the group is an important element requiring care. Rarely does a guest want to be called out in front of the group and asked to share information. The natural self-consciousness of teens results in shyness, which is compounded by being in a new space. One approach is to offer general welcome to multiple guests, encouraging our regulars to introduce themselves to those in their proximity or small group. As regular attenders extend a tone of welcome, the pressure of meeting and greeting is removed from the guest. To add a twist, invite regulars to introduce themselves to the guest and share a fun fact, perhaps a favorite breakfast food or Olympic sport, something lighthearted to break the ice. If a newcomer is brought by a regular attendee, the regular could be asked to introduce their friend and share two awesome things about them. This way, the regular attendee carries the focus of attention, and they have an opportunity to encourage their friend.

For some newcomers, a parent or leader might prepare the group for their participation ahead of time, with the newcomer's or parent's permission to share any sensitive information. For example, when I (Laura) was a preteen, my group at church had been praying for and supporting a peer named Michael, who had been badly burned in a house fire. When Michael was released from the hospital, he wanted to visit the kids who had prayed for him, sent him notes, and even purchased some things to replace what his family had lost. The boy was still bandaged in several areas, and in other areas, the scars from his burns were quite significant. The leaders of my group wanted to prepare members for Michael's visit by explaining what they would likely see and allowing questions ahead of time in a safe space. This preparation equipped the group to respond more readily with warmth when Michael arrived. We knew what his bandages would look like, and the process of his healing had been explained to prevent anyone from being frightened by what they saw.

Before my (Laura's) son graduated from the children's ministry to youth group, I talked with the middle schoolers about autism and what were the best ways to engage my son. This preparation proved to be quite timely, as over the next few months, two other boys with autism also joined the group. I remained available to answer questions from leaders and peers and to model engagement with my son for several weeks before leaving him in this new setting.

Sometimes youth leaders receive advance notice that a youth on the margins will join their group. That time can serve as a valuable preparation period for asking questions of the parents, conducting research, and preparing volunteers and the other teens. Consider the story of my (Laura's) preparation to welcome a new student shared in chapter 10. Within one afternoon, plans were in place, and the team was not caught off guard by the significant needs of their newcomer.

Unfortunately, we do not always have warning about the needs of a guest prior to their arrival, so often we do the best we can with the information we have and build from there. Be intentional about catching a parent or guardian in the parking lot after youth group, or follow up with a phone call the next day. Affirm the teen's participation with phrases like "We are very glad your teen attended" and asking for parental expertise to best include them.

It is important to be mindful during groups, discussion, games, and activities. Place teens with higher levels of need alongside teens who can respond with much grace. In some cases, it can be helpful to pull a teen aside and affirm their gifts ahead of time as you explain how you hope they can minister to a peer without taking away from their youth group experience. My (Laura's) daughter, who works to manage her ADHD, was made a school bus helper in charge of the two other children at her bus stop who are two years younger than her. On a crowded bus at the end of the day, it is her job to make sure the younger children get off at the right stop. Her job takes just a few minutes, but these are important minutes where her maturity is encouraged. The bus driver affirmed the potential in my daughter, and I continually celebrate it at home, giving my daughter affirmation in her growing abilities alongside her challenging diagnosis. Note, as in this story, pairing should not be done to "pawn off" a "problem kid" to a high-performing teen. The responsibility begins with the adults and should incorporate the entire youth group.

While no church can prepare for every possibility, many opportunities exist to be intentional in building a culture and ethos. When that ethos is naturally warm and grace-filled, we offer the best possible space for a teen on the margins to enter in. When we study the ministry of Jesus, we begin reflecting it back to one another. Then when guests come, we begin by offering an intentional ethos and slowly learn more about their unique needs, adjusting as we learn and grow together.

14

Teaching and Preaching Inclusively

Several decades have passed since I (Laura) taught my first Sunday School class, but one of the early lessons I learned still hangs clearly in my mind. The children were in preschool, all ages three or four, and it was nearly time for dismissal. I reminded the group to gather their things because "moms and dads" would be arriving soon to pick them up. Kate quickly interjected, "I live with my aunt and uncle. They will be picking me up." Immediately I was reminded of the error in my words. Kate and her four siblings had recently been removed from their birth parents by Child Protective Services and placed with her aunt and uncle. The removal had been difficult, and Kate bore the weight of a tumultuous three years. It was important to Kate to be seen that morning in Sunday School.

Verbiage matters to children and teens, so it is important not to assume that each lives with a biological mom and dad. Statistics vary among communities, but nationally almost 30 percent of all children and teens do not live with both biological parents.[1] The next time you have the opportunity to serve with a group of children or teens you know, scan the group. Note those who live with a single parent because of divorce, death, deportation, or a measure of

1. United States Census Bureau, "Census Bureau Releases New Report on Living Arrangements of Children," news release, February 3, 2022, https://www.census.gov/newsroom/press-releases/2022/living-arrangements-of-chldren.html.

choice. Note those who bounce between two households following a divorce. Note those who have been adopted internationally, domestically, or from foster care. Note those who are still in foster care, waiting for permanency. Note those who might have a parent regularly deployed for military service. Additionally, you might have children or teens who live with extended family members temporarily or permanently for a variety of reasons. It is helpful to refer to their guardian or to simply avoid labels and titles in group settings.

Because we cannot assume the living situation of a child or teen in our church, it is important to gather accurate and helpful data when registration is completed. Adding lines for the first and last names of the adults the child or teen lives with is important. A church should not assume everyone in the household has the same last name. It would be wise to include a line for custody information in case a church needs to know a co-parenting schedule or information regarding who is not allowed to pick up, so a staff member can call 911 should a birth parent who is not allowed to do so come to the door at pickup.

In foster care training, adults are encouraged to allow children and teens to take the lead in choosing what to call those adults. The church should also practice following the teen's lead. Some children and teens call their foster parents by their first names. If the children are younger, they might call them mom and dad, particularly if other children in the home use those titles. Younger children are often not bothered by having more than one "mom" or "dad" in their life. Sometimes nicknames suffice. I (Laura) have friends who are older but foster and go by "Mimi and Papa," affectionate names as they are of grandparent age. Some children and teens are comfortable acknowledging their foster parents for what they are, but others prefer to keep their personal information private. A friend of mine has a foster daughter who refers to her as her "grown-up" in social situations. The church should not make assumptions about whether a child is a member of a family based on the youth's and adults' apparent races. In some contexts, the racial background of the child or teen is different from that of their foster family, often making it apparent that the family is not the birth family, while in other families, the foster child or teen looks surprisingly similar to the family with which they are placed. My oldest son looks like me, so we are never questioned about our relationship. However, my youngest is a different race, so the substitute school bus driver recently hesitated to release her at the bus stop.

Another consideration when crafting our language is the way a child or teen views their family situation. Some children and teens in foster care are happy and thriving in a safe environment. They may desire to be adopted and remain with that family. Others grieve the loss of their birth family and pray to return to it, even if the situation was not healthy. Still others feel torn because they love both families and struggle with feelings of disloyalty to their biological family. A child or teen may raise a prayer concern specific to their open child-welfare case, praying for their birth parent, praying to return to their birth family, or praying to be adopted. In response, we need to validate the feelings of the children and teens we serve while treading cautiously. It would be wise to maintain dialogue with the foster family to confirm information being shared. A foster parent may be able to describe the current permanency plan of a teen thereby confirming a prayer request of a foster child without breaking any level of confidentiality. We can also direct our prayers with words like "healing," "peace," and "safety" for each person involved. If a teen shares in a small group about an upcoming court hearing for their case, we might pray for wisdom for the judge as decisions are made or for the teen's safety, whatever the outcome.

All these variables affirm that those who minister to teens need to be sensitive to the diversity of the families we serve. A simple rule is to "always ask before assuming." Asking provides the appropriate names, titles, and living arrangements. In our teaching and preaching, we need to be inclusive in the words we use, making sure that each child and teen's context is affirmed and validated. As we teach about the value of each child and teen to God, we can model that by including each of their family contexts in the terminology we use.

15

Pictures, Permissions, and Caseworkers

Foster Care Legal Issues

When a child or teen enters foster care, standards are put in place to protect the child, their foster parents, and sometimes their birth parents as the child-welfare court case remains open. It is helpful for youth workers to have a basic understanding of the system and what implications could carry over to a ministry setting. While certain issues concerning foster care vary from state to state, the major pieces are consistent across the United States.

A child or teen comes into foster care through a removal by Child Protective Services (CPS) following or during an investigation of abuse, neglect, or both. Initially, social workers explore placement with relatives. If this effort is unsuccessful, social services next explore a kinship placement with a non-related adult with whom the child has a relationship, like a teacher, coach, or family from church. The term "kinship placement" refers to an adult known to the child or family of the child: It does not have to refer to a relative. In kinship placement, the family can become a licensed foster home, which opens avenues for financial subsidy from the state as well as other resources such as Medicaid or counseling. When a child or teen is placed with an already-licensed foster family, it means that no suitable relative or kinship placement was available to them. Foster families are screened and trained, but they are initially strangers to the child. Effort is made to keep a child or teen in their home community so that school placement is not disrupted. However, there are times when "beds are not available" in the specific community or when an available relative or kinship placement is in another town, necessitating that the child or teen move schools. Licensed foster families receive a daily stipend to offset costs for care. Children and teens in foster care often immediately qualify for Medicaid, which covers all medical, dental (but not always orthodontics), and basic vision services, and a stipend is available for daycare if the foster parents work.

Once a child-welfare case is open and the child or teen is removed from their birth home, a judge and social worker outline a service plan asking the birth parent or parents to complete specific services as part of their effort to reunify. These services can vary widely but can include addiction treatment, anger management classes, job coaching, parenting coaching, and much more. Except in extreme cases, an effort is always made to reunify the child with their birth family. In a case of neglect, birth parents might be asked to complete psychological evaluations to rule out untreated mental health concerns and to take parenting classes. The birth parents might be asked to complete addiction counseling, attend a drug or alcohol rehabilitation program, or secure appropriate housing. In the majority of cases, the child or teen in foster care has regular visits with their birth family, initially supervised. If things progress positively, their visits become longer and unsupervised as they move closer to reunification. If the birth parents are not in compliance with their required services, a judge will consider terminating parental rights, making the child or teen available for adoption. All cases are reviewed on a schedule set by the state. While social services often sets a goal to achieve permanency for a child or teen within one year, that rarely happens because judges are cautious to give birth parents adequate time to benefit from the support and services offered to them.

While in foster care, children and teens are not allowed to have any identifying photographs posted publicly, including on social media. So if a picture is taken at youth group and the face of a teen is visible, the youth pastor may not post it on the youth group web page without blurring out the face of the teen in care and anything else that could identify them. When one of my (Laura's) sons was in kindergarten, the local United Way was doing a campaign for which it took a picture of each elementary school principal alongside a child from their school to place on billboards throughout the community. I was approached to have my son photographed for a billboard, but I had to decline because of its public nature. Additionally, my child's birth parents had a history of domestic violence, so I was working hard to keep my last name, address, and place of work, as well as the name of my child's school, private.

In the church where I served, a foster child "borrowed" the last name of her foster family to use while at church. While it was not a legal name change, it identified her as part of the family she was placed with and provided a layer of protection from her volatile birth family.

Every child or teen in foster care is assigned a caseworker to manage the paperwork required by the state and to serve as their advocate, as the child or teen is a temporary ward of the state. Caseworkers are required to see each child and teen on their caseload in person regularly. Because such a child or teen is considered a temporary ward of the state, they need to receive permission to travel out of the state. Ideally, this permission comes from their birth parents but can come from a judge as well. In an amicable situation, a teen who wishes to travel with a youth group to an out-of-state camp must secure paperwork from their caseworker for their birth parents to sign, giving the teen permission to travel. This process can take a few weeks, so it is best to start early. If birth parents are angry or unsupportive of church participation, they may be unwilling to provide permission. In these cases, the caseworker can take the request before a judge, who determines whether participation is in the teen's best interest. The signature of a judge overrides the wishes of a birth parent and can grant permission for a teen to attend youth camp. Some states require birth parent notification, not necessarily permission, as well as a judge's signature.

Children and youth in foster care must be supervised by adults who have been screened for safety purposes to provide a safeguard against further harm while they are in care. Licensed foster families are thoroughly screened and background checked. Any babysitter needs to be background checked and have their information on file with the child or teen's caseworker. Some states do not allow the child to be left with any caregiver who is not fully foster certified. I (Mike) have attended many playdates because I was unable to leave my foster child at the house of an adult who was not certified as a foster parent. In most states, minors, or those under twenty-one, or those uncertified, are not allowed to babysit for anyone in foster care. For school, church, sports leagues, and scouting activities, most states assume that these organizations have already taken measures to ensure the safety of their staff and volunteers and the children who participate. Even as a volunteer soccer coach for my (Laura's) daughter's recreational league, I must be background checked and complete several online training courses.

Layers of protection provide "prudent parenting" to allow foster parents the ability to leave their child or teen in the care of a Sunday School teacher, youth worker, soccer coach, or scout troop leader. "Prudent parenting" allows foster parents to give basic permissions for things like attending a youth event or participating in a sports league. Foster parents are assuming that churches have done their due diligence in screening staff and volunteers to make sure the adults supervising their foster children have been well vetted. The minimal requirement for vetting all volunteers and staff working with minors involves running a triple background check at federal, state, and local levels, and, in addition, checking the sex offender registry. This is true for all minors, not just for foster children. Organizations working with teens can run confidential background checks in all four areas for a small fee. A number of businesses and nonprofits serve churches in this area. All volunteers and staff in a ministry or church should have these checks run regularly. Consult with your insurance agency for recommendations on how often they should be renewed. It is necessary to read your organization's child protection policy carefully, evaluating whether it protects staff and teens and children who are part of vulnerable populations such as those in foster care or those experiencing disability.

16

Boundaries

Boundaries are tricky: They can both cause harm and create safety. For youth on the margins, boundaries play an important role in creating a meaningful ministry experience, but they can be hard to put in place initially.

Imagine a child in a playpen. Within the confines of the four "walls" are toys and soft blankets appropriate for the age and stage of the child. The child can explore safely without harm, but that freedom has limits. Each of the four "walls" prevents the child from venturing farther. The child may perceive the boundaries as limiting rather than as part of a space of intentional freedom.

When I (Laura) was a child, I had limits regarding where I could ride my bike independently. Each year, my parents evaluated the limits and adjusted them based on my age, the neighborhood, and my maturity. While I always pushed for less restrictive limits, I also knew that my mom had created intentionally safe space that mapped my limits according to relationships we had built with safe neighbors.

My (Laura's) son was a "bucket baby." This is a term for infants who are always in a seat, crib, or playpen and are not allowed to freely explore their environment. In his case, his birth mom was trying to protect him from the thousands of LEGO bricks and other small toys that belonged to his older brothers. Their home was small, so it wasn't possible to create a playroom or separate toy space. She was doing the best she could under the circumstances, but when my son was removed and came to live with me at twenty-two months of age, he could barely walk. His development had been so delayed by the lack of opportunity to explore that while the baby seat had kept him safe from small toys, it had hindered his ability to reach milestones.

Used for good, boundaries create safe space, but used poorly, boundaries hinder the same good. Without enforced limits, children can become tentative. Imagine the true story of a school playground and field next to a busy road. The playground did not have a fence, so the children would cluster near the building, avoiding the field because they did not know what was safe or allowable. Once the school added a fence, the children were able to use and enjoy the entire play area. The boundary both expanded their freedom and reduced their anxiety.

Youth on the margins often require more boundaries because they lack the level of social skills necessary to navigate their environment. My (Laura's) son is quite friendly. He strikes up conversations everywhere we go, inviting grocery clerks to his birthday party and waitstaff to sit down and have dinner. His intent is good, but the social implications become complicated quickly.

If someone speaks kindly to my son, he assumes they are the best of friends, and he expects that level of engagement and then some. If someone speaks kindly to him one Sunday, then the next Sunday he assumes they should also be hugging and making plans to hang out. The person who simply spoke kindly is caught off guard, and in the context of the church, it is difficult to act in a way that might be perceived as unloving.

Youth and adults in the church need to be taught ways of loving with their words and interactions while also communicating a boundary to youth on the margins.

"Yes, I am glad to see you, but no, you may not hug me in that way."

"Yes, I am glad to see you, but I am going to sit with another friend tonight."

"Yes, I am glad to see you, but I am going to finish this game of air hockey. I would love to hear about your week in five minutes."

And yes, in many situations, it is acceptable and even loving to set a timer. This tactic allows someone to give love and attention while preventing them from overextending themselves with a youth on the margins who may be prone to take and take and take.

Boundaries help my son, and others on the margins, to organize and make sense of their world. Not extending invitations to others without my permission is a huge rule and boundary for my son that is very important in our context. Following this rule helps keep my son safe from strangers, and it helps protect others from awkward exchanges.

The church is a place where many hugs are exchanged, but sometimes youth on the margins struggle with physical contact, either desiring too much or wanting to avoid it altogether. This drives the importance of having conversations, led by caregivers or youth staff, and clearly explaining appropriate and inappropriate physical contact in the youth group setting. Some school classrooms use greeting-option posters that offer ideas like "wave," "handshake," and "hive five"; each student points to their preferred greeting when they arrive each morning to let the teacher know how to greet them. Churches could use a similar approach.

When physical touch is appropriate, a general rule of thumb is to prohibit touch anywhere a bathing suit would be. Using this guideline, staff and volunteers, for example, should not give piggyback rides or allow a teen to sit in their lap. For hugs, clarify if, when, and what kind of hugs are appropriate, making sure that everyone is on board. Youth group leaders should take special care to emphasize that kids can *always* say they do not want a hug or that they want a hug to end, and that this must be respected.

While there will always be boundary testers in the crowd, most people feel safer with boundaries in place. Boundaries assure us of safety in a world of unknowns. Boundaries can also communicate safety to kids on the margins. For a youth who has grown up in a tumultuous home situation, perhaps never knowing when they would be hit next or where the next meal might come from, knowing the parameters at church provides a sense of safety not found at home. When youth feel safe, they can shift their attention from survival to growth.

When setting up and using boundaries:

Assume compliance. The organization assumes that students and adults will adhere to the policies and guidelines of the organization. Everyone is expected to comply.

Transitions mark territory and cue behavior. Going straight from dodgeball to silent prayer is likely not going to work.

Have clear rules and expectations. For example, "You cannot sit around the tables at the back of the room."

Affirm the good.

Address the boundary violation; do not attack the character of the teen.

Avoid the following:

Public discipline or confrontation that is win-lose.

Lecturing the whole group.

Having lots of rules.

Manipulative praise.

Power struggles or waging war (instead, offer choices). Students seek power over their lives. Thus, winning a power struggle can be more important to them than making good choices.

Warning—instead just give the logical consequence of their action.

Reacting—consequences can follow sometime later. Give the teen time to respond. My (Mike's) favorite line is "I am not sure how I want to respond to this right now; let's talk in a few minutes after we think."

17

Behaviors at Youth Group

Many times, one of our former teens or college students will reach out with the same preface: "I have this kid in my youth group . . ." What usually follows is "and they remind me of one of your kids. Could you give me some ideas for managing their challenging behaviors in youth group?" Both our (Mike's and Laura's) children frequently become classroom illustrations as we train youth pastors in college. Our kids have visited our college classes on the children's snow days or early release days, so over the years, our students become familiar with them, their behaviors, and the tools we use. Unfortunately, there is no one-size-fits-all formula for managing behaviors in youth group, but tools and practices exist that can help us craft a plan to nurture the adolescents we are called to serve.

My (Laura's) son, who is on the autism spectrum, attends middle school youth group with his peers. He made a slow transition to the program, beginning with short visits at which I was present. It was important that he understand the differences between youth group and the children's ministry he was familiar with. I prepared him ahead of each visit with conversation, explaining what he would experience and what behavior he would need to show during that time. A specific leader was designated as his "buddy"; this leader shadowed my son and me during those visits to see how I provided guidance and boundaries. Once my son had visited each "piece" of youth group successfully with me, he was allowed to attend with his leader buddy while I remained available nearby. After a few months, the need for me diminished, and now he attends regular youth group independently with his leader buddy.

Because my son presents with cognitive and social delays, he finds some aspects of youth group challenging; for him, there can be a fine line between what is attainable with effort and what is out of reach. For example, he does not enjoy sitting for the twelve to fifteen minutes of teaching, but he is capable of doing so. It is important to hold him to his ability. To assist with this, a behavior chart has been established. This originated in children's ministry and has been adapted for youth group. Each week, the chart lists seven or eight behaviors to aim for and for which he can earn a check mark. A specified number of check marks translates into a reward. In the children's ministry, the rewards could be earned every six to eight weeks; in youth group, the rewards occur about once every three months. Each semester, the youth group leaders and I review the chart and adjust it as some behaviors become natural and new challenges arise. At the end of each youth group meeting, my son fills out the checklist with his leader buddy. His most recent reward was a trip to the junkyard with his leader buddy. My son has developed an interest in cars shared by his leader, so this outing was like Christmas morning for both of them! The cost for gas was minimal, but the trip was motivating to my son for months.

Sometimes the behavior plan needs adjustment. Imagine a teen who is failing at the basic plan "homework before video games." With the help of a therapist, I (Mike) worked out an hourly system for a teen I was responsible for. For every forty-five minutes of homework the teen did, I rewarded them with fifteen minutes of free time. The weekly or daily goals seemed outside their reach, but incremental rewards were effective.

On the topic of behavior, the public school system is ahead of the church with more years of intentional experience navigating the behaviors kids bring to the classroom. Looking to a public school model for guidance can be wise and helpful. Practically, if special education teachers are in your congregation, they can be a resource for consultation! Meetings at school are set in a positive context where everyone gathers to pursue the best support for a child's success. The church can do the same.

Behavior is communication, so the challenge for a church is to unravel the message in the behavior a youth is exhibiting and to respond in a way that meets the expressed need in a healthy way. For example, once one of my (Mike's) youth group worship team members refused to leave the stage after leading worship. The teen proceeded to noisily take apart the equipment while the sermon was being given. After being physically escorted out of the building, he finally explained that his teenage garage band had just disbanded that night. In his distress, he was going to dismantle and give away all his equipment, even if it disrupted the entire worship service. The disruption was an opportunity to hear and meet this teen, even while needing to maintain proper respect for the entire group.

It is wise to begin youth group each season with a reminder of the expectations. I (Laura) would do this each September as I kicked off the new year. Some rules related to building use and others to respecting one another. Many years, this was the only time rules were addressed. The bar of expectation was set high, the kids were supported by loving leaders, and the expectations were met. At other times, a teen would enter the equation with challenging behaviors. The task then became unraveling the behavior to understand the need and then to find a healthy way to meet that need.

The following are some questions and pieces of advice that we try to keep in mind regarding behaviors:

What are the factors at play here?

What are some (potential) underlying issues not necessarily visible on the surface?

What might be driving this behavior?

What knee-jerk reactions would be inappropriate or unhelpful in addressing the behavior?

The less we do the more the teen has to do—do not solve or rescue. Teens should be allowed to own their behavior and the solutions to their problems.

Shift thinking from "What do I do?" to "What do I say?"

Here are a few values to guide our actions:

Never argue with a teen who is emotionally invested.

Protect people's dignity.

"The dumber you are, the smarter the people around you are." Let teens come up with solutions and act on them.

Three basic rules are important when addressing disruptive behavior:

1. Use enforceable limits.

   Tell the child what you are going to do: "I will drive the van as soon as everyone is wearing a seat belt."
2. Provide choices within limits.

   "Feel free to stay and join us or . . ."

Always provide choices you like. Otherwise, the child will inevitably pick the one you do not want.

3. Apply consequences with empathy.

   People see God in us. The tone of the conversation should be caring and sensitive to heightened emotional states in the child.

   Children are sensitive to emotions and social signals from others. If you are angry, they will get caught up in the anger.

   If a child is angry at you, they will not blame themself for a consequence you give them.

Perhaps a teen acts out because they want attention and are not getting it at home. Understanding a family situation could provide clarity, and offering regular one-on-one time with a caring leader, while following the church's abuse-prevention policy, might go a long way in meeting the need for attention. Maybe another teen pushes the boundaries of the youth group rules. Understanding their family situation might reveal a home where an overwhelmed parent has few rules, so the teen is used to freedoms that have also led to insecurity. Pairing this teen with an engaging leader who hangs with them throughout the duration of youth group can provide a positive role model who can frame the intent of boundaries in real time as the teen challenges them. Another possible scenario is a teen overwhelmed by the sensory stimuli at youth group: loud music, a colorful room, excited teens, a sugary snack, and so on. Sometimes we need to help our teens learn to self-regulate by intentionally planning times of transition into our schedule where the high-energy game ends, the music calms, a lighthearted interesting video pops onto the screen, and water is provided. At other times, we might need to adjust the level of stimuli.

Sometimes unraveling the message of a behavior can take time and multiple attempts toward a resolution. Sometimes we might need the support of parents, trained classroom teachers, and even licensed counselors. We may never erase a particular behavior, but we can help the kids we serve to grow in healthy and positive ways through the support and example we provide.

18

Barriers in the Pursuit of Professional Counseling

Recently, I (Laura) had opportunity to catch up with my "first friend" for the first time in over thirty-five years. When we were young, she moved in across the street from me shortly before she turned three. I was four, and she became my first regular playmate. We had hundreds of playdates back and forth across the street, sleepovers, and trips to my family cottage.

Sadly, both of our families experienced traumatic events. We each lost a parent early in life, and between our families, we experienced drug and alcohol abuse, witnessed domestic violence, and observed unhealthy coping mechanisms. We both moved after one of our surviving parents had to testify against the other in court. We lost contact. Then, after connecting on social media, we found ourselves sitting across the table at a diner halfway between our homes. It felt like receiving a missing piece of my childhood, not only in her friendship but because she was so intertwined with my early years. She said the same of me. We caught up and each shared pieces of our stories the other did not know. We both sat in awe that despite so much, we have each grown into successful adults managing professional careers and families. We wondered aloud why we had not been in counseling for our unique traumatic family situations, but we knew that in the era and community where we grew up, "You just didn't do that."

In recent decades, the practice and acceptance of professional counseling has grown significantly. A greater level of comfort exists in accessing therapeutic care. In particular, the disruption COVID introduced in employment and community, alongside uncertainty about the future, brought many latent mental health issues to the surface. This led to an increased awareness of and wider acceptance for seeking support. Still, there are pockets and people groups in the United States within which individuals are hesitant to pursue professional counseling and its benefits. A well-meaning youth pastor might encourage a family to pursue therapy for their teen and be met with resistance. For this reason, it is important to consider and name some of the barriers commonly present in seeking clinical advice, therapeutic counseling, or mental health resources.

An individual's age may contribute to their comfort level with therapy as professional counseling continues to emerge as a profession. The Silent Generation (1928–45) grew up during the Great Depression and World War II. Families fought to provide them with essentials. I (Laura) grew up hearing stories of my grandpa eating lard sandwiches, so clearly there was no money for anything extra. Because of their upbringing, my grandparents remained resistant to outside help for emotional health throughout their lives. Private insurance companies funded limited services of any kind following World War II, but the Affordable Care Act, passed in 2010, expanded opportunities, particularly for preventive mental health care.

My (Laura's) parents were Baby Boomers (1946–64) who were raised by Silent Generation parents proud to be giving their children a life with more stability. Boomers' resulting affluence and self-sufficiency sometimes led to pride as they surpassed their parents in education and earning potential. As a member of Generation X (1965–80), I grew up as professional counseling established itself as mainstream. More helpful views of counseling began to replace older images from television of lying on a couch speaking to someone who was "shrinking" one's head. During my lifetime, I have watched the field emerge and become a common resource for navigating life challenges.

Another factor contributing to comfort level with counseling is ethnic background. In Black and Hispanic circles, community and extended family typically are highly valued. Individuals are often more connected, living in a wider circle of support. In foster training, this was emphasized with the statistic that while White children made up about 50 percent of our (Laura's) local school district, 90 percent of children in foster care in the same community were White. Black and Hispanic families "took care of their own." If a parent was struggling, typically a grandmother, auntie, or matriarch would step in and care for the children. White families often exist as a nuclear unit, sometimes living far from extended family. Within Black and Hispanic communities, extended family often can provide a natural support structure for someone experiencing grief or processing trauma. Research shows that ethnic minorities in the US are vastly underrepresented in participation in therapy and in research on therapeutic methods.[1] This study demonstrates that outside help is sought far less outside of White populations than within them and that the prevalence of mental health disorders is greater in Hispanic and Black Americans. This could indicate that members of the latter communities may tend to have hesitancy regarding sharing personal matters with people outside their extended family or ethnic circle.

In some communities, a person processing a traumatic experience may simply be told to pray more. While some Asian families live as multigenerational units or near other Asian Americans, which provides them with natural support, there are some Asian Christians who view mental health exclusively as a spiritual concern. The spiritualizing of mental health can also be seen more in the southern United States. In the Bible Belt, we often find families of lower economic status who are accustomed to praying that God will supply all their needs. If we pray to God for the provision of bread, why would those prayers not extend to cover an uncle's depression? Prayer certainly has a powerful role to play in supporting an individual walking through a difficult time, but prayer need not stand alone. Trained and caring professionals may be the answer to the prayers.

The church has an opportunity, and even a responsibility, to help further normalize professional counseling and other mental health supports. Parishioners come to pastors with matters of concern regularly, and a pastor needs to understand where their boundary needs to end. Pastors are not trained therapists, nor do they have time in their schedule to consistently meet with every individual needing counseling. However, a pastor could continue regular check-ins alongside professional counseling. Chapter 19 more fully explores when and how to refer a person to a counselor.

Pastors and churches should all have an established relationship with counselors in their community, so when, not if, the need to refer occurs, they can confidently facilitate a connection. When my (Laura's) church purchased property adjacent to our building and had several vacant offices, it made sense to offer space to three counselors from our congregation. They would receive free space, and the church staff could refer anyone to them for a free initial session. The counselors periodically visited church staff meetings, reminding staff of their areas of specialty and helping us to know them, building our level of

1. Robinson De Jesús-Romero, Amani R. Holder-Dixon, John F. Buss, and Lorenzo Lorenzo-Luaces, "Race, Ethnicity, and Other Cultural Background Factors in Trials of Internet-Based Cognitive Behavioral Therapy for Depression: Systematic Review," *Journal of Medical Internet Research* 26 (February 1, 2024), e50780, https://doi.org/10.2196/50780.

confidence in making a referral. One of the counselors was particularly gifted in working with teens, and I would often take the opportunity in the hallway to get her take on an individual or situation in the youth ministry where I led.

Pastors can also find appropriate opportunities to speak about professional counseling from the pulpit. One of the pastors I (Laura) worked with, who was in his early fifties, had a heart attack on the way home from a church mission trip. He required emergency triple bypass surgery at a hospital several hours from home. The experience shook him deeply, and he found his recovery to be challenging at multiple levels. He sought the support of a counselor alongside his doctor, physical therapist, and spiritual director. When he returned to the pulpit, several of his sermons explored his experience, normalizing the value of seeking support from a team of individuals.

There are times when economics impact a family's ability to pursue counseling. Perhaps a parent is out of work, or an insurance plan is limited. These are times when the church having a relationship with a local counselor can be helpful to work out a sliding scale or an agreement for the church to cover several sessions. If someone is uncertain about the relevance of counseling in their context, the church might budget funds to help members get started and understand the value of the service. Low socioeconomic status is a major predictor of not being offered mental health or psychiatric treatment or receiving treatment in many developed countries.[2]

A youth pastor might accompany a family or teen to their initial counseling appointment, providing a comforting presence or helping with the logistics of transportation. At times, the pastor might participate in the session, helping a struggling teen to articulate an experience, but more likely, once the ice has been broken, the pastor can step back.

As professional counseling grows in mainstream acceptance, youth pastors need to consider these factors, or layers of several factors, as they encourage families to pursue counseling. Oftentimes a pastor's role in helping a family is logistical: The pastor can help the family think through next steps or assist them in overcoming barriers. Pastors might consider themselves bridge builders who help laity make important connections to support healing and a holistic spiritual life.

2. Helen Niemeyer and Christine Knaevelsrud, "Socioeconomic Status and Access to Psychotherapy," *Journal of Clinical Psychology* 79, no. 4 (2023): 937–53, https://doi.org/10.1002/jclp.23449.

19

Referral

Involving Professional Counselors or Caseworkers

Knowledge about making referrals may be one of the most important skills of a youth worker.[1] A referral is when a pastor or other caregiver connects a teen and their family to a more skilled or resourced provider. Referral typically involves a professional counselor or mental health assessment. If we were your youth ministry professors, we would ask you to memorize both when and how to refer. If you are a paid youth worker, there will be a test, and it will likely be a life and death situation in the life of a teen.

When to Refer

The following four areas are automatic referral situations, and each will be explained in further detail:

1. Danger to self or others
2. Beyond capacities, experience, or expertise
3. Specialized treatment needed (suicide, addiction)
4. Caregiver is over-immersed or too connected

1. We would like to acknowledge with gratitude Dr. Jane Jung from Meier Clinics for much of the content included in this chapter.

Refer as Soon as You Believe the Person You Are Helping May Be Dangerous to Themselves or Others

Any threat of harm to others or suicidal ideation should immediately be referred, likely through a hospital emergency room intake. Emergency rooms can keep the person safe and provide a mental health assessment. Immediately refer to a trained professional for the following issues:

- Self-harm (intentional cutting, burning, pulling hair, bruising of self)
- Suicidal ideation (thinking about suicide; does not require plans to kill self)
- Homicidal ideation (thinking about killing others, with or without plans)
- Abuse (neglect or sexual, physical, or emotional abuse)
- Psychosis (disconnection from reality, hearing voices, or experiencing hallucinations or delusions)

Refer as Soon as You Sense a Situation Is Beyond Your Capabilities, Experience, or Expertise

Many situations can be handled by parents or pastors; however, not everyone has the experience or expertise to handle every concern. When you are beyond your depth, you should refer the teen to someone with greater experience or expertise in the relevant area.

Refer as Soon as You Believe Specialized Treatment May Be Needed

The Christian community and pastoral care can often address mild cases of trauma, grief, depression, anger, or anxiety. Specialized treatment needs that should be referred can include issues needing medical care, addiction, suicidal ideation, prolonged worsening function, and so on. Refer a teen who is engaging in poor coping skills, such as the following:

- Use of drugs, alcohol, or food to self-medicate
- Engaging in behaviors that have a potential for danger (for example, sneaking out at night, having sex)
- Spending entire days playing videogames, on social media, or watching television or movies as a form of escape

Refer When the Issues They Are Struggling with Hit Close to Home for You

You should refer a teen if you are experiencing trauma in helping that teen or if your own mental or physical health issues are being exacerbated by working with the teen. When your own concerns become triggered, you are not able to provide careful and objective care. Refer the teen if any of the following are occurring, for example:

- You are in the midst of struggling with a similar issue.
- The issue reminds you of your own issues in the past that still have a hold on you.
- You notice yourself becoming more emotionally involved or stirred up.

How: Guidelines for the Referral

These four guidelines are helpful in the process of referring a teen. Each is explained more fully in the following sections.

- Be direct: Engage the parent and teen.
- Have information available: Anticipate questions.
- Walk with the teen: Do not just hand off!
- Reassure: They are not beyond help.

Be Direct: Parents and Referral

If a teen is experiencing an automatic referral issue, you must inform the parents or guardians. The parents should then call a mental health facility, which will help them determine the right level of care for their teen. Should a teen be at imminent risk of harming themself or another person, any party involved should refer to the nearest emergency room.

If the teen is *not* experiencing an automatic referral issue but is experiencing one of the other issues listed above, you should engage the teen and their parents or guardians about counseling.

- Explain why you think professional counseling could be helpful at this time.
- State what you have noticed or observed.
- If relevant, ask whether the situation or behavior is also occurring at home.
- Ask if they have thought about getting additional help.

Have Information Available and Anticipate Questions

When a student is in danger or a parent is urgently seeking information, it is a poor time to begin your research. Before a crisis can occur, compile a list of counselors and their contact information; keep copies of the list where they are available to distribute as needed. Know the types of therapy and specific areas of treatment that each counselor specializes in. Be able to describe or provide the following items prior to being asked:

- The counseling intake process
- The general nature of therapy
- How insurance, sliding scales, and ministry financial help may work
- Contact information for multiple therapists

Walk Alongside

Because you care about the teen and their family, it is crucial that you maintain your connection to and support of them while they are obtaining and using services.

- Tell the teen directly that you are not handing them off to a therapist.
- Emphasize that you will not be removing yourself from the situation but are helping them expand the team of people helping.
- Once the teen is in counseling, ask how things are going with therapy.
- Use active listening skills: Reflect. Empathize. Validate.
- Ask them how they are connecting with the counselor.
- Encourage the teen to tell the counselor directly if they have any misgivings or misunderstandings.
- Sometimes finding a good therapist is about finding a good match. Trying out different therapists is okay.

Reassure

Individuals and much of our society have biases against counseling. The teen and their parents will need reassurance when pursuing a referral. Therapy is not for "crazy" or "broken" people. I (Mike) often tell the story about how we celebrate broken arms by signing casts but hide our mental health issues. An arm will not heal well without a doctor and treatment. This is true of our nonphysical health concerns as well.

Every youth leader we know has, at some point, been surprised by a crisis and needed information about and a process for a referral. Knowing this information and reviewing it periodically is part of our duty of pastoral care.

20

Glass Children

Siblings of Those with Disabilities

A healthy kid who has a sibling with chronic health needs is known as a glass child. Alicia Meneses Maples tells a poignant story of her childhood years prior to age twelve. Her younger brother had autism and would break every one of her books, toys, and treasures in some way. He would bite her daily, hit her, and put holes in the walls. Several years later, her youngest brother was born without an immune system. While her father cared for her middle brother and tried to control him at home, her mother spent four years primarily at the hospital, caring for her youngest brother. Maples states that she was a good child because that was her job, and that is what her parents needed from her. When her youngest brother died, she was eleven. Age eleven was when she first began to attempt to take her own life. She relates that no one knew how much she was hurting: not her parents, other family, or teachers. She felt invisible and made herself as invisible as glass. Glass children are perceived as having no problems and present as being compliant or perfect children, if they are seen at all.[1]

Maples encourages parents to pay close attention to the emotional health of their children. All the difficult pain, loss, stress, and emotions that an adult would face in losing a child or caring for a disabled child are felt by the healthy sibling. But the healthy sibling experiences this situation with the coping skills of a child. When a glass child says they are "fine," adults should not believe

1. Alicia Maples, "Recognizing Glass Children," TEDx Talks, San Antonio, TX, December 27, 2010, 5:00–5:10, https://www .youtube .com /watch?v =MSwqo -g2Tbk.

them. They are not fine if they experience what the adults around them are experiencing, but as a child.

Glass children are siblings of disabled or chronically ill children who often become invisible or hidden as parents are consumed by the needs of their disabled or ill child. A foster placement, a chronic illness, or a disability can place immense and various stresses on a family. Chronic illness or issues could involve a child with criminal history, long-term or short-term disability, cancer, mental health concerns or addiction. The physical, emotional, and financial difficulties that often accompany these stressors sometimes mean the sibling's needs are not met emotionally, physically, or socially. This phenomenon can also occur for biological children in families that foster or adopt, especially when significant behavior disorders or other challenges are present.

Glass children are not glass as in "fragile": rather, they are often strong, resilient, and self-sufficient. As Maples explains, "The reality is glass children are some of the strongest children there are: we have to be to survive some of the things we have to survive."[2] Glass children often suffer from a form of benign neglect, even intentionally presenting themselves as invisible to allow parents to focus on the "greater needs" of their siblings or foster siblings.

Prevalence

According to an analysis by Mhairi McKenzie Smith and colleagues, "Approximately 7–17% of children have a sibling with a chronic illness," which the study's authors define as "encompass[ing] both physical and mental health disorders."[3] It is likely that everyone knows a family that includes a child with a chronic illness—which means that you and everyone you know are probably acquainted with a glass child.

Issues

Glass children often feel that any issues they face are insignificant in comparison to their siblings' and parents' challenges. Thus, they become caretakers of not just their siblings but also their family. They experience high levels of

2. Maples, "Recognizing Glass Children."

3. Mhairi McKenzie Smith, Snehal Pinto Pereira, Lynette Chan, Charlotte Rose, and Roz Shafran, "Impact of Well-Being Interventions for Siblings of Children and Young People with a Chronic Physical or Mental Health Condition: A Systematic Review and Meta-Analysis," *Clinical Child and Family Psychology Review* 21 (February 15, 2018): 246–65, https://doi.org/10.1007/s10567-018-0253-x.

isolation and a lack of social support, and they carry the caregiver role into other situations like church and school.

> Unlike those with a disabled parent, who are more readily identified as young carers in need of support . . . children and young people with a disabled or chronically ill brother or sister are less likely to be perceived as a population with significant and specific vulnerabilities and needs . . . with the impact of their complex experiences often being overlooked.[4]

Parents are so consumed with the needs of glass children's siblings that "when they look at us they look right through us as though we are made of glass."[5]

Interventions

The following is a list of interventions that can help glass children.

Common fate: Teens in these complex family situations need to experience what is known as "common fate." If they are connected to other teens in similar situations, they learn they are not alone. Meeting others through support groups or networking can give them hope, identity, and a group with which to belong.

Caregiving: Youth ministry leaders should work to prevent glass children from becoming ongoing caregivers or spokespeople for their siblings in the ministry. Leaders should help them find the ability to step away from social protector roles that they likely play at home and at school. They need ways to step away from the "I take care of my family" role. Parents' Night Out events also offer an opportunity to give nondisabled siblings a night off. Dedicated buddies at church for the disabled sibling can remove the glass child's responsibility for several hours and allow the teen to leave the caregiver role.

Support for parents: Parents' Night Out activities or specialized camps can give space to parents to breathe again. Support or recreation for parents might allow them to move out of a survival or triage situation and become more aware of other vital needs in their own family. If the parents are healthy, the children will be vastly healthier.

Adult mentors: Present and active adults who reach out to the teen may dispel isolation. An adult who takes a teen out for ice cream may give a small respite to a teen from family chaos or instill a sense of value back to the teen. Someone who sees them and hears their story. This should not be done

4. Imogen Hanvey, Aida Malovic, and Evangelos Ntontis, "Glass Children: The Lived Experiences of Siblings of People with a Disability or Chronic Illness," *Journal of Community and Applied Social Psychology* 32, no. 5 (2022): 937.

5. Maples, "Recognizing Glass Children," 5:10–5:20.

because of their home life situation but because of their independent value as a teen in the image of God. Ask glass children not about their sibling but about themselves.

Activities: A separate activity, like meeting with a mentor for ice cream or a frisbee game, is healthy. A corporate family activity, like a camp or family games night with dedicated and trained staff, can allow the family to integrate around their relationships instead of a diagnosis.

Training and counseling: Glass children need a safe place where they can receive counseling and develop coping skills. Often, the sibling attends special programs or therapies. The types of resources that make the sibling's programs possible should also be used and made available to benefit the glass child, if that is a possibility. A foster placement often provides resources that facilitate counseling for the foster child. This benefit of the foster system usually can also be used for family therapy, which can include the family's other children individually.

Communicate love and value: Glass children are likely "easy maintenance kids": ones who conform well to social expectations, never rock the boat, and stay attuned to the needs of others while making their own needs invisible. They can be prone to legalism, and they may believe that their worth lies solely in their contributions to others. They need clear words and actions that communicate they are loved, accepted, and valued for who they are irrespective of their contributions to their family or their youth group.

Family pairing: Healthy families should invite teens as well as their entire family into their common life, to dinner, to vacations. Momentary calms in a glass child's chaotic life can bring great relief, hope, and healing. Recruit families to come alongside glass children with regular dinners at their house.

21

Transience

Seth was one of my (Mike's) favorite students of all time. He would show up every week at youth group and pester me, trying to figure out if we were playing dodgeball that night. As a middle schooler, he had already experienced serious life challenges. When he was a junior, Seth told me that "dodgeball definitely saved my life." As he came to youth group to play the game, he heard the message that he was known and cared for by God and our church community.

One night, when he was a sophomore in high school, Seth returned home in the evening to his mother's apartment above an auto-repair garage. He found his mother's new boyfriend cooking drugs in the middle of the living-room carpet. Seth's little sister was home. He yelled at the guy until the boyfriend left the house, and Seth told his mom to never let him come back.

The next day, when Seth returned home from school, the entire apartment was cleaned out. The only things left in the entire apartment were in his room. He did not have a phone or internet, so he packed up all of his belongings into two large garbage bags and walked several miles, abandoning what he could not carry. This began a period of couch surfing between different homes, moving from house to house until he could locate a more permanent solution. Living-location changes disrupted his schooling and his friendships. He worked hard, but the challenges were overwhelming.

By the time he was a senior at age seventeen, he was traveling on international mission trips and making plans for college, both of which he had never dreamed would be possible. At one point Seth had to choose whether to go on a mission trip with his youth group, take care of some medical issues, or buy a laptop so he could take college classes in the fall. My (Mike's) church was able to donate the mission trip expenses, help him with schooling, and connect him to state services. In addition, a doctor in the congregation saw him at the clinic for free. Our church was not the only factor in Seth's success, but he still says dodgeball saved his life.

Students are significantly mobile in the US and the world. Student mobility, known as "transience," dramatically threatens teenagers' health, education, relationships, and a host of other factors.[1] While educational systems are actively struggling and researching this issue, there seems to be little to no direct research on the effect of transience on youth discipleship or evangelism.

Definitions and Prevalence

Runaways, homelessness, immigration, unaccompanied minors, housing insecurity, and "couch surfing" are all forms of youth transience. These situations can often overlap in the life of a teen. There are many definitions of which to be aware. More than 1.6 million teens are runaways or "thrown away" from their homes yearly.[2] A "thrown-away teen" is one who is asked to leave their home. As Matthew Morton and colleagues explain, "Approximately 3.0% of households with 13- to 17-year-olds reported explicit youth homelessness (including running away or being asked to leave), and 1.3% reported experiences that solely involved couch surfing, resulting in an overall 4.3% household prevalence of any homelessness, broadly defined."[3] "Homelessness" and "housing insecurity" are similar ideas but refer to different levels of severity. Housing insecurity refers to unstable or unaffordable housing that causes transience or threatens homelessness. Another term, "unaccompanied minors," may refer to those who are abandoned, thrown away, or run away. Housing insecurity or immigration affects millions each year and can also cause significant disruption at all levels of the teen's life.

1. Michael Severe and Mark Senter, "Forty Years of Youth Ministry," *Christian Education Journal: Research on Educational Ministry* 17, no. 3 (2020): 449–67, https://doi.org/10.1177/0739891320943900.

2. Matthew H. Morton, Amy Dworsky, Jennifer L. Matjasko, et al., "Prevalence and Correlates of Youth Homelessness in the United States," *Journal of Adolescent Health* 62, no. 1 (2018): 14–21, https://doi.org/10.1016/j.jadohealth.2017.10.006.

3. Morton, Dworsky, Matjasko, et al., "Prevalence and Correlates of Youth Homelessness," 14.

Causes and Issues

"Immigration and migration, poverty, foster care, and parental job transitions are the four greatest factors that affect student mobility."[4] High transience has a negative effect on a teen's health care, food stability, education, mental health, and relationships. For example, according to Kimberly Bender and colleagues, "approximately 75% of homeless youth report being emotionally, physically, or sexually abused by their families and note these issues are key reasons for running away."[5] Studies note that homeless youth who now meet the diagnostic criteria for substance abuse have prior PTSD at the rate of 40 percent.[6] While a potential chicken-or-egg scenario, trauma and abuse experienced in childhood is a major factor driving teens into homelessness and substance abuse. And once a teen is homeless or facing housing insecurity, they experience far greater levels of trauma.

Bender and colleagues report that youth who experience trauma and disability are at higher risk of being homeless, and that youth who experience housing insecurity are at a higher risk of mental health issues and other concerns.[7] In the homeless population, 83 percent "report exposure to at least one form of victimization."[8]

In public education, smaller classrooms, better trained teachers, better school programming, and better facilities are "irrelevant" for impacting students who are experiencing student transience.[9] Church work with youth faces the same challenges. Better facilities, better staff, and better programs housed in traditional formats tied to a location or attractional model fail for the world's transient youth population. Some school districts find that transience is so prevalent that they must align the curricula of every classroom in the entire district. Teens who must move from couch to couch are likely to attend several different schools within a district over the course of a semester or school year. This strict curricular alignment within the district allows a teen who is moving between schools to maintain continuity of study. Even

4. Severe and Senter, "Forty Years of Youth Ministry," 464.

5. Kimberly Bender, Kristin Ferguson, Sanna Thompson, Chelsea Komlo, and David Pollio, "Factors Associated with Trauma and Posttraumatic Stress Disorder Among Homeless Youth in Three U.S. Cities: The Importance of Transience," *Journal of Traumatic Stress* 23, no. 1 (2010): 161, https://doi.org/10.1002/jts.20501.

6. Kurt D. Johnson, Les B. Whitbeck, and Dan R. Hoyt, "Substance Abuse Disorders Among Homeless and Runaway Adolescents," *Journal of Drug Issues* 35, no. 4 (2005): 799–816.

7. Bender et al., "Factors Associated with Trauma," 168.

8. Bender et al., "Factors Associated with Trauma," 161.

9. Sarah D. Sparks, "Student Mobility: How It Affects Learning," *EducationWeek*, August 11, 2016, https://www.edweek.org/leadership/student-mobility-how-it-affects-learning/2016/08.

with this herculean effort by schools, however, high mobility is still disruptive to education.

Trauma and disability are significant factors affected by youth transience and homelessness. When youth are experiencing some form of housing insecurity, they are at heightened risk of experiencing further victimization and mental health disorders. Parents, school officials, pastors, and health care providers should be aware that "residential mobility in the past five years may indicate increased odds of depression among adolescents even among adolescents whose housing stability has improved in the past year."[10]

Interventions

Trauma and disability heighten the risk of homelessness and transience. Conversely, teen transience heightens the risk of trauma and abuse. Trauma is often the cause of homelessness, and homelessness often causes trauma. Simply finding stable housing very often solves neither the problem that resulted in the transience nor the long-term impact of it. A church involved in the life of a transient teen would do well to connect with local social services, which can coordinate medical, job, education, and other vital resources across multiple areas as the teen moves from location to location. We may need to collaborate with other churches, connecting teens to faith communities and mentors in each of their new temporary locations.

One of my (Mike's) ministry students tells of having lived in over a dozen foster homes when they were a child. At the age of twelve they were invited to church and attended without their foster family. This church became their family throughout their adolescence, even though they never lived with a church member. Time continually brought the student new foster home placements, but the church continued traveling to pick them up, sometimes across multiple counties.

While youth homelessness is beyond the scope of this book, we must be aware that mental health, disability, homelessness, and trauma are often comorbidities: coexisting conditions that complicate intervention and may cause one another.

10. C. Glasheen, V. Forman-Hoffman, S. Hedden, T. Ridenour, J. Wang, and J. Porter, "Residential Transience Among US Adolescents: Association with Depression and Mental Health Treatment," *Epidemiology and Psychiatric Sciences* 28, no. 6 (2019): 691.

22

Juvenile Justice and Incarceration

As I (Mike) write, my adopted son is in a medical program. It is a "lock down": similar to juvenile detention but medically focused instead of punitive. I can see my son, but he lives behind metal detectors and never goes outside. To see him, I must pass through double steel doors opened remotely from a secure control booth. I know many more police, lawyers, probation officers, and social workers than I imagined possible.

There are few difficulties that break a parent's heart like the incarceration of their child. It is unpleasant to have an officer call on your house for a curfew violation or underage drinking charge. It is heart-wrenching to repeatedly go to court and powerlessly watch your child descend further into the justice system. Adolescent probation, incarceration, and confinement can drain finances and create inordinate stress, and other siblings can disappear in the chaos (see chapter 20, which addresses glass children).

Prevalence

Most teens do not get entangled with criminal offenses. Some teens perform what is known as status offenses. These offenses are based on the teen's "status" as a minor and cannot apply to adults. Status offenses are not criminal but can lead to probation or other serious consequences. The five most common status offenses are as follows:

- truancy (skipping school)
- underage drinking
- running away
- violating curfew
- acting out (also known as ungovernability, incorrigibility, or being beyond the control of one's parents)[1]

Teens who commit status offenses rarely progress to more serious crimes or behavior.[2] It is likely that isolated incidences of the above are part of normal adolescent development for many teens and pose little to no current or future risk. That is good news for parents: Don't panic! If you are a youth pastor, help parents in your church not to panic.

Issues

Here is the bad news. Teens on the margins are disproportionately involved in juvenile probation or the justice system. The behaviors that stem from some mental health concerns, mental disorders, or foster care place teens at risk of drug use, victimization, engagement in risky behavior, and overall increased potential for physical and mental health issues, including substance use disorders. While cause and effect are sometimes difficult to disentangle, these conditions can lead to juvenile probation and criminal issues and ultimately a form of "confinement" such as jail, detention, or placement in a residential program.

Interventions

Youth pastors may find the following interventions effective ways to support youth involved in or at risk of becoming involved in the juvenile justice system or probation.

- Visit local emergency teen shelters or shelter care, detention centers, adolescent hospitals, or foster group homes. A significant variety of programs are likely to exist across your area. One large complex thirty minutes from my (Mike's) house contains thirteen types of distinct programming ranging from detention to teen group foster homes.

1. The Annie E. Casey Foundation, "What Are Status Offenses and Why Do They Matter?," April 6, 2019, https://www.aecf.org/blog/what-are-status-offenses-and-why-do-they-matter.
2. Development Services Group, "Status Offenders," literature review, Office of Juvenile Justice and Delinquency Prevention, last updated September 2015, https://ojjdp.ojp.gov/sites/g/files/xyckuh176/files/media/document/status_offenders.pdf.

- Make a connection with the local detention or shelter chaplain. They can provide a tour, explain intake processes, and even coordinate volunteers for their chapel or mentoring for confined teens.
- Go to court. Experience the system in action. Know how to connect with the court, probation, and lawyers prior to a family experiencing a crisis in this area.
- Talk to probation officers about how you can help. I (Mike) once worked in a town with a teen court. Teens would be peer judges and pass community service sentences for repeat teen status offenders. I would mentor an offender and supervise them for ten hours a week of community service in the church for weeks at a time. Lots of window washing led to opportunities for conversations and breaks at the local ice cream shop.
- Get to know the resource officers in high school and middle school. These police officers are assigned to a particular school and maintain a constant presence. Resource officers are the first to investigate an issue and are often trusted by teens in their school. They can help explain, navigate, or connect you.
- When you are supporting a particular youth, keep tabs on that youth's parents. Juvenile probation and justice system processes move very slowly, often intentionally. Many probation officers will not meet a teen for weeks or months after an offense just to see if the behavior is repeating or a single incident. A parent may still be dealing with a probation issue a year after the court hearing, many months after everyone else at church has forgotten about the concerns and prayer requests.
- Encourage the parents of a teen in juvenile probation or the justice system. They often feel failure and fear the ruin of their child. Both are far from true. The shame and stigma for juvenile offenses make most parents keep silent; many will not come to the church for help. If you were involved in the teen's life prior to their involvement in the system, the parents are more likely to reach out to you for help.
- Visit kids in confinement. Pastors can have access in many places where even a grandparent cannot call or visit. Note that some teens never receive visits while in a shelter, hospital, detention, or jail: Two or three pastoral visits can change their lives and their view of God.

The legal system is incredibly complex. When factors such as mental health, disability, or foster care also affect a teen involved in that system, it is usually nightmarishly convoluted. Navigating the system differs by county and state. Do not navigate it without a guide. Someone like a caseworker, probation officer, or lawyer in your congregation can be vital.

23

Youth Ministry as Respite Care for Parents and Providers

I (Mike) once took foster placement of three children in a sibling group. Instant chaos: figuring out the beds, whose socks went where, school transfers, and so on. I had to navigate a very different set of behaviors and expectations among the children. I needed to set boundaries involving acceptable levels of screaming and violence, and I grappled with one child's irrational fear of trees. And then there was the trauma. The situation was wonderous and overwhelming. As the placement progressed, the children became adoptable. I wanted to show them that I was "all in and never going to abandon them." I believed at the time that always being available equated to stability. The nature of the kids' trauma meant that any night, school day, or event might bring new chaos, incidents, and problems. Difficult phone calls with nurses, principals, police, and others were near-daily occurrences. "Intense" cannot begin to describe the never-ending barrage of inexplicable problems. Helping a fifth grader write a report on the Constitution, I discovered they could not read at the first-grade level. One child would run away and thought it was funny to hurt others. Another would hide for hours behind our couches for no apparent reason. I was exhausted but unable to know it in the crisis.

The children's caseworker suggested respite. Respite is given to caregivers like foster parents or in-home medical providers as a quick period of rest and rejuvenation. I suspected it would further traumatize the children and just prove that I was ready to leave them like their biological family had. I found

I was wrong on two counts for resisting respite. First, I could not create calm and stability if I was burned out and empty. Second, always being there for the kids is a lie and mistake. It creates unmanageable expectations driven by fear and guilt in the parent. I started doing weekend respites once a month, and it revolutionized my life and made me a better parent.

The Defense Zones of Respite

Some foster care placements are difficult and long-term. Caring for a family member with a chronic health issue such as a mental health or physical disability can be as well. Many of us know that these types of care may involve stress and sleep deprivation well beyond those experienced by a parent with a newborn. As a result, it is necessary for the caregiver of a person with a chronic health issue involving high-support needs to also receive care. Three major defense zones—programmatic, social, and individual—can be covered to help keep a caregiver healthy, and each must be engaged to some extent.

Programmatic

The programmatic approach to respite is centered around events run by a church or ministry that give a break to caregivers. These events are common for disability ministries; examples include date nights and Christmas shopping opportunities for the caregivers while the children or others they have been caring for are dropped off at a secure location staffed with well-trained volunteers. These programs may be crafted to let attendees engage in service, fun, or social engagement while allowing caregivers such as parents or foster parents to take a breath. Sometimes the parents stay in the building for a separate activity such as a training, Bible study, or fellowship. MomCo, formerly Mothers of Preschoolers (MOPS), runs this kind of ministry for women with young children. While the central program is often Bible study, we suspect a period of adult interaction paired with respite from caring for needy young children is the real home run. Disability camps for the individual child or for the whole family often provide intentional respite over multiple days. Many parents testify that a week of disability camp as a family saved their marriage. Programmatic options include the following:

- Parents' night out
- Adult small groups with provided childcare for each group, or centralized childcare at the church for all small groups meeting at the same time
- Sunday morning disability programming

- Support groups, parent training, or a service project with supplied supervision

As a youth pastor, when I (Mike) was asked if we offered a parent ministry, I would often joke that "we have a middle school youth group where we take your kid completely for two hours a week." Respite ministry is parent ministry.

Social

The social respite approach involves two families, one with and one without a child or other dependent who has a chronic health condition. One family invites the other to visit both for a meal and for necessary social interaction. If the child or other family member with the chronic health condition has behavioral issues or elevated physical needs, this may require the assistance of a babysitter or other respite caregiver with specialized training. This hospitality allows one family to participate in another family's day-to-day interactions. This activity can be like a playdate where parents can interact with parents while children interact with children. Often these kinds of social events are the only time a caregiver can connect with an adult or spend time in a broader social setting in an entire month. An example of a larger version of these types of events is described in the pizza and park scenario near the beginning of chapter 3. Social respite requires networking and supporting these types of activities. The church may need to connect people, encourage small groups to participate together, or develop a ministry that organizes informal visits and gatherings of these kinds.

Individual

During a particularly difficult placement with two young children, I (Mike) had two college students who would watch my kids weekly. I could not leave because of state regulations for certified caregivers, but I would go watch a show in my bedroom. The college students played with all the kids and took payment by using the laundry machines. Once we had a local youth pastor who would take a child on the margins out by themselves. A simple one-on-one. Other adults would be in the ice cream shop to protect the child and staff, following child protection protocols. This would allow me space to sleep, do laundry, or do something special with another sibling who is often ignored among the urgent chronic issues in our home (see chapter 20, which addresses glass children). Imagine the relief for a new mother when grandma comes for a few days to help. I once cried in relief when I was alone for an hour for the first time in months.

The following are a few ideas for individual respite:

- A mentor could meet individually with the child. Regularity is even more effective.
- Invite the teen on the margins to participate in service, deliver food to homeless community members, or work at the church.
- Invite a family to swim and watch the children for two hours a week through the summer.

Note that these respite options can focus on the child with a disability or trauma, on the parent, or on the whole family. It is likely that a combination of these respite types and focuses is necessary for holistic and regular rejuvenation.

24

Camps, Retreats, and Overnights

A staple of youth ministry is the opportunity for extended time together during camps, retreats, and overnights. For teens on the margins, these extended stretches of time, opportunities to strengthen relationships or develop new ones, and new environments can bring added challenges. A teen on the margins often relies on additional internal and external supports to navigate their day, and those supports are often not naturally available away from home.

All of my (Laura's) kids have attention deficit hyperactivity disorder. ADHD involves difficulty with executive function, the ability to plan and carry out tasks of daily living. For a teen with ADHD to attend a camp, retreat, or overnight, extra steps of support are needed. The following list is designed to assist parents in helping their teen engage in a camp or retreat, whether or not the teen has ADHD.

Packing and Items

Before the teen leaves home, it is a good idea to provide them with a packing list to help them remember essential items. Including soap, a towel, and deodorant on the list communicates an expectation of hygiene. For winter camp, including extra gloves, hats, snow pants, boots, and lip balm on the list is important so that the teen will be able to participate fully. One of my (Mike's) foster kids argued that he did not need a Bible or notebook for camp precisely because it was not on any list, so those items are also important to include.

I (Laura) have found it helpful to have my own teen pack his bag for trips under supervision. The first time he did overnight camp, he forgot he had extra socks and wore the same pair, night and day, for four days. This experience did not end well. So moving forward, the practice of him packing his bag with the piles of items we assembled together helped him remember the items he was bringing to camp and where he could find them. Most importantly, it is critical to ask families to put their child's name on everything. One of the most significant challenges with executive function is keeping track of one's items. This can already be challenging at home in one's bedroom, and the tight quarters of a cabin or the chaos of a church gymnasium raises the bar.

Expectations and Schedule

Providing a printed schedule, either in a booklet given to participants or on a page posted on a gathering-space wall, allows everyone to pace themselves, knowing what is next. A printed schedule can be helpful for teens who have issues with executive function, who are on the autism spectrum and struggle to transition, who have experienced trauma, or who struggle with anxiety. Existing outside of one's routine and comfort zone can be scary, but knowing what to anticipate can ease fear. If a program is meant to be flexible or incorporates a surprise, you may need to make an exception for particular kids or to provide a careful buddy who will prep them and walk them through variations in camping due to weather or changes in the plan.

Socioeconomics

Not every program may be for every kid, but money should not be a determining factor if participation is appropriate. Take into consideration the finances needed when you consider kids on the margins and the already-stressed budgets of their caregivers. Often, families on the margins have extra medications, therapies, and educational expenses to pay for, lower incomes, or a combination of these items. Some teens may lack the necessary gear to attend camp. A teen in foster care or from a family with a limited income may not have a sleeping bag, winter boots, or snow pants. My (Laura's) church once welcomed a family displaced by flooding in another state. Their teen had lost all their personal belongings. After visiting youth group for several weeks, they wanted to join the upcoming retreat but needed several items in order to participate. Leaders can often source these types of items from other church families as hand-me-downs or through visits to a local thrift store. All items should be washed and in good condition. If a church is frequently supporting teens in this way, a youth pastor might keep a camp closet where church families can regularly contribute needed items. It is important to build the price of scholarships into the yearly budget or trip budget so that everyone can attend.

Junk Foods

Teens are notorious for seeking junk food, especially away from the watchful eye of parents. While junk food can be fun, a retreat or camp full of junk food will often impact the mood and behaviors of the teens, and this is often doubly so for teens with various conditions, ADHD, or trauma. Limit the intake of soda and sugar. Sometimes it is OK to unplug the pop machine or limit the number of items purchased at the camp canteen. Provide options of fruit and vegetables, granola bars, and protein-packed snacks for energy. Avoid snacks with food dye. Encourage hydration, especially during increased activity. I (Laura) would bring cases of bottled water and write the name of each teen on a bottle, providing an inexpensive short-term option for a reusable water bottle for each teen. During the first night of camp scavenger hunt to help teens find their bearings, one of the tasks was for campers to locate drinking fountains so they would be equipped to refill. One camp required kids to drink a full glass of water at every meal before juice, lemonade, or bug juice would be made available.

Nursing and Medication Management

Many of our teens take regular medication, and extended hours away from home necessitate that church leaders dispense that medication. A doctor or nurse from your church congregation is always the first choice to take as a camp nurse, but if one is not available, it is helpful to choose the most nurturing leader for this task. Depending on the number of teens participating, this might be the only task for this leader. Aside from dispensing medication, this adult will be providing the ice packs and mosquito cream, pulling the splinters, and staying with the teen who throws up. As youth pastor, I (Laura) quickly realized the importance of outsourcing this task, so my energies could remain focused on leading the group. Parents or guardians should fill out a form for each teen taking prescription medication with information about dosage and indicate whether the teen has authority to adjust dosage. This information should be transferred to a master list so the camp nurse knows who needs medication at what time. A log should be kept indicating each time a teen takes their medication.

Youth groups should carry a well-stocked first aid kit for the location and should place one in each vehicle. Buy a few for any church or personal vehicle used on an outing. When I (Laura) began in youth ministry, the first aid kit was a backpack. As the years progressed and I discovered the need for more items, this "nurse bag" evolved into the nurse tub. Parents were asked to put their teens' medication in a resealable plastic bag along with their signed instruction form. The baggies could be added to the tub to keep everything in one location. Prescription medications should be sent in prescription bottles and collected at departure. My church asked teens to bring no medication in their personal luggage aside from quick-action medications like EpiPens and rescue inhalers for asthma, and we assured them and their families that common items like ibuprofen and adhesive bandages would be provided. Prior to my coming on staff, some of the teens in my youth group had brought a significant amount of cold medicine with a form of alcohol in it as an ingredient. Claiming to have colds, they self-medicated beyond the recommended dosage, creating difficult behaviors and uncomfortable phone calls to parents.

Mood Management

Extended time together as a youth group can be a rich blessing. It can also be overwhelming for a teen managing a mental health condition, trauma, autism, or a tendency toward overstimulation. Offering breaks from high-energy activities, places where teens can go for a quiet reset, and blocks of supervised free time during daylight can be helpful. Traveling for extended periods of time in a tightly packed vehicle can also be overwhelming. When I (Laura) was a teen in youth group, before seat belts were widely used, I once became overstimulated riding shoulder to shoulder in a tight minivan as we were driving across several states. At a rest stop, I asked for permission and rearranged the vehicle interior to create space to lie on top of the luggage at the very back. While in retrospect we know this was quite unsafe, at the time, it showed I recognized my need to re-establish my "body bubble." My peers saw how comfortable the makeshift bed looked, and we all took turns stretching out. Having one fewer teen in the seats of the minivan provided more space for everyone. While of course this is no longer acceptable inside a vehicle, it helps demonstrate how the arrangement of a space can help produce a less stressful environment within a camp or retreat setting.

Overstimulation

Large-group chapels or times of worship with teens are often loud and overstimulating. While a teen may be able to tolerate a single worship session during weekly youth group while they are rested, they may struggle more when away from home and operating on less sleep and unfamiliar food. Leaders should pack noise-canceling headphones, and alcohol wipes for cleaning them, and should be sensitive to teens who prefer to sit away from speakers or take a short walk in a designated area during worship. A buddy can help a particular teen navigate sensory issues if necessary.

Hygiene

Moving through tasks of daily self-care and hygiene can be difficult for teens away from their home routines. When a teen knows there is a game or friend waiting, it is easy to skip washing their face or applying deodorant. This is where a helpful leader can come into play, making sure that everyone has ample time to get ready and a scheduled time in the shower. A leader can organize spaces for everyone to store toiletries and hang wet towels and can devise a system for separating dirty clothes. My (Laura's) youth group's nurse tub included hotel-sized soaps and shampoos. Additionally, I brought travel-sized deodorants, toothbrushes, and a few extra towels to ensure hygiene was supported. My son recently attended a retreat where hygiene items were given as "prizes" for games. Many teens feel uncomfortable changing in a shared bathroom space, and a teen with ADHD may not conceive a way to maintain modesty in unfamiliar space. A cabin leader can explain systems and processes that allow teens to change privately, utilizing a timer that gives each person a solo time in the bathroom. Hygiene and showers should be part of the daily routine.

Partial Participation

Some teens need significant enough help with daily care and routines that participating fully with their youth group on a retreat is not feasible. This could be true for teens with certain physical disabilities or potential trauma responses, or for foster children with prohibitive legal restrictions. Options for such a teen include welcoming them for a limited number of hours if the camp is in proximity and parents or guardians agree to provide transportation. My (Laura's) son on the autism spectrum just participated in three hours of a twenty-four-hour lock-in with his youth group, and for him, that was the right amount of time. Camps, retreats, and special events can be transformatively powerful for a teen on the margins.

25

Aging Out

Graduation, Transition, or Continuing in the Program

Joddie experiences a genetic disorder similar to Down syndrome as well as autism. She received a certificate of completion from high school at the age of twenty and, in her state, will continue to receive academic support through age twenty-one. Her program focuses on life skills, without the typical high school discussion of Shakespeare or precalculus. While Joddie cannot manage money or drive a vehicle, she competes in Special Olympics and enjoys the social component of her classes and activities.

One of Joddie's family friends is inviting Joddie's whole family to their church, but the church has a difficult roadblock. The church has a clear rule: No one attends youth group once they have graduated from high school. Joddie's area has intensive early graduation programs that mean many kids who are sixteen have graduated, so they are not able to attend youth group. Joddie, though she has not completed her schooling, has her certificate and so is also not able to attend youth group. The church cannot offer Joddie or a sixteen-year-old early graduate any age-appropriate programming or access points into peer social connections.

Definition

"Aging out" refers to a youth's transitioning out of foster care or other system of support, usually at the age of eighteen. Teens leaving these support systems can face significant hurdles in housing, education, employment, and more. For teens from foster care, the struggles of aging out equate to higher risk factors including poverty, incarceration, and lower rates of high school and college graduation. While many US states offer ongoing medical insurance and social worker support, successful transition to adulthood is often elusive.

Traditional foster programs historically ended housing, schooling, and medical insurance at the age of eighteen. This loss of services caused a significant number of now-adult foster children to become immediately entangled in their state's department of corrections instead of college or careers. Today, many states have programs that provide schooling, ongoing Medicaid, transitional housing, and caseworker support. In states like Indiana, these programs continue through the age of twenty-five.

Aging out of youth group is tenuous for typical teens, many of whom find the transition to "adult church" difficult. Without age-specific teaching and programming, young adults can find themselves drifting from church in their twenties, instead focusing on important life skills like dating and establishing a career and probably managing laundry.[1] Those with trauma and disability are doubly challenged by aging out of programming. Most churches are struggling to offer disability programming or buddies for children. Teens are the new frontier we have been exploring here in this text, but adult disability programming is exceedingly rare, difficult, and beyond the vision of most ministries and churches.

Prevalence

Aging out or transitioning is ubiquitous. All teens in foster care, and all teens with disabilities, will eventually face the end of their youth group time just as other teens will. If a church has a child or teen with a disability, that church will eventually face the question of how to address the needs of the student as they age or graduate.

Issues

Youth ministries must avoid the "one-eared Mickey Mouse" problem in which the youth group operates separately from the rest of the church, like a lone Mickey Mouse ear on a Mickey Mouse hat, where the main part of the hat represents the rest of the church. Mark DeVries notes that some churches

1. Tim Clydesdale and Kathleen Garces-Foley, *The Twentysomething Soul: Understanding the Religious and Secular Lives of American Young Adults* (Oxford University Press, 2019), 63.

provide age-specific ministry and staff for teens but do not connect adolescents to the overall church body or community of believers.[2] It was originally thought that this unhelpful model was the cause of youth abandoning the church in high numbers; however, this migration appears to be occurring in all forms of ministries and prior to graduation. Nevertheless, DeVries's insight is important: Many teens are connected to the church through only a single program or person such as a youth pastor or youth group. When that program or person is disrupted, or the teen ages out of the youth programming, the teen may struggle with integrating into the entire church family.

Now imagine a disability ministry or a youth ministry that is "margin sensitive." That program could be the only connection a foster child or a teen with a disability has to the faith community. When that teen on the margins ages out, the funding ends, or the program leader changes, the teen could be lost from the community of that local church or ministry.

Many churches find it challenging to integrate a person experiencing severe cognitive disability or delay. The challenge becomes more acute if that person is beyond the typical age span of their youth group but has been held in a bubble of programming or care that does not intersect with the rest of the congregation. Not only is there no available formal programming, but there is also no scaffolding of support beyond youth ministry. How does a foster teen, now nineteen, who has not graduated from high school and has no biological family relationships, engage in a typical church setting? The vast majority of churches have no young adult or college and career-specific programming. Attempting to engage an "aging out" teen in the same way as an average forty-year-old with kids is problematic.

Additional complexities come to the fore when a youth with a disability turns eighteen. Does an eighteen-year-old who has emotional and mental characteristics similar to those of a twelve-year-old stop attending and graduate to adult programming? Many young adults with cognitive disabilities will never gain adult competencies. These concerns and issues highlight the problem of ableism we outlined in chapter 1.

Interventions

With these concerns in mind, for teens with disabilities involving higher support needs, there are three main options: graduation, transition, or stay in the program.

2. Mark DeVries, *Family-Based Youth Ministry: Reaching the Been-There, Done-That Generation* (InterVarsity, 1994), 42.

Graduation

A church or ministry may choose to graduate all or the majority of disabled students to non–youth group programming. The teen becoming an adult joins adult programming through a buddy or integration approach as described in chapter 7. Some churches may wish to join others across denominations to provide socialization and more comprehensive programming. One church we know has a Best Buddies program, in which teen or adult buddies do small-group activities with disabled churchgoers once the disabled churchgoers leave youth group. Buddies would take out these transitioning teens to go bowling or to the movies and attend their Special Olympics events.

Transition

Churches that offer transition to members with disabilities who have been attending youth group and have higher support needs often have established programming and a larger population of disabled members. Transition options can be varied, but they basically offer adult programs for people with disabilities in the church. These programs can be as simple as irregular social events or as robust as weekly programming with specialized facilities intended to serve these adults their entire lives. Many churches using this approach not only create specialized programming but also integrate adults in this group into specialized service areas within the church. Working at the church food bank or taking part in an adult choir are examples of options. Disabled adults with higher support needs need not be separated into their own choir: More effective is integration into a welcoming and appropriate ministry in the church that engages all members in its service.

Continued Participation

A continued participation approach is most common in smaller or less resourced churches and in churches that have smaller populations of members with disabilities involving higher support needs. It can also be common in Hispanic churches. Here the new adult experiencing the disability remains part of the youth group until their capacity is at or above the adolescent level, at which point they can join the adults in the church. Many Hispanic churches view youth groups as "everyone not married": It would not be uncommon to see people in their late twenties there, as well as members with high support needs continuing indefinitely as participants. Keeping an adult in youth programming creates legal and child protection risks. Whether this approach is viewed as normal or inappropriate is often culturally dependent.

Ultimately, the true success of any of these options relies on an integrated approach. A ministry that simply tries to hand off disabled young adults with higher support needs to a another ministry without planning, care, and coordination will fail. A youth ministry that ages out foster children with no support structure, programming, or care will be harming that teen at a significantly vulnerable point in their life. Churches can lean into their resources and dream of ways to continue including young adults on the margins. As youth age out of youth group, the body of Christ can continue to offer everyone a seat at the table.

Index